Redesigning Schools
to Be Antiracist

Redesigning Schools to Be Antiracist

A Systemic Change Approach for School Counselors and Other Leaders

Stephen Sharp

Foreword by Cheryly Holcomb-McCoy

CORWIN

A Sage Company

FOR INFORMATION

Corwin

A Sage Company

2455 Teller Road

Thousand Oaks, California 91320

(800) 233-9936

www.corwin.com

Sage Publications Ltd.

1 Oliver's Yard

55 City Road

London EC1Y 1SP

United Kingdom

SAGE Publications India Pvt. Ltd.

Unit No 323-333, Third Floor, F-Block

International Trade Tower Nehru Place

New Delhi 110 019

India

SAGE Publications Asia-Pacific Pte. Ltd.

18 Cross Street #10-10/11/12

China Square Central

Singapore 048423

Vice President and
  Editorial Director: Monica Eckman

Senior Publisher: Jessica Alan

Senior Content Development
  Editor: Mia Rodriguez

Project Editor: Amy Schroller

Copy Editor: Lynne Curry

Typesetter: C&M Digitals (P) Ltd.

Cover Designer: Scott Van Atta

Marketing Manager: Olivia Bartlett

Library of Congress Cataloging-in-Publication Data

Names: Sharp, Stephen (School counselor), author.

Title: Redesigning schools to be antiracist : a systemic change approach for school counselors and other leaders / Stephen Sharp.

Description: Thousand Oaks, California : Corwin, [2025] | Includes bibliographical references and index.

Identifiers: LCCN 2024039345 | ISBN 9781071875834 (paperback ; acid-free paper) | ISBN 9781071875841 (epub) | ISBN 9781071875865 (epub) | ISBN 9781071875872 (pdf)

Subjects: LCSH: Educational change—United States. | Educational counseling—21st century. | System design. | Anti-racism—Study and teaching—Evaluation. | Student counselors—In-service training—Technological innovations. | Student counselors—Training of—Technological innovations.

Classification: LCC LA217.2 .S527 2025 | DDC 370.11/50973—dc23/eng/20241119

LC record available at https://lccn.loc.gov/2024039345

This book is printed on acid-free paper.

SUSTAINABLE FORESTRY INITIATIVE
Certified Chain of Custody
At Least 10% Certified Forest Content
www.sfiprogram.org
SFI-01028

25 26 27 28 29 10 9 8 7 6 5 4 3 2 1

CONTENTS

Foreword   ix
by Cheryl Holcomb-McCoy

Publisher's Acknowledgments   xi

About the Author   xiii

Introduction: Starting Systems   1

PART I. HISTORIC DESIGN

1. Colonial United States, Prototype for a Nation   9
   Early Colonial America   9
   Early Virginia Colonial Law   10
   Massachusetts Early Colonial Law   14
   Early Colonial Massachusetts Origins of American Education   16
   Virginia – Partus Sequitur Ventrem (1662)   16
   Virginia Slave Code of 1680   17
   The First Race in Maryland and Virginia   18
   Virginia Slave Code (1705)   20
   Maryland Slave Code (1715)   21
   Pennsylvania Slave Code (1725)   22
   South Carolina Slave Code (1740)   23
   Colonial Education   25
   The Road to the American Revolution   26
   The American Revolution (1776)   27

2. Early United States: Launching a New Country   33
   The Constitution of the United States (1787)   33
   The Census and Naturalization Act 1790   35
   Missouri Compromise (1820)   36
   Common Schools—Education and Early United States:
   Public Education Prototype (1852)   38

Dred Scott vs. Sanford (1857)   38

The American Civil War (1861–1865)   41

Reconstruction and the Freedmen Bureau (1865)   44

Black Codes   46

Civil Rights Act (1866)   49

Fourteenth Amendment (1868)   51

Fifteenth Amendment (1870)   52

Civil Rights Cases of (1883)   52

Plessy v. Ferguson (1896)   54

The One Drop Rule and Jim Crow   59

The Committee of Ten (1892)   61

3.   The Evolving America: Systems and Scientific Racism   65

Eugenics   65

World War II and The GI Bill (1944)   73

Brown v. Board of Education (1954)   77

Civil Rights Act (1964)   80

Elementary and Secondary Education Act (1965)   86

Green v. School Board of New Kent County (1968)   87

Swann v. Charlotte-Mecklenburg (1971)   89

Milliken v. Bradley (1974)   91

No Child Left Behind (2001)   99

*Students for Fair Admissions, Inc. (SFFA) v. President &
Fellows of Harvard College (Harvard)* (2022)   101

**PART II. UNEQUAL FUTURES: THE RISK
OF INEQUALITY IN SYSTEMS**

4.   Present and Future Inequality   113

Unequal Futures   114

Analyzing Inequality   115

Systems of Inequality   117

Education Solutions for Unequal Future   118

PART III. SYSTEMIC CHANGE

5.   The Dynamics and Complexity of Systems   123

Systems Characteristics   124

Systems Behavior   125

Human Hurdles in Systems Thinking   125

Limited Information 125

Unintended and Counterintuitive Consequences 126

Systemic Change Challenges 126

Policy Resistance 126

Tragedy of the Commons 127

Increasing Returns 127

Goal Calibration 127

Systemic Change 128

Conventional Problem-Solving to Systemic Change 128

Mental Models 129

Systemic Storytelling 131

Listening Languages 132

Systems Mapping 133

Graphing Over Time 133

Stock and Flow Models 134

Causal Loop Diagram 135

System Modeling and Simulation 139

Systems Leverage 140

Leading for Systemic Change 142

PART IV. DESIGNING EQUITABLE FUTURES

6. Reverse Engineering Racism and Equitable Designs 147

The Systems of Racism 147

Implementing Change 147

Modeling Equity 151

Youth Participatory Action Research (YPAR) 153

Reverse Engineering Racism 156

Stroh's Four Stages of Leading Systemic Change 160

Five-Stage Design Thinking Process With Equitable
Principles 165

Aligned Equitable Systems Framework 166

Bias to Critical Consciousness 170

Discrimination to Equality 172

Privilege to Cultural Humility 173

Segregation to Belonging 174

Poverty to Equity 176

Oppression to Justice 178

7. Human Design: Future Systems   181
        A Thin Layer Across the Water   181
        The Language of Our Humanity   182
        Education Ties to Our Futures   183

Glossary   187

References   189

Index   203

FOREWORD

"*Antiracism means anti-white.*" This is a familiar and untrue statement that I hear frequently when discussing "antiracist" practices in schools. To me, it distracts from the real issue—our unwillingness to *change*. Antiracism causes educators to "change" normal behaviors and to ensure that every stuedent, parent, and family—regardless of background, race, income, ability, or experience—matters. Antiracism is far from being anti-white. It is an active approach to ensure that racism and all of its "ugly" characteristics, including racist beliefs and practices, are no longer present in schools and communities.

Most importantly, antiracism requires us to examine our day-to-day school practices and policies for underlying racist beliefs about people. Who matters and who doesn't? These faulty beliefs of "mattering" often misguide our behavior and result in institutionalized unequal practices. Racist, biased, and unfair practices that place more value on some groups than others are entrenched in the DNA of schools. And harmful, racist policies such as fraught gifted and talented policies, racially discriminatory hair policies, and policies that criminalize Black, Brown, and Indigenous students are pervasive in today's schools.

In *Redesigning Schools to be Antiracist*, Stephen Sharp gives his audience hope that there is a way for school counselors and other educators to play a vital role in stamping out racism and oppressive practices in schools. He also spends time walking us through the long-standing history of racism and colonialism in this country. This historical context is fundamental to our understanding of redesigning schools, and Sharp gives us a template from which to work. Although we have fought for civil rights, women's rights, and LGBTQ+ rights, minoritized students still suffer from unequal chances for a quality education. So, redesigning schools is a worthy action for school counselors to delve into.

Sharp spends time explaining "unequal systems" that illuminate the presence of racism in schools and communities. From the banning of books to excessive punishment, minoritized students and their families continue to face systems that destroy their chances of living productively. Rather than helping students escape the cruel realities of being poor and oppressed, schools often emulate and repeat these dynamics. For instance, it is indefensible that only 17% of Black students, 21% of Latino students, 11% of students with disabilities, and 10% of multilingual learners can read proficiently by fourth grade (NAEP, 2019). These statistics are maddening, and every school counselor should be asking how they can turn this trend around. Fixing "unequal systems" is, in my opinion, the most important aspect of a school counselor's job. If she doesn't concentrate on correcting societal ills, she is part of the problem rather than a solution! School counselors must not kowtow to the rants of some who profess that antiracism is "anti-white." Remember, that is just a distraction from the real issue at hand.

And lastly, Sharp makes a rallying cry for school counselors to wake up and do something! Although I agree that "redesigning schools" is critical, I suggest that school counselors must "reverse" their roles in schools too. Rather than being a protector of the status quo, school counselors must act boldly to change it. The history of racism in schools and educators playing a "passive role" in advocating for minoritized youth is long and disappointing (Pine & Hilliard, 1990). I compare school counselors' silence to the "moderate" in Dr. Martin Luther King, Jr. *Letter from the Birmingham Jail*:

> "I have almost reached the regrettable conclusion that the Negro's great stumbling block in the stride toward freedom is not the White Citizen's Council-er or the Ku Klux Klanner, but the white moderate who is more devoted to "order" than to justice; who prefers a negative peace which is the absence of tension to a positive peace which is the presence of justice; who constantly says "I agree with you in the goal you seek, but I can't agree with your methods of direct action;" who paternalistically feels he can set the timetable for another man's freedom; who lives by the myth of time and who constantly advises the Negro to wait until a "more convenient season."

Dr. King's words still resonate. Antiracist school counselors must be devoted to **justice** rather than negative peace. Antiracist school counselors understand that their work will cause some tension, but they work through it because the outcome is equality for all. Antiracist school counselors "walk the walk" rather than "talk the talk." And unapologetically, antiracist school counselors live up to the promise of a multiracial democracy and ensure that every child has opportunities to achieve their dreams—without divisive distractions.

I'm excited about Stephen Sharp's book because it will spur much-needed discussion among school counselors about their role and responsibility to those who need their support the most. I'm pleased that this book will challenge school counselors *to do something!*

Cheryl Holcomb-McCoy, PhD

PUBLISHER'S ACKNOWLEDGMENTS

Corwin gratefully acknowledges the contributions of the following reviewers:

Sarah N. Brant-Rajahn
Assistant Professor
Messiah University
Harrisburg, PA

Eva M. Gibson
Associate Professor
Austin Peay State University
Clarksville, TN

Alicia Oglesby
Associate Director of College Counseling
American School Counselor Association
Pittsburgh, PA

ABOUT THE AUTHOR

 **Stephen Sharp** is a school counselor and best-selling author. He has worked to provide students with the knowledge and skills to be healthy and successful in the twenty-first century. Stephen has served on the governing boards of both his local, state, and national school counseling organizations. Stephen completed his MEd at Millersville University of Pennsylvania and BA from Lycoming College.

Steve is a best-selling author, and he is a co-founder of the Leadership Summit, a community-based social justice network to provide students the language and tools to understand and combat the many forms of oppression.

Stephen is a nationally certified school suicide prevention specialist and worked with the Commonwealth of Pennsylvania to pilot an electronic behavioral health screening for schools. He works tirelessly nationwide to provide education and training on mental health, substance abuse, and inequality.

Stephen frequently presents and writes on school counseling practicees, leadership, technology, emerging career skills, mental health, and race in education. Stephen was named the 2017 Pennsylvania Middle School Counselor of the Year.

"A system of education is not one thing, nor does it have a single definite object, nor is it a mere matter of schools. Education is that whole system of human training within and without the school house walls, which molds and develops men."

—DuBois (1903), "The Talented Tenth"

INTRODUCTION

Starting Systems

The school year starts. In August 2023 at Dearington Elementary, school students entered the aging building. The shuffle of new sneakers and Crocs, the jostling of new backpacks, fresh haircuts, and new clothes created a cascade of flowing colors entering the school system with a mixture of excitement and anxiety. Still, this has been announced to be the last school year for Dearington Elementary, following its recommendation for closure (Gordon, 2023). Lynchburg, Virginia, home to Dearington and to many educational institutions, was also noted historically with its many Black schools and a troubled past with desegregating (Gaebe, n.d.). Dearington Elementary, the predominantly Black school, was not alone in the anticipated closure. Experts predict a rise of school closures in the next decade (Redelmeier, 2023), with race being the strongest predictor of school closure (Blad & Najarro, 2023) Other education trends were increasingly concerning. Over forty states in recent years have introduced bills to ban the teachings regarding race or racism. Black students comprised, according to available research, 40 percent of the K–12 school suspensions (Love, 2023) and there is concern of a growing impact of the pandemic on learning, particularly for students of color. Suicide rates for Black children now doubled that of their white peers (Hopkins, 2023) Uncertainty in higher education grew to an all-time high, following the Supreme Court decision to strike down affirmative action.

Still, the intersection and interconnectedness of race and education is far from new. In 2014, my antiracist and equity work and impetus of the book was shaped. While speaking to a graduate class of prospective counselors, one of the students asked my opinion after a grand jury didn't indict the police officers following the ruled homicide of Eric Garner. I shared my disappointment and frustration with both the verdict and noted the reforms needed for racial equity went far beyond policing. Our schools were gateways through which everyone passed but seemed to reproduce inequality as often as it was a tool for equality and freedom. The acknowledgment and outcry of Eric Garner's death echoed over schools where race and opportunity seemed to distance themselves under the shadow cast most recently from the education policy of No Child Left Behind. I answered a few more questions and left for the evening. The next day, the same graduate student reached out to me and asked if we could talk more about race in education. I met with the student and two of her friends, and what began as a casual conversation became brainstorming and then deep research into the practices and understanding of race in education. What became apparent was that there was little information or programming directed at K–12 students that focused specifically on understanding and addressing racism.

Through weeks of research, interviews, and meetings, a new program was developed, the Leadership Summit. Our group and meetings were distributive in nature: K–12 students, community organizers, educator administrators, higher education officials, parents, graduate students, K–12 educators, business owners, clergy, and more participated in the design and implementation. One trainer with the YWCA asked a question during an early planning meeting, "Do you just want to just talk about race, or do you want to change the lives of these kids and the conditions they go through every day?" The question fundamentally changed the focus and direction, not just for planning but my life's work. Talking about race doesn't change any of the conditions of racism that students face. Additionally, simply talking about racism could easily distill the focus to Black and white and not recognize how racism is a system that damages everyone, just not equally. Curriculum was designed, funds were raised, and dozens of people were trained to work with youth and facilitate group discussion on race. We shifted away from traditional titles, roles or leadership structures, placing the focus strictly on the youth we hoped would benefit from our efforts. The transition extended beyond simply talking about our values: We put our values into action. Collectively, we took shared values of connectedness, equity, hope and youth empowerment and designed them into systems.

The Leadership Summit was an antiracism training session focused on teaching secondary (middle and high school) students the language, vocabulary, and big ideas of antiracism, and providing them with networking and additional resources. In our first year (2015), we had every school district in our region send students to the event. The event expanded to seven counties and would have over one thousand students participate by the end of the program (due to the pandemic). The program provided students with large group instruction about the big ideas of antiracism. There were small group discussions led by trained facilitators to explore reflections, insights, and feelings. Finally, there were focus sessions using the arts (music, fine arts, drama) or high interest areas (media, politics, etc.) to provide focused discussion and exploration through the lens of race. Values of understanding, engagement, and action would pass through the curriculum, through training, into group discussion and be reflected in our students who would add it to their own lived experiences. The program would run, be replicated, and re-replicated independently, like other prototypes and systems. Each session would be analyzed, showing students growing in areas of empathy, identity development, and motivation to take systemic action.

OPPRESSION CYCLE

While working for years with the Leadership Summit, we heard firsthand the views of racism and race as teens and adults shared their thoughts, fears, hopes, and lives. Always, almost like a magic trick, patterns and connections would emerge. We'd see this happen between groups at each session and from one year to the next, as teens and adults would grow, graduate or change. One common tool we used to create a shared language of race and systems was the **Oppression Cycle**. Originally developed by Schmidt (2011) while at Texas A&M, it is a framework to help people deconstruct concepts of race and create common shared language and definitions.

We applied an adapted version of the Oppression Cycle, introducing it to group analysis of cartoons. We could analyze the historical cartoon, *Snow White*. 1937's *Snow White and the Seven Dwarfs* was a technological marvel for its time, the first full-length animated feature film. Using state of the art technology, models were turned into animated characters. Analyzing the characters, so important to the history of film, shows much about the nature of design.

Describing one of the dwarfs, you'd need only pause during a "Heigh-Ho" and describe the image of one of the characters. A wide grin, blue pants, and large round belly may detail the contented Happy; a slim build and furrowed brow with red slacks may reflect the discontented Grumpy. The oversized clothing, full cheeks, big ears, large wide eyes, and slouched posture could describe Dopey. Each of the seven characters was unique, but it was not by birth; rather, it was by design that each was created. Each of the seven designs wasn't created to aid a sleeping princess but instead it was done to communicate messages in a for-profit story. The messages, while passed in colors, cell shading, and lines, are defined in each name, like Dopey. The use of design isn't exclusive to the Disney feature film. Many of the design characteristics of Dopey specifically were found in depictions of Blacks during the era in both print and film. A notable example was the now-banned cartoon parody of *Snow White*, called Coal *Black and De Sebben Dwarfs*, which was prohibited in 1968 from further airing or distributions for its racist minstrel era-like depictions of Blacks.

Shifting from cartoon imagery, we can talk about the underlying power of messages and the interconnections to other ways of understanding race, racism, and oppression. Stereotypes, the inherent messages that a person may carry about groups of individuals, may lend itself to prejudice. Prejudice, the prejudgments, beliefs, or cognitive processes of groups of people, could lead to discrimination. Discrimination is action against individuals or groups of people. Oppression is the summation of prejudice and discrimination combined with power and time. More clearly stated by Schmidt (2011) is that power is more than political or monetary but systemic. Systemic through this lens is found in the systems such as institutions, practices, policies, or even laws. Racism, a form of oppression, often is described ubiquitously as negative beliefs, attitudes, or actions based on race; however, embedded in institutions are practices, policies, and laws spanning time that create advantages and disadvantages based on race, leading to divisive and harmful impacts on individuals.

FIGURE 1   THE OPPRESSION CYCLE

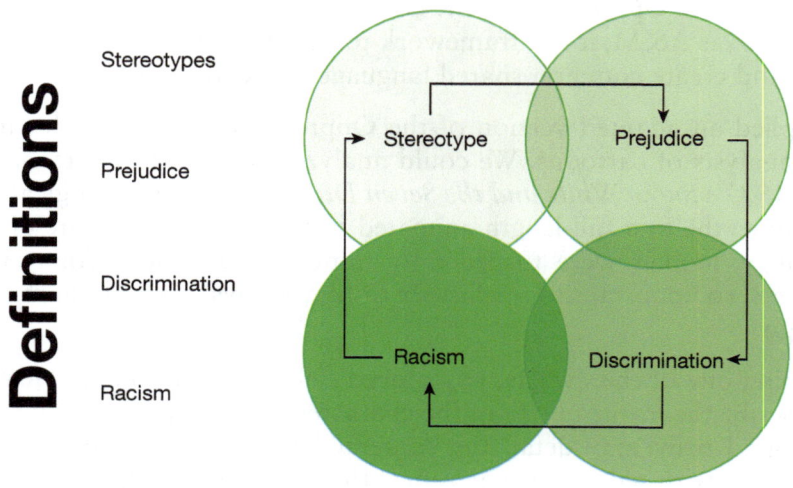

Often stereotype, prejudice, discrimination, and racism are used interchangeably. Clearly, each concept carries its own weight, scope, and power. The terms are sometimes conceptualized and even taught as being part of a dosing effect. If one carries enough Stereotypes, they may become Prejudice. If Prejudice goes unchecked, one may Discriminate. As implied in the name, the Oppression Cycle reflects the interconnected nature of the core concepts, but the directionality is nonlinear. Racist practices, policies, or laws may originate not out of racial animus but rather greed or political power. Still, institutional or systemic racist practices, while not spurned by bias, result in racially biased repercussions. The case that systemic racism gives rise to racist ideas, more than the reverse, was best illustrated in the 2016 National Book Award winner for nonfiction called *Stamped from the Beginning*. Through *Stamped from the Beginning (2016)*, Dr. Ibram X. Kendi deconstructed the origins of racist ideas through an examination of American history, repeatedly demonstrating with precision that systemic structures (practices, policies, and laws) drove and further developed racist ideas, and the solution was antiracism.

The Oppression Cycle shifts many understandings of how race and racism work. Most approaches focus on the biases, the human interactions. The framework helps shed light to why systems remain unchanged despite intensive self-discovery and learning.

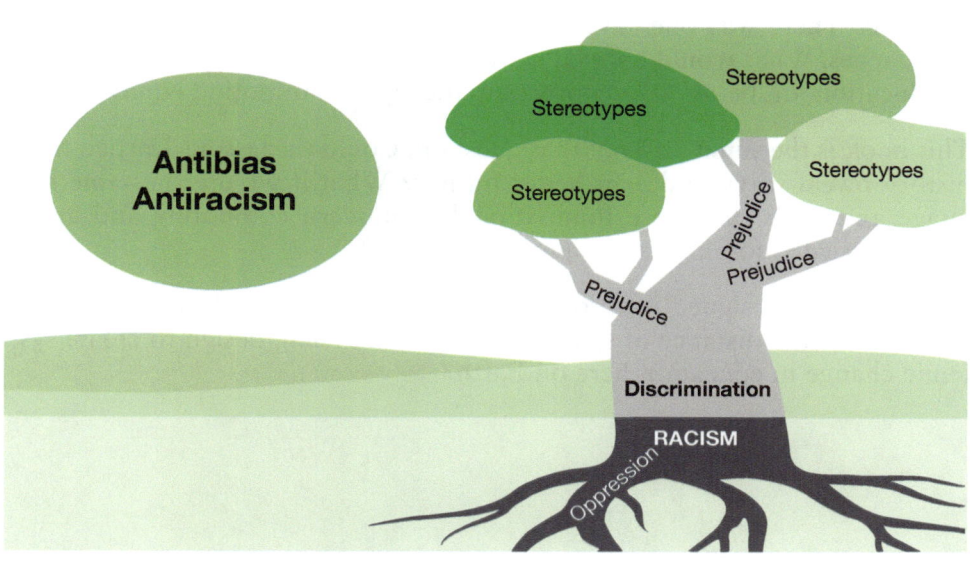

The Oppression Cycle helps to guide action. Thinking of the actions to address racism, we can use a metaphor of cutting down a tree. The work addressing the Stereotypes and Prejudices would be helpful. The Antibias work of analyzing and interrogating Stereotypes and Prejudices would be like trimming back the limbs of a tree. This wouldn't cut down the tree or change the roots of the tree, or the roots of oppression. Trimming back the limbs of the tree would make subsequent work on the trunk of Discrimination or uprooting Oppression (or racism) easier. Antiracism is the systems level work, the foundational work, the work at the roots.

In my work with students, I collaborated with them to develop the readiness skills for the rapidly changing twenty-first century world of work. This included advising regular clubs in computer coding and computational design and connecting them with local technical professionals. These efforts led me to an organization called Counselors for Computing, focused on equipping underrepresented people in careers in computing—women and people of color,—through educating and training school counselors.

While working with Counselor for Computing, I had an opportunity to visit a Google office. I stood in front of a massive screen, looking at Earth with its calm blue ocean waters and sprawling continents. I zoomed in to find cities invisible from space, finally locating the school building where I worked. I walked through the Google office and saw endless collaborative spaces, white boards, and social spaces, with relatively few computers. I left realizing that the highest achievements of computing and innovation were drive by human interaction. It also became clear that the process of transforming the imaginary—dreams, ambitions, and aspirations—into real-world results was a common function of both education and the computer scientists. There was one caveat: We used dramatically different tools and approaches. What would happen if we adopted a more systematic approach in education, or, better yet, focused specifically on promoting equity?

This book is the summation of that question. Could the lessons learned from history reveal ways to design better futures? What if we use the same language and tools that were foundational to modern computing and apply them to create more just and equitable systems?

Just as people designed interconnected systems that helped me to view my school from the distance of space, could we use system design to create systemic change in education here on Earth?

PART I

·················

HISTORIC DESIGN

CHAPTER 1

....

COLONIAL UNITED STATES, PROTOTYPE FOR A NATION

To understand racism as a series of interconnected systems, one needs to simply look at the changing definition of race and how it was applied throughout history. Many of the concepts and practices regarding race were constructed over time from European and also strictly American roots.

Seeing how race is encoded and recoded overtime is to better understand the structures, patterns, and behavior of the systems of racism and to develop a more equitable future.

The source material (original text, manuscripts, laws, and other documents) are provided directly. Small edits were made to spelling for clarity, but the original language is provided for the reader to make their own inferences.

The history of racism and race in America is interwoven with the history of education in America, too. The parallel stories provide the backdrop for how much of modern America is understood and defined. The deeper understanding of these histories, and by nature the architecture of two systems, racism and education, create a deep and textured map of each system, their aspirations, faults and legacies. Through careful reading of the ways race and racism was constructed, encoded, and applied in the many systems of America and throughout education, we can see the patterns and structures which we can use to redesign a more equitable system.

EARLY COLONIAL AMERICA

The construction of race and racism was carried on many of the same ships that founded the earliest colonies that preceded the United States. In the centuries prior to European colonization and the rise of the transatlantic slave trade, there was expansive trade, bartering, cultural exchange, and conflict between many of the states, nations, and empires of both Europe and Africa. Following Portugal's expansion down West Africa, there was a rise in colonies to support the wealth from the development of sugar, tobacco, rice, and cotton. There was also a rise in the use of enslaved Africans, as Portugal's number of colonies grew and other European countries modeled the practices.

EARLY VIRGINIA COLONIAL LAW

Jamestown was the first permanent British settlement in North America. As noted in 1619 by Jamestown's John Rolfe, the colony of Virginia's secretary and recorder of history, "about the last of August, there came to Virginia Dutchman of Warr that sold us twenty Negroes." Although there are records of Black people in the Americas prior to the British colonies, the first record of "negros" in the British colonies also tied to servitude. Angolan Africans were captured and boarded on a ship bound for Veracruz on the coast of present-day Mexico. While in the Gulf of Mexico, the ship was seized, along with the Angolan Africans, who were subsequently sold to the British colony in Jamestown, Virginia in 1619 (McCartney, 2020).

FIGURE 3   LANDING NEGROES AT JAMESTOWN FROM DUTCH MAN-OF-WAR, 1619

During this period of time, written records referred to individuals from their country of origin or perceived country of origin. British colonials were referred to as "English-born." The term Negro was likely a reference to Negroland, a designation used to describe the geographical region of Western and Central Africa as early as the mid-1100s (Cooley, 1841).This region is where the Portuguese were already enslaving Africans to send to the Caribbean and other parts of the world, and was the point of origin of the ship with the Jamestown Angolan-Africans (McCartney, 2020).

FIGURE 4 NEGROLAND AND ADJACENT COUNTRIES 1693-1767

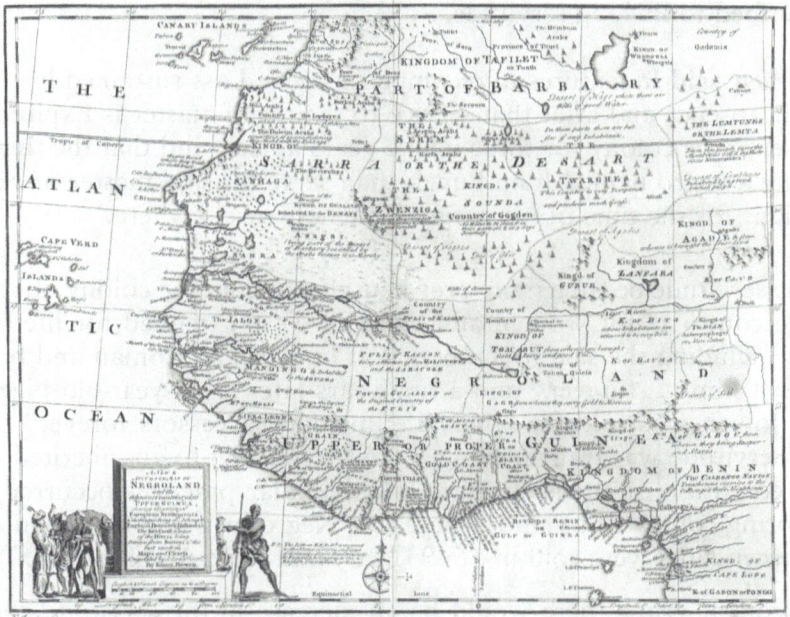

SOURCE: Bowen, Emanuel, 1693. Retrieved from the Library of Congress.

Coded: *Negro coded as "from the continent of Africa."*

The actual servitude status of the twenty Africans, though not fully clear as either indentured servitude or enslavement, would reflect a series of definition and redefinitions of both the term "negro" and nature of servitude in the years to follow (McCartney, 2020).

Colonial Virginia laws would initially codify "negros" as those the colony would not permit to have access to firearms in Act X of the Virginia Acts (1639):

> All persons except negroes to be provided with arms and
> ammunition or be fined at pleasure of the Governor and Council.

Coded: *Negro is code in Virginia for "unable to own guns."*

Negroes were again redefined as those with separate servitude conditions. John Punch, a Negro indentured servant, would have his service contract extended to a lifetime of servitude, while the English-born servants simply had three years of service added to their contract for attempting to run away. The verdict (General Court, 2020) also had Punch's descendants (assigns) also ascribed to lifelong servitude.

> By their said Indentures in recompense of his Loss sustained by their absence and after that service to their said master is Expired to serve the colony for three whole years apiece, and that the third being a negro named John Punch shall serve his said master or his assigns for the time of his natural Life here or elsewhere.

Lifetime servitude became more prevalent throughout the colony of Virginia. Notable contracts for women and children were extended for lifetimes or forever, including the sale by Francis Pott of a Negro woman and boy "for the use of him . . . forever," and a few years later a ten-year-old Negro girl named Jowan was sold for "their lifetime and successors forever" (Simba, 2022). Servitude was transforming a service contract to an inherited or biological condition on a case-by-case basis. Similar practices occurred in the neighboring colony Maryland, where two Negro men and a woman and all their descendants were sold in 1649 (Maryland State Archives, 2000).

In subsequent years, there would be an increase in the servitude contracts extended to lifelong service, increasingly rapidly after the Virginia General Assembly passed ACT XXII (Virginia General Assembly, 2020):

> WHEREAS there are divers loytering runaways in the collony who very often absent themselves from their masters service, And sometimes in two or three monthes cannot be found, whereby their said masters are at great charge in finding them, And many times even to the losse of their year's labour before they be had, Be it therefore enacted and confirmed that all runaways that shall absent themselves from their said masters service shall be lyable to make satisfaction by service at the end of their tymes by indenture (vizt.) double the tyme of service soe neglected, And in some cases more if the comissioners for the place appointed shall find it requisite and convenient. And if such runaways shall be found to transgresse the second time or oftener (if it shall be duely proved against them) that then they shall be branded in the cheek with the letter R. and passe under the statute of incorrigible rogues, Provided notwithstanding that where any servants shall have just cause of complaint against their masters or mistrises by harsh or unchristianlike usage or otherways for want of diet, or convenient necessaryes that then it shall be lawfull for any such servant or servants to repaire to the next comissioner to make his or their complaint, And if the said commissioner shall find by good and sufficient proofes, that the said servant's cause of complaint is just, The said comissioner is hereby required to give order for the warning of any such master or mistris before the comissioners in

their seuerall county courts, where the matter in difference shall be decided as they in their discretions shall think fitt, And that care be had that no such servant or servants be misused by their masters or mistrises, where they shall find the cause of complaint to be just. Be it further also enacted that if any servant running away as aforesaid shall carrie either peice, powder and shott, And leave either all or any of them with the Indians, And being thereof lawfully convicted shall suffer death as in case of felony.

Additional laws were passed to make a further distinction between Negro servants and English-born servants. Initially, this was done by adding years to the English-born servants caught running away with a Negro servant in the An Act to Discourage English Running Away with Negroes, 1660/1 (Henig, 1819). servitude

BEE itt enacted That in case any English servant shall run away in company with any negroes who are incapable of makeing satisfaction by addition of time, Bee itt enacted that the English so running away in company with them shall serve for the time of the said negroes absence as they are to do for their owne by a former act.

The law was amended less than a year later in the March 1661/2-ACT CII. Run-aways. The statute increased penalties for English-borne servants for running away with Negro servants. The law appeared to indicate Negroes were "incapable" of serving additional time, as all Negro servants would appear in this and subsequent Virginial colonial laws to be enslaved for life.

Coded: *Negro coded as slave, servant for life.*

Not only was there an increased frequency and prevalence of lifelong servitude. There were growing tensions with Indigenous people of the region. The Powhatans, the indigenous tribe of the region, who were involved in regional conflicts and escalation, were found in indentured servant roles, often becoming "lifelong servants." Following the Third Anglo-Powhatan War, the English required tribal children, be taken from their homes and families.[11] While the English stated the boarding was for educational purposes and religious conversion, many of the children were sold in servitude. Article 10 of the Treaty Ending the Third Anglo-Powhatan War (General Assembly, 2020d) noted the following:

it is further enacted & consented, That such Indian children as shall or will freely and voluntarily come in and live with the English, may remain without breach of the articles of peace provided they be not above twelve yeares old.

Another Article (IX) in the Treaty Ending the Third Anglo-Powhatan War, written for the return of "Indian servants," was used as legal rationale to rapidly expand the capture of Indigenous people (and Negroes) and their lands throughout the region:

> all such negroes and guns which are yet remaining either in the possession of himselfe or any Indians, and that here deliver upon demand such Indian servants as have been taken prisoners and shall hereafter run away, In case such Indian or Indians shall be found within the limitts of his dominions; provided that such Indian or Indians be under the age of twelve years at theire running away.

Coded: *In Virginia, Indian coded no right to family.*

Coded: *Indians are slaves.*

Virginia, as the first permanent British settlement for the continent, would serve as a model for other colonies. Maryland and New York would adopt similar laws bonding Negroes and to lifelong servitude.

MASSACHUSETTS EARLY COLONIAL LAW

Massachusetts had early records of enslavement, as early as 1637. Following the Pequot War, Governor John Winthrop noted the death and capture of several hundred of the Pequot tribe. Over a dozen of the Pequot people were sent to Bermuda (only to ultimately land in the Bahamas). In return, the company received the following year (1638) some cotton, tobacco, enslaved Africans, and other goods (Triber, 2024).

Years later (1641) Massachusetts would publish Bodies of Liberty (1641), providing rationale and legal justification for slavery and other forms of servitude. While defining and ensuring the freedoms and rights of the colonists . . .

> No mans life shall be taken away, no mans honor or good name shall be stained, no mans person shall be arrested, restrained, banished, dismembered, nor any ways punished, no man shall be deprived of his wife or children, no mans goods or estate shall be taken away from him, nor any way damaged under color of law or Countenance of Authority, unless it be by virtue or equity of some express law of the Country warranting the same, established by a general Court and sufficiently published, or in case of the defect of a law in any particular case by the word of God. And in Capital cases, or in cases concerning dismembering or banishment according to that word to be judged by the General Court.

. . . the document also represented the first British colony in the Americas to legalize the enslavement of Africans and Indigenous Peoples (Ward, 1641).

> There shall never be any bond slavery, villinage or captivity amongst us unless it be lawful Captives taken in just wars, and such strangers as willingly sell themselves or are sold to us. And these shall have all the liberties and Christian usages which the law of god established in Israel concerning such persons does morally require. This exempts none from servitude who shall be Judged thereto by Authority.

Bodies of Liberty established both freedom and servitude as being established, and thus justified by God.

Coded: *Slavery is divine right.*

As the rapidly expanding Puritan plantation colonies of Massachusetts, New Plymouth, Connecticut, and New Haven continued to grow, they soon joined together to form the United Colonies of New England or the New England Confederation under the Articles of Confederation of the United Colonies of New England in 1643.

In addition to noting that the settlement of the colonies was one of Divine right, the Articles of Confederation of the United Colonies of New England (1643) established a series of treaties and other wartime agreements between the colonies, and a framework for civil law. Significantly, the Articles of 1643 created the first fugitive slave law in the colonies (Thorpe, 1909).

> . . . It is also agreed that if any servant run away from his master into any other of these confederated Jurisdictions, that in such case, upon the ceritficate of one magistrate in the Jurisdiction out of which the said servant fled, or upon other due proof; the said servant shall be delivered, either to his master, or any other that pursues and brings such certificate or proof. And that upon the escape of any prisoner whatsoever, or fugitive for any criminal cause, whether breaking prison, or getting from the officer, or otherwise escaping, upon the certificate of two magistrates of the Jurisdiction out of which the escape is made, that he was a prisoner, or such an offender at the time of the escape, the magistrates, or some of them of that Jurisdiction where for the present the said prisoner or fugitive abideth, shall forthwith grant such a warrant as the case will bear, for the apprehending of any such person, and the delivery of him into the hands of the officer or other person who pursues him. And if there be help required, for the safe returning of any such offender, then it shall be granted to him that craves the same, he paying the charges thereof.

Connecticut would legalize slavery shortly after in 1650.

> **Coded:** *Slavery is law across New England.*

EARLY COLONIAL MASSACHUSETTS ORIGINS OF AMERICAN EDUCATION

During this time, the Massachusetts Bay colony also created and passed the Massachusetts School Law, the first education laws in the new colonies in 1642. Under the new law, all children ages six through sixteen years old needed to be taught to read and write. Towns in the colony with more than fifty families were required to provide public education. Larger towns with more than two hundred families were required to appoint at least one teacher (Blackwell, 2023).

All heads of households were required to teach the English language and the laws of the land to their children and other dependents, including their servants. Initially, most families would provide the education themselves or hire a third party. "Selectmen," locally elected officials, would now be in charge of supervision of the growing education systems rather than clergy (Blackwell, 2023). Further described, in the follow-up education law, the Old Deluder Act of 1647, the selectmen were asked to surveil and monitor their neighbors to ensure the children, servants, and apprentices were being educated and trained, including vocational skills (New England Historical Society, n.d.) If heads of the household failed to educate their dependents or the children had difficulty learning the skills, the selectmen would take them from the homes and place them with new masters to provide new education and discipline (New England Historical Society, n.d.). Similar laws were passed in the other New England colonies in the years to follow.

VIRGINIA – PARTUS SEQUITUR VENTREM (1662)

Following a suit by Elizabeth Key Grinstead, a woman who sued for her freedom and won, there was a response in colonial lawmakers to the legal victory. Elizabeth was the child of a free, white Englishman and an African servant (Robinson, 2016). She and her husband sued for her freedom, as under English common law at the time, the legal status of the father determined the legal status of the child (Morgan, 2018). In response to legal victory, the Virginia Assembly passed Act XII (1662) Partus Sequitur Ventrem, which meant in Latin "offspring follows belly."

> Whereas some doubts have arisen whether children got by any Englishman upon a negro woman shall be slave or free, Be it therefore enacted and declared by this present grand assembly, that

all children borne in this country shall be held bond or free only according to the condition of the mother—Partus Sequitur Ventrem. And that if any Christian shall commit fornication with a negro man or woman, hee or shee soe offending shall pay double the fines imposed by the former act.

This was a new law contorting standing English common law. The Virginia assembly would apply the same rules they use for livestock to those enslaved. The enslaved black woman's child would now also be enslaved. No longer would the father have responsibility for caring for the child financially or otherwise, parting from historic practice (Morgan, 2018). Children fathered through rape or coercion would also add to the enslaved population.

Slavery would now be inherited for life; slavery was tied to the Negro and was now biology.

Coded: *Negroes are slaves. Slavery is hereditary.*

VIRGINIA SLAVE CODE OF 1680

Following Bacon's Rebellion (1676), Jamestown was raided and burned. In 1680, the Virginia General Assembly (2020a) reconvened in the colony, still rebuilding from the rebellion. The rebellion was a coalition of people from a wide range of servitude (indentured and enslaved), reflecting many different countries of origin. Following the rebellion, the servants and slaves of African descent became the primary focus of forced and coercive labor; in part this was due to Bacon, himself, being a former servant (Tiffany, 2017). The Virginia Assembly passed its own comprehensive slave law, "An act for preventing Negroes Insurrection," with key elements modeled from the Barbados Slave Code. Following a rebellion on Barbados, that British colony drafted a series of comprehensive slave codes (General Assembly, 2020b), which later colonies modeled. The law now defined Negro slaves as those who would be unable to congregate, carry anything perceived to be a weapon, travel from plantation grounds without permissions, or have equal protection of law ("presume to lift up his hand in opposition against any Christian"). The law not only described different forms of permissible violence against the enslaved people but also permitted kidnapping and public violence against Negroes unaccompanied by planters:

WHEREAS the frequent meeting of considerbale numbers of negroe slaves under pretence of feasts and buriaills is judged of dangerous consequence; for prevention whereof for the future, Bee it enacted by the kings most excellent majestie by and with the consent of the generall assembly, and it is hereby enacted by the authority foresaid, that from and after the publication of this law, it shall not be lawfull for any negroe or other slave to carry or arme himselfe with any club, staffe, gunn, sword or any other weapon of defence or offence, nor to goe or depart from of his masters ground without a certificate from his master, mistris or overseer and such permission not to be granted but upon perticuler and necessary occasions; and every negroe or slave soe offending not haveing a certificate as aforesaid shalbe sent to the next constable, who is hereby enjoyned and required to give the said negroe twenty lashes on his bare back well layd on, and soe sent home to his said master, mistris or overseer. And it is further enacted by the authority aforesaid that if any negroe or other slave shall presume to lift up his hand in opposition against any christian, shall for every such offence, upon due proofe made thereof by the oath of the party before a magistrate, have and receive thirty lashes on his bare back well laid on. And it is hereby further enacted by the authority aforesaid that if any negroe or other slave shall absent himself from his masters service and lye hid and lurking in obscure places, comitting injuries to the inhabitants, and shall resist any person or persons that shalby any lawfull authority by imployed to apprehend and take the said negroe, that then in case of such resistance, it shalbe lawfull for such person or persons to kill the said negroe or slave soe lying out and resisting, and that this law be once every six months published at the respective county courts and parish churches within this colony.

At the same time, more broadly across the British colonies, enslaved people were clearly identified as goods (property) rather than persons as noted in the ruling of *Butts v. Penny* (1677) (Slavery Law and Power, n.d.). While the ruling was in response to a suit in Barbados, regarding "10 and one half Negroes," it came from the King's Bench, the highest common law court, rippling throughout the British empire and colonies.

Coded: *Slaves are restricted in travel.*

Coded: *Slaves no right to defense.*

THE FIRST RACE IN MARYLAND AND VIRGINIA

The Black population continued to increase in the colonies. The Black populations in the colony of Maryland rose from approximately twenty in 1640 to 760 twenty years later (Maryland State Archives, 2000). The first appearance of "race" began in 1664 with Maryland's anti-miscegenation laws. The law was a transition for previous marriage laws prohibiting the intermarriage of "English and Freeborn" women to men of African descent (Battalora, 2013). The Maryland General Assembly wrote the following in 1681 (Maryland State Archives, 2000):

> for as much a[s] diverse Freeborne English or Whitewoman sometimes by the instigation Procurement of Conievance of theire Masters Mistres or dames, and always to the Satisfaction of theire Lascivious and Lustfull desires, and to the disgrace not only of the English but also of many other Christian Nations, do Intermarry with Negroes and Slave.

Prior to the common prevalence of racial language, people were associated with the country and not preferred biological traits. With the 1681 law, new language emerged prohibiting the marriage of "English and other WHITE women" to men of African descent. The law is the first clear reference of race in the Americas and created race as defined as being English-born, Christian, and heterosexual. The colony of Virginia adopted similar language. In An act for suppressing outlying slaves (1691), the law said the following (Virginia General Assembly, 2020):

> And for the prevention of the abominable mixture of the spurious issues which hereafter may increase in this dominion, as well as by negroes, mulattoes and Indians intermarrying with English or other white women, as by their unlawful accompanying with one another, Be it enacted by the authoritie aforesaid, and it is hereby enacted, that for the time to come, whatsoever English or other white man or woman being free shall intermarry with a negroe, mulatto, or Indian man or woman bond or free shall within three months after such marriage be banished and removed from this dominion forever, and that the justices of each respective countie within this dominion make it their perticular care, that this act be put in effectuall execution. . . .

White, as the first race, was inherited, giving hierarchical privilege (making prospective romantic partners limited to legally defined whiteness), and creating legal social boundaries to protect the "new" social class. Violation was clear—those who did not ascribe to these newly defined roles of sexual partnership would be banished or removed from the community.

Coded: *White is heterosexual, Christian and English-born.*

Coded: *White controls land and occupancy.*

VIRGINIA SLAVE CODE (1705)

Consolidating the previous decades of laws and codes written regarding Blacks, indentured servants and slavery, the Virginia General Assembly wrote sweeping legislation called An act concerning Servants and Slaves" (1705). In part a reaction to the continued rise in populations of enslaved Africans, and possibly in response to growing anti-slavery sentiments (like to *The Selling of Joseph* by Samuel Sewall, written in 1700), the laws expanded on those previously passed. Sewall's writings made clear that slavery was antithetical to Christian principles, although the Curse of Cham, a narrow Old Testament interpretation of why Black people were Biblically placed into bondage, was the colonial Christian validation of enslavement (Sewall, 1700).

All non-Christian servants were declared slaves for life, regardless of the amount of time left on their service contract. Enslaved people would no longer be able to carry firearms or any perceived weapon. They would be subject to physical assault or even murder without reprisal. The words white and Christian were used interchangeably in the law, establishing different service conditions based on religions and skin color. Those enslaved were not permitted to travel long from the plantation. Intermarriage was punishable by imprisonment for white men and women, and fines for the officiant. Additional hierarchical language in the Slave Code was clear regarding those who escaped enslavement. Article XI (1705) of the Slave Code noted the following (Virginia Assembly, 1814–1823):

> And for a further christian care and usage of all christian servants, Be it also enacted, by the authority aforesaid, and it is hereby enacted, That no negros, mulattos, or Indians, although christians, or Jews, Moors, Mahometans, or other infidels, shall, at any time, purchase any christian servant, nor any other, except of their own complexion, or such as are declared slaves by this act: And if any negro, mulatto, or Indian, Jew, Moor, Mahometan, or other infidel, or such as are declared slaves by this act, shall, notwithstanding, purchase any christian white servant, the said servant shall, ipso facto, become free and acquit from any service then due, and shall be so held, deemed, and taken: And if any person, having such christian servant, shall intermarry with any such negro, mulatto, or Indian, Jew, Moor, Mahometan, or other infidel, every christian white servant of every such person so intermarrying, shall, ipso facto, become free and acquit from any service then due to such master or mistress so intermarrying, as aforesaid.

Blacks captured while trying to escape would likely face death. Those assisting the capture would be rewarded, and planters whose escaped servants died during capture would be given reparation payments. The notion of payment due to slavers and annual payments to the Crown and clerks for the overarching system of slavery diminished the lives and well-being of Blacks in the region to shilling and a few hundred pounds of tobacco.

Service would be explicitly slavery and explicitly Black, as "white" would now be used for the first time to contrast differences between indentured servants and those enslaved, and differences in marriage and childbearing.

Coded: *Slaves are all non-Christians.*

Coded: *Negro is slave.*

Coded: *Whites are freemen.*

MARYLAND SLAVE CODE (1715)

Following the Virginia Slave Codes, comparable comprehensive codes were expanding throughout the British colonies. Maryland passed its own version of a slave code in the Proceedings and Acts of the General Assembly, Vol. 30 (1715). Black people were seized if traveling without a pass and could face enslavement or six months in prison. Enslaved people would not be afforded a jury trial, like the colonist, presenting before one of two justices.

The Maryland law would again reiterate making all Blacks as slaves:

> And be itt alsoe Enacted by the Authority that all Negroes and other Slaves Already Imported or hereafter to be Imported in this province and all Children now born or hereafter to be born of such Negroes and Slaves shall be Slaves dureing their naturall lives.

The expanse of slavery was matched by the expanse of the new *racialized* Slave Codes, as populations of those enslaved continued to expand across the southern colonies. In Maryland, the Black population was nearly one-third to one-half of the total colony's population in the years prior to the American Revolution (Maryland State Archives et al., 2020). Race, no longer region or religion, would be the tool of categorizing humans and service.

Coded: *Black is slave.*

Coded: *Black unable to travel.*

Coded: *Black unequal justice.*

PENNSYLVANIA SLAVE CODE (1725)

The expanse of slavery was even noted in other colonies, such as Pennsylvania. An Act for Better Regulating Negroes in the Province was enacted 1725–1726 (Statutes at Large of Pennsylvania, n.d.). Similar to other colonies, legal rights for those enslaved were limited through the Act.

The law limited intermarriage, and even cohabitating, between enslaved Negroes and whites, punishable for all parties, including the clergy, involved. Free people, men and women who were found lying with a white person, would be enslaved, while their partner would face the penalty of local adultery for fornication laws.

Those enslaved were limited on how or where they could travel. Negroes were banned from traveling more than ten miles from their master or finding additional work. The enslaved were also barred from drinking in or near a liquor shop and had a 9 p.m. curfew.

As there was a broader mix of freed Blacks, enslaved people and whites, the Slave Codes of Pennsylvania also laid a foundation of Codes for Black and those of mixed-race separate from those enslaved. Those enslaved were banned from any transaction with freed Black. A freed Black could also be placed into bond (indentured servitude) if that were thought to be "unwilling to work," or unable to pay fines. Free Blacks were described in the law as noted in the following:

> And whereas 'tis found by experience that free negroes are an idle, slothful people and often prove burdensome to the neighborhood and afford ill examples to other negroes:

> Therefore be it enacted by the authority aforesaid, That if any master or mistress shall discharge or set free any negro, he or she shall enter into recognizance at the respective county court with sufficient sureties in the sum of thirty pounds to secure and indemnify the city, township or county where he resides from any èharge or'incumbrance they may bring upon the same in case such negro by sickness or otherwise be rendered incapable to support him or herself, 'but until such recognizance be given such negroes shall not be deemed free.

The Pennsylvania Slave Codes carried on much of the racially divisive language of other slave codes, but expanded in assigning dehumanizing characteristics in law to all people of African descent.

Coded: *Black – intermarriage means enslavement. Black means burdensome.*

Coded: *Black means limited travel.*

Coded: *Black means conditional and costly freedom.*

SOUTH CAROLINA SLAVE CODE (1740)

The South Carolina General Assembly drafted language for the Bill for the better ordering and governing of Negroes and other slaves in this province (1740), also known as the Negro Act of 1740. The bill swept in language in the encoding race from many aspects of life and was likely in response to many growing regional and global pressures regarding slavery and colonial expansion.

As Spain and Britain became entangled in war, the Spanish Royal Decree of 1733, declared that any who escaped from enslavement in the British colonies to Florida would be granted both freedom and sanctuary (Landers, 1984) The Decree increased tension throughout the southern colonies, especially Georgia and South Carolina.

In 1739, nearly fifty enslaved people rebelled in Stono, South Carolina. The rebellion stormed and burned one of the armories, and led to many deaths for Blacks and whites. The rebellion was stopped by the colonial militia prior to reaching Florida (Niven, 2016).

The following year, the South Carolina Assembly enacted the bill. The bill was more restrictive for all Negroes and Indigenous people of the region, enslaving all and any future generations (South Carolina Slave Code, n.d.):

> Be it enacted, that all negroes, Indians, (free Indians in amity with this government, and negroes, mulatos and mestizos who are now free excepted) mulatos or mestizos, who now are or shall hereafter be in this Province, and all their issue and offspring born or to be born, shall be and they are hereby declared to be and remain for ever hereafter absolute slaves, and shall follow the condition of the mother; and shall be deemed, should, taken, reputed and adjudged in law to be chattels personal in the hands of their owners and possessors and their executors, administrators and assigns, to all intents, constructions and purposes whatsoever.

The law would further clarify and expand the legal powers inherited by whiteness as whites would be the only individuals permitted to provide testimony as witness. White individuals could travel freely individually or in the company of Black people without being stopped or assaulted. A white person could capture and assault any groups of Negroes with more than seven individuals. White people were free to capture, assault, and even kill any Black people found off of a plantation.

The value and style of clothing would also be ascribed in the racialized code. The code would clearly and narrowly define and reiterate the only attire suitable for the enslaved: "negro cloth, duffils, coarse kerseys, oznabrigs, blue linen, check linen or coarse garlix or callicoes, checked cottons or Scots plaids."

Similar to other slave codes, blacks and other enslaved people could not travel freely in the colony and needed special tickets to leave the plantation. The law would remain unequal for the enslaved of South Carolina: If they were perceived to assault a white person, it could result in death.

Expanding previous codes, enslaved people would no longer be allowed to rent or purchase any homes, grow food, or learn to read and write.

In the southern colonies, these would be the first compulsory education laws, the banning of Black and Indigenous people in literacy and writing English language.

Shortly after the 1740 law, two enslaved men were purchased by the Society for the Propagation of the Gospel in Foreign Parts and began training to become instructors in 1741. The following year in 1742, the Society opened a school in Charleston, South Carolina. The school had three instructors, including the two Black enslaved men, with thirty students. The school was permitted to operate, claiming that Christian education made the enslaved more obedient and that the education was focused more on apprenticeship. The Charleston Negro School would remain in operation for over twenty-two years, following the death of the last remaining Negro instructor (Comminey, 1999).

Coded: *White, enforcer of the laws.*

Coded: *Slave separate fashion.*

Coded: *Slave banned from education.*

Coded: *Slave unable to own a home.*

Coded: *Slave limited access to food.*

COLONIAL EDUCATION

As the education systems continued to grow along with the colonies, most education across the British colonies was a localized effort and often informal. The majority of education occurred in the home and focused on basic literacy, practical skills, and religious education. There was no established system for funding any formal education. While few regions had tax-subsidized education, most formal education would be tuition driven or rely on charitable donations, such as fuel contributions (Kober & Rentner, 2020).

While the scope and structure of the theologically-focused Massachusetts and New England education system were already noted, the other colonies had different models. The colonies in the mid-Atlantic (Delaware, New Jersey, New York, and Pennsylvania), while often run by local churches, had less of a religious focus than the New England colonies. Charities also established free schools for the poor and working class (Roos, 2022). Quakers would establish schools for Black children throughout the first half of the 1700s in New Jersey, New York, North Carolina, Pennsylvania, and Virginia (despite Quaker opposition to slaveholding) (Black Teacher Archive, 2023). In New York, the Manumission Society opened a free school for Blacks (The Education of African Americans, n.d.).

Southern colonies focused on private tutors, English boarding schools, or field schools (a community-funded schoolmaster and school). A schoolmaster might also include during the early colonial days bondsmen and indentured servants (Roos, 2022).

Georgia Slave Code (1755)

By Royal decree in 1751, slavery was enacted in the Province of Georgia following a request by the Trustees, a group of elected officials identified in the colony's charter to govern the colony from England. The practice of slavery had originally been banned when the colony was founded in 1735 (Wood, 2021).

By 1755, the Trustees of Georgia petitioned the crown to allow for slavery in the colony. An Act for the Better Ordering and Governing Negroes and Other Slaves and to prevent intermingling or carrying away slaves from their Masters or Employers was passed in 1755.

Similar to South Carolina's sweeping restrictive education laws, teaching of writing would be banned in the Province of Georgia for enslaved people. Those enslaved could not congregate in groups, or administer medicine or treatment to anyone else enslaved. There could be no sales of alcohol to the enslaved. They were not allowed to own a home.

Enslaved people were no longer allowed to leave the plantation without written permission, to assemble in groups, or purchase their own homes.

They were also banned from carrying a firearm and could face death if they ever struck a white man.

If an enslaved person were to be maimed or disabled while being trying to be apprehended, the Act stipulated the appropriate cost of that enslaved person's able-body was five shillings. Similarly, if a constable failed to administer his duty to capture an escaping, enslaved individual, the constable would owe a sum of twenty shillings.

The most significant change in the Georgia Slave Code was the blurring of the line between race as a condition of servitude and the broader set of imposed preferred biological traits, which would be further expanded through subsequent Georgia Slave Codes. All free people of color (free Blacks, free Indigenous people and any of noted mixed heritage) "shall be proceeded and tried by the justices and freeholders appointed by this act for the trial of slaves, in like manner in herby directed for the proceedings and trial of crimes and offences committed by slaves" (Georgia, 1978).

Coded: *Black is unequal in the law.*

Coded: *Slave banned from healing.*

Coded: *Slave banned from celebration.*

Coded: *Slave banned from community.*

THE ROAD TO THE AMERICAN REVOLUTION

As the British colonies in America drifted closer to revolution and ultimately, independence, tension also rose regarding enslavement and the ideals of liberty and freedom driving the patriotic movement. In Pennsylvania, Quakers banned their members enslaving individuals or participating in the slave trade. At the same time, Virginia, the Carolinas, and other colonies began to ban British goods that were taxed as a result of the Townshend Acts (1767). The British transatlantic slave trade was explicitly noted in the boycott in the various nonimportation agreements, which would continue as political tensions and economic pressures would continue to rise (Smith, 1940; Charleston Nonimportation Agreement, 1776).

Tensions were visible even in the streets of colonies. In Boston, the occupying British soldiers used to collect and enforce taxation and other British law led to the Boston Massacre, leading to the deaths of several colonists by the British, including Crispus Attucks. The Townshend Acts also led to the Tea Act of 1773, an attempt to encourage more colonists to purchase teas taxed under the Townshend Act, ultimately, resulting in the Boston Tea Party (Chaffin, 2000).

The Tea Party led to the Crown passing the Coercive Acts of 1774. The oppressive acts, particularly in the north, were creating increasingly challenging conditions. The Boston Port Act closed Boston Harbor until the lost tea was reimbursed; other acts like the Administration of Justice Act freed British officials from the jurisdiction of colonial laws, leading some to call it the "Murdering Act."

The Quartering Act of 1774 allowed the British to inhabit unused buildings. However, due to unclear reporting and administration of the law, it is likely that the implementation resembled the practices of past Quartering Acts, which often resulted in British soldiers seizing private establishments and requisitioning supplies (Gerlach, 1966). The conditions were likened to slavery throughout the colonies to build resistance momentum against the Crown (Little, 2022). The comparisons to slavery were neither fair nor accurate. As the colonies expanded from economic conflict like nonimportation agreements banning British taxed goods, they would transition to outright warfare, as concepts of race, slavery, and servitude would continue to evolve. The Declaration of Independence would enshrine values of liberty, equality, and opportunity into the identity of the developing nation, while those they enslaved would seek to fight for the British at a chance for emancipation. By the end of the American Revolution, Vermont and Massachusetts all abolished slavery, with Pennsylvania, New York Rhode Island, and Connecticut establishing plans for gradual emancipation.

Drawing parallels to the enslaved pointed a trajectory for freedom for the colonies. The encoded races were similar but slightly different in each colony as systems of slavery. The tension of slavery, freedom, liberty, and tyranny set the stage for the new nation.

THE AMERICAN REVOLUTION (1776)

As much as there had been economic and overt conflict happening in the colonies, the Declaration of Independence was the foundation for our new governments, a new country, a new system. The Declaration encoded many of the values, beliefs, and aspirations for the colonies as it served to sever ties with Britain. As the Continental Congress affirmed the document crafted by a five-person design team, including John Adams, Benjamin Franklin, and

Thomas Jefferson, the adoption of the Declaration was a landmark for the ideals of democracy and the creation of a new independent country (National Archives, n.d.a.). The Preamble of the Declaration of Independence noted (National Archives, n.d.b.) the following words:

> We hold these truths to be self-evident, that all men are created equal, that they are endowed by their Creator with certain unalienable Rights, that among these are Life, Liberty and the pursuit of Happiness.–That to secure these rights, Governments are instituted among Men, deriving their just powers from the consent of the governed, –That whenever any Form of Government becomes destructive of these ends, it is the Right of the People to alter or to abolish it, and to institute new Government, laying its foundation on such principles and organizing its powers in such form, as to them shall seem most likely to effect their Safety and Happiness.

As the Declaration concludes, it lists twenty-seven grievances against King George III. These grievances reveal the encoding of race and highlight the tension in the new nation's founding documents between the ideals of liberty and contemporary views of humanity. Among the grievances is this one, which reflects the colonists' perspective on conflicts with Native Americans and also includes language which today is considered to have racial biases of the time:

> He has excited domestic insurrections amongst us, and has endeavored to bring on the inhabitants of our frontiers, the merciless Indian savages whose known rule of warfare, is an undistinguished destruction of all ages, sexes, and conditions.

The "domestic insurrection" was likely in reference to rebellions and revolts of the enslaved people, and to rising tension at the time with British promises to free those enslaved to join the British cause (Ostler, 2020). The irony should not be lost that in the same document that rejected rule and subjugation of Royal lineage, the final lines would uphold heritable servitude. Other passages in the Declaration challenging slavery had been struck by the Continental Congress (De Witte, 2020)

While the Declaration appropriated Haudenosaunee frameworks of democracy, the twenty-seventh grievance also assailed Indigenous peoples. The racist and imperialist language of "savages of our frontier" was a mischaracterization of the continued toll colonization took on Indigenous people and the financial impact the continued war campaigns and expressed genocide had on the British colonies turned fledgling states (Ostler, 2020).

Coded: *White has the rights of violence.*

FIGURE 5   THE ARTICLES OF CONFEDERATION (1777-1787)

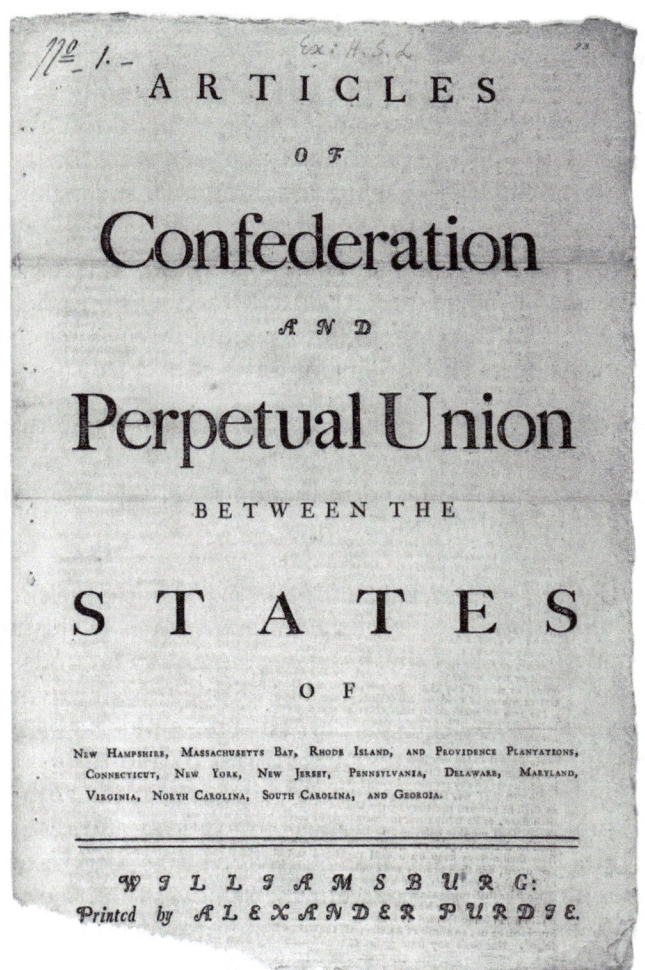

SOURCE: Retrieved from the Library of Congress.

Throughout the American Revolution and the years to follow, the newly birthed United States of America were guided by the framing documents known as the Articles of Confederation (Continental Congress, 1777).

> The United States, in congress assembled, shall have authority to appoint a committee, to sit in the recess of congress, to be denominated, "A Committee of the States," and to consist of one delegate from each State; and to appoint such other committees and civil officers as may be necessary for managing the general affairs of the united states under their direction - to appoint one of their number to preside; provided that no person be allowed to serve in the office of president more than one year in any term of three years;

to ascertain the necessary sums of money to be raised for the service of the united states, and to appropriate and apply the same for defraying the public expenses; to borrow money or emit bills on the credit of the united states, transmitting every half year to the respective states an account of the sums of money so borrowed or emitted, - to build and equip a navy - to agree upon the number of land forces, and to make requisitions from each state for its quota, in proportion to the number of white inhabitants in such state.

White as a race, an inherited biological condition, was assigned the full privileges of citizenship in the new country. Race was encoded in the foundational document, and the United States would be the first country to designate its composition, its citizens, around the concept of race.

The Articles made brief notes on slavery as well. As noted in British common law, especially in the case of *Butt v Penny,* which had been influential for nearly one hundred years, enslaved individuals were designated as goods or property. Article IV noted the following:

> Article IV. The better to secure and perpetuate mutual friendship and intercourse among the people of the different states in this union, the free inhabitants of each of these states, paupers, vagabonds and fugitives from Justice excepted, shall be entitled to all privileges and immunities of free citizens in the several states; and the people of each state shall have free ingress and regress to and from any other state, and shall enjoy therein all the privileges of trade and commerce, subject to the same duties, impositions and restrictions as the inhabitants thereof respectively, provided that such restrictions shall not extend so far as to prevent the removal of property imported into any state, to any other State of which the Owner is an inhabitant; provided also that no imposition, duties or restriction shall be laid by any state, on the property of the united states, or either of them.

The mention of property and securing its subsequent removal were in all likelihood referring to enslaved people escaping to northern states where those states were increasingly ending slavery practices both during and immediately following the war (Anastaplo, 1989). Fugitive slaves laws extended the reach of slavery beyond the lines of just slave holding states. Concepts like safety, security, and freedom for the enslaved would not be possible as slavery would have no borders. In the foundational documents of the United States slavery would be enshrined.

As the Articles did not give Congress the power to tax and attempts to amend the Articles to include taxation failed, the Articles were abandoned with the drafting of the US Constitution.

Coded: *The United States citizens are white.*

Coded: *Political power is white.*

Coded: *Slavery is national.*

CHAPTER 1 DISCUSSION QUESTIONS

- How did the early labeling of people based on geographical origin ("Negro" from Negroland) shape their legal and social status in the British colonies? How does this relate to the concept of identity and legal rights today?

- Analyze the significance of laws such as the Virginia Slave Code of 1680 and Maryland's anti-miscegenation laws of 1681. How did these laws codify racial distinctions and perpetuate inequality in the colonies?

- How did the early colonial practices in Virginia, Maryland, and Massachusetts set a precedent for the legal and social treatment of Indigenous people and people of African descent throughout the American colonies and later the United States? What are the lasting effects of these practices today?

- Compare and contrast the Virginia Slave Code (1705) with similar laws in other colonies like Maryland (1715), Pennsylvania (1725), South Carolina (1740), and Georgia (1755). What mechanisms were used to maintain these hierarchies, and what were their intended effects on enslaved people and free communities of color?

- How did the Declaration of Independence define and address issues of liberty and equality? Where did the Declaration fall short, particularly regarding enslaved individuals and Indigenous peoples?

- How did the educational and legal frameworks established during colonial times continue to influence social structures and systems of race and racism in America?

- In what ways did the ideals of liberty and freedom promoted during the American Revolution contradict the reality of slavery and racial oppression in the newly formed United States? How did these contradictions shape the nation's early development?

CHAPTER 2

....

EARLY UNITED STATES

Launching a New Country

THE CONSTITUTION OF THE UNITED STATES (1787)

As the new United States of America faced continued international pressures, financial strain, and discord, delegates from the thirteen states convened in Philadelphia to revise and create a new frame of government in 1787.

The product, a document seen by many as the model for modern democracy and an instrument to "secure the Blessings of Liberty," became a vehicle to enshrine the institution of slavery. Addressing the impasse between slaveholding and free states regarding both taxation and government structure, the three-fifths clause was established. The three-fifths clause counted each enslaved person as "three-fifths a person"; the ratio itself developed from the amount of taxable wealth an enslaved person produced in comparison to a free white man. (Perea, 2012). Article I, Section 2 of the Constitution reads as follows:

> Representatives and direct Taxes shall be apportioned among the
> several States which may be included within this Union, according
> to their respective Numbers, which shall be determined by adding
> to the whole Number of free Persons, including those bound to
> Service for a Term of Years, and excluding Indians not taxed, three
> fifths of all other Persons.

The new Constitution would also include a fugitive slave clause. The clause meant each state's enslaved people would remain enslaved and facing capture regardless of their geographic location. Federalizing a component of many colonies' slave codes created a Constitutional protection to slavery, expanding each state's definition of enslaved people of African or Native descent to be an interstate definition (National Archives, n.d.).

No Person held to Service or Labour in one State, under the Laws thereof, escaping into another, shall, in Consequence of any Law or Regulation therein, be discharged from such Service or Labour, but shall be delivered up on Claim of the Party to whom such Service or Labour may be due.

The ability for Congress "to provide for calling forth the Militia to execute the Laws of the Union, suppress Insurrections and repel Invasions," through the lens of the Declaration's Grievances, points to the (slave) militia's being formed to suppress (domestic) insurrections or resistance from the enslaved.

James Madison continued to believe enslaved people were necessary to the economy but acknowledged the underlying humanity that was being denied the last legacy of the Constitution. In the few short years following the drafting of the Bill of Rights, the founding father privately suggested the abolition of slavery and resettlement of enslaved people to Africa. He also proposed the sale of the Louisiana Purchase and other lands to fund the purchase and emancipation of all slaves (Feldman, 2017). This is in contrast to William Whipple, another founding father, wartime hero and signer of the Declaration, who simply freed those he enslaved to reflect the shared ideals of liberty in the new country. On the acts of emancipation, Whipple wrote (Glynn, 2011) the following, regarding enlisting of Blacks as soldiers in the wartime efforts, a part of a future vision for the country where all members would be free:

> "The last accounts from South Carolina were favorable. A recommendation is gone thither for raising some regiments of blacks. This, I suppose, will lay a foundation for the emancipation of those wretches in that country. I hope it will be the means of dispensing the blessings of Freedom to all humanity in America."

Despite evidence that just as the American system of government was being born, systems of slavery did not need to be upheld. Madison's private words highlighted what was the clear and lasting understanding of what race and slavery were in America, sweeping systems that existed in constant tension and somehow upheld, with consideration of the people impacted and effects only an afterthought.

Coded: *Slavery is part of the whole national economy.*

Coded: *Slavery was national.*

THE CENSUS AND NATURALIZATION ACT 1790

The first census categorization of race reflected that social and not biological nature of race. The 1790 census first racial categories were "Slave, Free White Males/Females" and "All other Free Person." This reflection made clear that there was no distinction in how the United States categorized its people. The terms citizenship, biology, and servitude were all intermingled and would continue to change over the years, the clearest illustration of the evolving definition of recoding of race.

The early 1800s saw the addition of "Free Colored Person" to the census, with "Black/Mulatto" not appearing until the mid-1800s, as "White, Black, Mulatto, Black Slave, Mulatto Slave and Indian." Racial categories would continue to expand through the century to include Japanese and Chinese, and Quadroon and Octoroon, those with a one-fourth or one-eighth trace of Black blood. The census categories would rapidly expand in the 1930s but would have few changes throughout the rest of the twentieth century. "African-American" would first appear in the census in the year 2000 (A. Brown, 2020)

FIGURE 6   A LEAF INSERT OF THE KENTUCKY CENSUS OF 1790

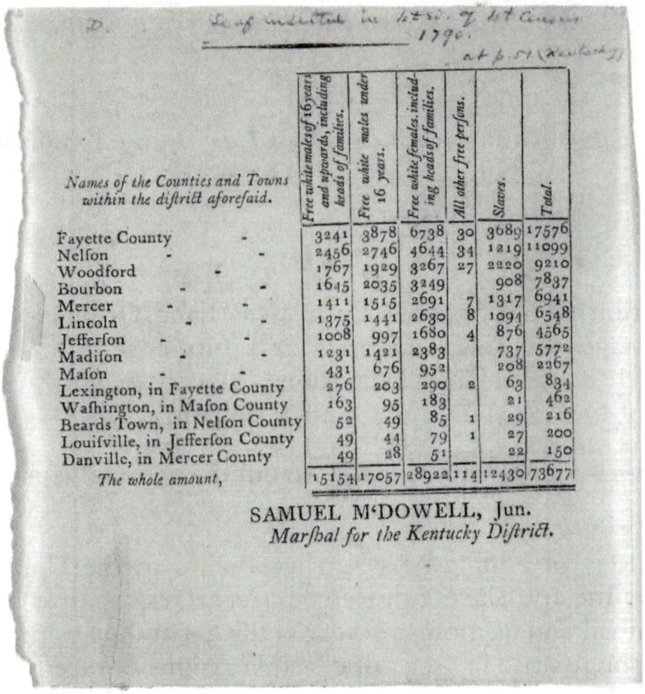

Names of the Counties and Towns within the district aforesaid.	Free white males of 16 years and upwards, including heads of families.	Free white males under 16 years.	Free white females, including heads of families.	All other free persons.	Slaves.	Total.
Fayette County	3241	3878	6738	30	3689	17576
Nelson	2456	2746	4644	34	1219	11099
Woodford	1767	1929	3267	27	2220	9210
Bourbon	1645	2035	3249		908	7837
Mercer	1411	1515	2691	7	1317	6941
Lincoln	1375	1441	2630	8	1094	6548
Jefferson	1008	997	1680	4	876	4565
Madison	1231	1421	2383		737	5772
Mason	431	676	952		208	2267
Lexington, in Fayette County	276	203	290	2	63	834
Washington, in Mason County	163	95	183		21	462
Beards Town, in Nelson County	52	49	85	1	29	216
Louisville, in Jefferson County	49	44	79	1	27	200
Danville, in Mercer County	49	28	51		22	150
The whole amount,	15154	17057	28922	114	12430	73677

SAMUEL M'DOWELL, Jun.
Marshal for the Kentucky District.

SOURCE: U. S. Census 1790. Retrieved from the Library of Congress.

During the late 1700s, the Naturalization Act was passed. The Naturalization Act of 1790 limited citizenship to only "free white persons." The law excluded Indigenous people, enslaved Blacks, and others from accessing citizenship (Lai & Medina, 2023):

> ". . . That any alien, other than an alien enemy, being a free white person, who shall resided within the limits and under the jurisdiction of the United States for the term of two years, may be admitted to become a citizen therefore."

The law marked a significant shift to tying citizenship to ill-defined Western European traits, moving away from laws explicitly based on an individual's country or region of ancestry present in laws nearly a century earlier.

As the century ended, the United States was still in early fragile development, with the encoding and recoding of race as a class of people given full rights of citizenship in the new country or bound to service being the most distinctive measure. The tension between the ideals of American liberties and the realities of American enslavement would grow in the following years.

Coded: *Black people were coded as property, not citizens.*

Coded: *Citizenship is for "white" or European immigrants.*

MISSOURI COMPROMISE (1820)

The new Nation would continue to grow as Land Ordinances would pass setting the stage for new territories and future states. The Northwest Ordinance of 1787 would limit expansion of slavery to Northwest Territories (Ohio, Illinois, Indiana, Wisconsin, and Michigan).

As the territories continued to expand, so did the national tensions regarding slavery.

As conversations of adding Missouri as a state to the Union continued, voices grew in the anti-slavery movement. As attacks against the systems of slavery continued and as more considered the expanding oppressive systems as morally wrong, a rise in "scientific" explanations of race began to spread as well. By 1820, the Missouri Compromise allowed Missouri to join as a slave-holding state, while Maine would join as a free state, continuing a balance between slave and free-holding states (Zeitz, 2000). The Missouri

Compromise of 1820 also banned slavery in the Louisiana Purchase Territory north of 36° 30′ latitude, except for Missouri (United States Congress, n.d.):

> "And be it further enacted, That in all that territory ceded by France to the United States, under the name Louisiana, which lies north of the thirty-six degrees and thirty minutes north latitude, excepting only such part thereof as included within the limits of the State contemplated by this act, slavery and involuntary servitude, otherwise than the punishment of crimes where of the party shall been duly convicted, shall be prohibited: Provided always, That any person escaping into the same, from whom labor or service is lawfully claimed in any State of Territory of the United States, such fugitive may be lawfully reclaimed and conveyed to the person claiming his or her labor or service, as aforementioned."

While the law did create a mechanism to promote freedom in new states, it further embedded and entrenched systems of race and slavery into the future of America, as all new southern states would now become slave-holding states.

Slavery spread across the southern states, while abolitionist and other liberations movements also continued to grow. Many different abolitionist organizations and supports would rise, increasing the volume of literature and resources. The first Convention of People of Color, the New England Anti-Slavery Society, the abolitionist newspaper the Liberator, and more would be creating systems of freedom and liberty, including an informal network that would be known as the Underground Railroad (Thirteen.org, 2018).

In slaveholding states, fear of rebellions rose following Nat Turner's rebellion in 1831, and southern states increasingly attempted to stifle antislavery activities and literature in the years that followed. In 1835, the House of Representatives passed the gag rule, a procedural measure that automatically tabled all antislavery business. In a society of coded race and servitude, no competing federal legislation was able to be introduced in the territories or District of Columbia regarding slavery, fugitive slave practices, African colonization, or abolition. The law would be renewed until it became a standing rule for the House, the Senate passed a similar rule (Hoffer, 2017).

Coded: *Slavery is part of America's future.*

COMMON SCHOOLS—EDUCATION AND EARLY UNITED STATES: PUBLIC EDUCATION PROTOTYPE (1852)

As the nation struggled over the role slavery would play in the still developing country, calls for education reform increased. Not only were there tensions over the future of slavery, the future of the United States was increasingly uncertain as waves of people immigrating from Germany and Ireland came to the "land of opportunity" to find their place only to find stratified social systems, creating strains. (Katz, 1976).

Horace Mann, the secretary of the Massachusetts State Board of Education, became an outspoken advocate, adding his voice to public calls for "free schools" (Reese, 2010). There would be a shift in systems from localized private schools, which were often exclusive and focused on religious education and academics skills, to publicly funded schools which focused on laws and promoting opportunity for everyone (Reese, 2010).

Massachusetts would pass the first compulsory attendance laws in 1852. New York would join Massachusetts in 1853, and the District of Columbia (1863) and Vermont (1867) would follow (Katz, 1976). Massachusetts law, which required students to attend twelve weeks a year (six weeks consecutively), was ineffective since no enforcement mechanism existed. As the nation grew and more states and territories adopted compulsory attendance laws (27 by 1890), they were ineffective regardless of the number of days students attended or the frequency they were present. There was no clear administrative mechanism to enforce attendance in any of the laws, a common census to track students (Katz, 1976), and limited tax support (Reese, 2010).

These schools would be the early foundation on which public education would continue to grow and develop. As the schools were being formed to be a unifying force in communities, the Nation would be divided across racial lines as the Supreme Court decided one of the most landmark cases in the nation's history.

DRED SCOTT VS. SANFORD (1857)

In 1853, an enslaved man, Dred Scott, filed a suit for his freedom and that of his family against John Sanford, a man who had inherited the Scotts a few years earlier. The case wound its way through various Missouri state courts and then the Federal courts before concluding with a ruling from the United States Supreme Court in 1857.

SOURCE: Fitzgibbon, J. H., photographer. (1857). Retrieved from the Library of Congress.

The Court (*Dred Scott v. Sandford,* 1857) posed a question for all those of African descent in the case, exploring the relationship of ancestry, citizenship, rights, and protection.

> Can a negro, whose ancestors were imported into this country, and sold as slaves, become a member of the political community formed and brought into existence by the Constitution of the United States,

and as such become entitled to all the rights, and privileges, and immunities, guarantied by that instrument to the citizen? One of which rights is the privilege of suing in a court of the United States in the cases specified in the Constitution.

The case was initially argued in April 1856 and the following December the case was reargued. The Supreme Court ruling would arrive in March 1857, seven to two against Scott. The ruling struck down the Missouri Compromise finding it to be unconstitutional as Congress did not have the authority to limit the expansion of slavery. Additionally, the federal government could not free those enslaved, with the court ruling that this violated the Fifth Amendment's due process clause, which stated that planters and slaveholders were required to have due process for the removal of their "property" (the people whom they enslaved) (Jackson, 2011). The ruling also set clear a priority of the humanity of people would be overshadowed by the perceived value and perpetuation of of the system.

The ruling also established that in the United States, those of African descent were not citizens and lacked citizens' rights. The ruling also clearly established a caste, an explicitly race-based hierarchy. The early use of the word "race" in a major US ruling was notable, specifically used to point to the dominant culture of white citizens. Justice Roger B Taney delivered the opinion:

> The words "people of the United States" and "citizens" are synonymous terms, and mean the same thing. They both describe the political body who, according to our republican institutions, form the sovereignty, and who hold the power and conduct the Government through their representatives. They are what we familiarly call the "sovereign people," and every citizen is one of this people, and a constituent member of this sovereignty. The question before us is, whether the class of persons described in the plea in abatement compose a portion of this people, and are constituent members of this sovereignty? We think they are not, and that they are not included, and were not intended to be included, under the word "citizens" in the Constitution, and can therefore claim none of the rights and privileges which that instrument provides for and secures to citizens of the United States. On the contrary, they were at that time considered as a subordinate and inferior class of beings, who had been subjugated by the dominant race, and, whether emancipated or not, yet remained subject to their authority, and had no rights or privileges but such as those who held the power and the Government might choose to grant them.

The ruling would create a national code of race, no longer dependent on state or local definitions, practices, or servitude status. Whiteness would equate into citizenship, while Blackness would be equated to "subordinate, inferior and subjugated," and without rights.

> **Coded:** *Whiteness is citizenship.*

> **Coded:** *White is dominant.*

> **Coded:** *Dominance as race is inherited.*

> **Coded:** *Black is subjugated.*

> **Coded:** *Black is subordinate or inferior.*

> **Coded:** *Racist systems will be prioritized over human conditions.*

THE AMERICAN CIVIL WAR (1861–1865)

The passing of the Kansas-Nebraska Act of 1854 contributed to the national strain between pro-slavery and anti-slavery movements. The Act allowed for voting white citizens of the territories to decide whether they would enter as free or slaveholding states. The Act nullified the Missouri Compromise and paved the way for the expansion of slavery. A precursor to wartime tensions, violent and bloody conflicts rose in Kansas, and a single-term congressman, Abraham Lincoln, rose to be president of the Union (Rawley, 1979).

Lincoln was from the newly formed Republican Party, an anti-slavery party that emerged in the aftermath of the Kansas-Nebraska Act. Both from party affiliation and his public stance during the Lincoln-Douglas debates, many slave-holding states were likely spurred by the election of Lincoln. South Carolina voted to secede from the Union in December 1860. Notably, South Carolina did not let its citizens vote for the president in the election prior to secession, nor did it hold a popular vote about secession (Loewen, 2011). The state then published the *Declaration of the Immediate Causes Which Induce and Justify the Secession of South Carolina from the Federal Union* (South Carolina Convention, 1860):

> The people of the State of South Carolina, in Convention
> assembled, on the 26th day of April, A.D., 1852, declared that the

frequent violations of the Constitution of the United States, by the Federal Government, and its encroachments upon the reserved rights of the States, fully justified this State in then withdrawing from the Federal Union; but in deference to the opinions and wishes of the other slaveholding States, she forbore at that time to exercise this right.

The South Carolina declaration was followed by similar declarations by Georgia, Texas, and Mississippi. Many other Southern states joined in passing Secession Ordinances (1861). Virginia, Texas, and Alabama specifically noted slaveholding in the decrees of secession (Digital History, 2021).

And as it is the desire and purpose of the people of Alabama to meet the slaveholding States of the South, who may approve such purpose, in order to frame a provisional as well as permanent Government upon the principles of the Constitution of the United States.

Whereas, the recent developments in Federal affairs make it evident that the power of the Federal Government is sought to be made a weapon with which to strike down the interests and property of the people of Texas, and her sister slave-holding States,

The people of Virginia in their ratification of the Constitution of the United States of America, adopted by them in convention on the twenty-fifth day of June, in the year of our Lord one thousand seven hundred and eighty-eight, having declared that the powers granted under said Constitution were derived from the people of the United States and might be resumed whensoever the same should be perverted to their injury and oppression, and the Federal Government having perverted said powers not only to the injury of the people of Virginia, but to the oppression of the Southern slave-holding States:

In April 1861, Confederate forces would fire on Fort Sumter and the United States would erupt into Civil War. Wartime efforts would include the passage of the Confiscation Acts (1861 & 1862), which allowed for the seizure of rebel "property" (enslaved people) and supported that any enslaved person who escaped the confederacy would be free (United States Senate, 2023). During the debates, Lincoln made clear his support of a racial hierarchy and in published articles stated his goal for Emancipation was primarily to maintain the Union; moral or other justification of liberation of enslaved people was not noted (Kendi, 2017). The Preliminary Emancipation Proclamation (Lincoln, 1862) and then the formal Proclamation 1863 was helpful in bolstering the Union's wartime efforts, freeing enslaved people in any state. The Proclamation did free people in occupied slave-holding states, but many others remained enslaved in border states and other exempted areas (Kendi, 2017). The Proclamation did assist people to free themselves and seek refuge in the north or with Union armies.

As the war came to an end in 1865 with the final land and sea battles, the passage of the Thirteenth Amendment, ending slavery, was seen as a conclusion to a wartime goal, a goal only realized while fighting for maintaining the Union (National Archives, 2022).

> Section 1: Neither slavery nor involuntary servitude, except as a punishment for crime whereof the party shall have been duly convicted, shall exist within the United States, or any place subject to their jurisdiction.

> Section 2: Congress shall have power to enforce this article by appropriate legislation.

The conditions of forced servitude would be *mostly* repealed; but the Amendment did not remove any of the other coded benefits and restrictions that had been written in by the colonies, states, and or nationally for people black and white. Slavery would continue as an extension of the state's legal systems. The legacy of slavery, and the continuation of the other systems of oppression would be evident in the new name for the formerly enslaved, "freedmen." Rather than returning to the universal application of the older names like Negro, or better yet simply citizens, the formerly enslaved would continue to be tied to the old systems as the United States looked for new beginnings.

Coded: *Black is freedmen, formerly enslaved.*

RECONSTRUCTION AND THE FREEDMEN BUREAU (1865)

At the end of the Civil War, and prior to the Thirteenth Amendment, Congress established the Bureau for the Relief of Refugees, Freedmen and Abandoned Lands in March 1865 to assist the recently freed enslaved people in establishing housing, hospitals, labor, and other legal assistance. An Act to establish a Bureau for the Relief of Freedmen and Refugees (1865) noted the following (United States Congress, 1865):

> Be it enacted by the Senate and House of Representatives of the United States of America *in Congress assembled*, That there is hereby established in the War Department, to continue during the present war of rebellion, and for one year thereafter, a bureau of refugees, freedmen, and abandoned lands, to which shall be committed, as hereinafter provided, the supervision and management of all abandoned lands, and the control of all subjects relating to refugees and freedmen from rebel states, or from any district of country within the territory embraced in the operations of the army, under such rules and regulations as may be prescribed by the head of the bureau and approved by the President. The said bureau shall be under the management and control of a commissioner to be appointed by the President, by and with the advice and consent of the Senate.

The Freedmen's Bureau, as it came to be known, served as a major foundation for not only Black education, but public education as well through the establishment of Freedmen's Schools (Claybaugh, 2010). As noted, schools for Negro education had been established well before the Civil War and Reconstruction; the Freedmen's School marked a concerted effort to build public education on a systemic basis. The schools were built and maintained through a system of established and growing engagement from Black communities, federal contributions, charity and local taxes.

Freedmen's schools were structured in a variety of models from traditional models to evening and "Sabbath schools" (Stowe, 1879). There was public

FIGURE 9 AN ACT TO ESTABLISH A BUREAU FOR THE RELIEF OF FREEDMEN AND REFUGEES

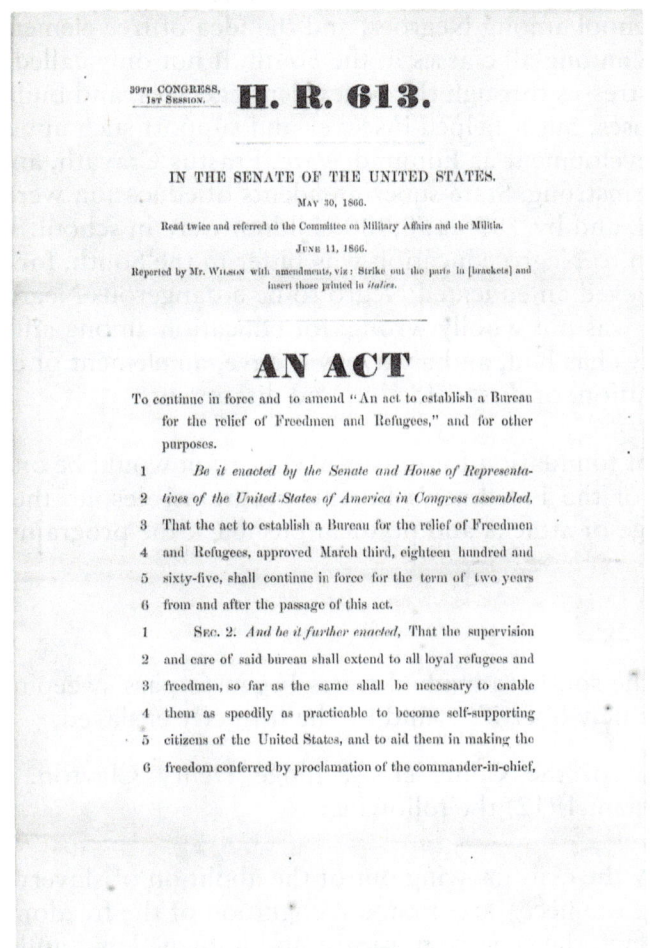

SOURCE: Records of the U.S. Senate, June 11, 1866, RG 46.

resistance from poor whites and former planters with indifference and opposition noted toward public education at that time (Anderson, 1988). Despite public resistance from many southern whites for any public education initiatives, by 1865 fourteen states would start 575 schools, employing nearly 1,200 teachers for nearly 72,000 students in attendance, Black and white (Anderson, 1988).

The schools would serve as models for future education institutions in their structure, funding, and delivery. University education shifted from a lofty dream to an evolving realized universal right.

Du Bois (1901) noted the following:

> The greatest success of the Freedmen's Bureau lay in the planting of the free school among Negroes, and the idea of free elementary education among all classes in the South. It not only called the schoolmistresses through the benevolent agencies, and built them schoolhouses, but it helped discover and support such apostles of human development as Edmund Ware, Erastus Cravath, and Samuel Armstrong. State superintendents of education were appointed, and by 1870 150,000 children were in school. The opposition to Negro education was bitter in the South, for the South believed an educated Negro to be a dangerous Negro. And the South was not wholly wrong; for education among all kinds of men always has had, and always will have, an element of danger and revolution, of dissatisfaction and discontent.

The significant foundation for universal education would be one of the most lasting parts of the Freedmen's Bureau programs, despite the uncertainty, regular barrage of attacks and political pushback the programs received.

BLACK CODES

Throughout the south, individual states began to pass sweeping legislation, restricting the new liberties found by the formerly enslaved.

Major-General of the Confederacy, Judge Henry Clayton, summarized, noted (Goodman, 1912) the following:

> To remedy the evils growing out of the abolition of slavery it seems two things are necessary: first, a recognition of the freedom of the race as a fact, the enactment of just and humane laws, and the willing enforcement of them; secondly, by treating them with perfect fairness and justice in our contracts, and in every way in which we may he brought in contact with them. By the first we convince the world of our good faith, and get rid of the system of espionage (Freedmen's Bureau), by removing the pretext for its necessity; and by the second, we secure the services of the negroes, teach them their places and how to keep them, and convince them at least that we are their best friends . . . we need the labor of the negro all over the country, and it is worth the effort to secure it. Besides all this . . . do we owe the negro any grudge? .That has he himself done to provoke our hostility? Shall we be angry with him because his freedom has been forced upon him? . . . He may have been the companion of your boyhood . . . you may be bound to him by a thousand ties which only a southern man knows, and which he alone can feel in all its force. It may be that when, only a

few years ago . . . you went to meet the invaders of your country, you committed to his care your home and your loved ones; and when you were far away upon the weary march . . . many and many a time you thought of that faithful old negro, and your heart warmed toward him.

The southern approach as summarized captures a few distinct sentiments. First, it showed that the recently emancipated Black were perceived either with animosity or as an inconvenience due to no longer being enslaved. Second, there was clear resentment toward Union forces and the continued ripple effect of the Civil War. Finally, public sentiment leaned toward creating the perception of peace and civility while returning to re-utilizing Black labor and removing the Union presence.

Mississippi's state legislature (Black Codes of Mississippi, 1865) passed their Black Codes shortly after the establishment of the Freedmen's Bureau and prior to the ratification of the Thirteenth Amendment. These codes were modeled on the previous slave codes, recoding the earlier systems. Blacks were permitted to be sued and sue, hold property, although there were limitations on the ability to actually rent and lease land. People of color were permitted to marry, but they were not allowed to marry a white person.

Freed young Black youth who were orphaned were remanded into the courts for apprenticeships, with preference given to their former masters for placement. If the child ran away from "the master," the planter was permitted to both pursue the child and have a justice of the peace remand the child into forced servitude.

For free Blacks, unemployment or employment without a state issued work license in Mississippi would have them identified as "vagrants," a crime that would result in fines and imprisonment, which would also result in permissible forced servitude under the Thirteenth Amendment. Notably, the inability to pay fines would also result in imprisonment. The decision of the court was sweeping, and trial by jury in Mississippi was not an option for Blacks.

A list of broad and expansive "crimes" would also be punishable by fines and imprisonment, including these examples: "insulting gestures, exercising the function of a minister of the gospel without a license from a regularly organized church, or any other misdemeanor."

South Carolina enacted similar laws to Mississippi in December 1865. Language detailing the responsibilities of house servants to be available twenty-four hours a day for all seven days of the week was added to the South Carolina laws. Blacks were banned from owning firearms by the ordinances. Marriage was only to be recognized between people of color, and children could be remanded by the courts into servitude contracts. Children were required to receive education in servitude at least six weeks a year, as long as the school was a convenient distance (Goodman, 1912).

Vagrancy laws also could lead to imprisonment and forced servitude. In addition to unemployment, unlicensed musical or theatrical performances, and people who lived "idle or disorderly lives" could be ensnared by the law. Simply being unemployed or in poverty was enough to classify freedmen and their families as vagrants under these laws. And even if people found work, they often faced low wages and coercive labor agreements, which could lead to vagrancy entrapment.

Louisiana passed a final version of its Black Codes in December 1865. Blacks were not allowed to preach or hold congregations. Every (white) citizen was to "act as a police officer for the detection of offenses and the apprehension of offenders." The increased surveillance and policing contributed to the rise of threats, violence, lynching, and other forms of domestic terror during the era. Blacks were not allowed out in the town after 10 p.m. and were banned from living within the limits of towns unless they were servants. Blacks were also prohibited from doing commerce within towns' limits. The Louisiana Codes made more explicit the practice of sharecropping (Police Regulations of Saint Landry Parish, 1865).

> Be it further ordained, That every negro is require to be in the regular service of some white person, or former owner, who shall be held responsible for the conduct of said negro.

The agricultural labor contracts were not like typical labor contracts, and the forced servitude of the antebellum slave system gave way to the coercive sharecropping system. The contracts signed included family members, particularly children. Steep fines would be added for "disobedience" (swearing or impudence) and for "absences from the home." Wages were skewed with half the wages agreed to be paid in regular intervals, while the other half could be held until the end of the contract (or not paid at all due to illness, abandonment or "idleness"). Should a worker refuse to work for more than three days, the offender was to be reported to the justice of the peace and was to be forced to labor on the roads, levees or other public works without remuneration until he should consent to return to the service of his employer. Those contracted were forced to work nine hours a day in the winter and ten hours a day in the summer (Goodman, 1912).

Other states including Alabama, Georgia, Florida, and Virginia would also have apprenticeship and vagrancy laws (Goodman, 1912). As noted by Army Command General Alfred H. Terry in Virginia at the time, the wages received by the formerly enslaved were "wages utterly inadequate to the support of themselves and families," with poverty criminalized with punishments like imprisonment and forced servitude (Tarter, 2020). General Terry summarized the following:

> "The ultimate effect being a practical re-establishment of slavery, if not a worse condition of servitude than that from which the slaves

had been emancipated. The ultimate effect being a practical re-establishment of slavery, if not a worse condition of servitude than that from which the slaves had been emancipated."

In the aftermath of the passage of the Civil Rights Act of 1866 and the Fourteenth and Fifteenth Amendments, Black Codes were made unconstitutional. The codes were simply maintained or, following the end of Reconstruction, renewed or reintroduced on what would become known as the Jim Crow laws.

Coded: *Black are laborers.*

Coded: *Black servant to whites.*

Coded: *White to surveil and police.*

Coded: *Blacks unable to have religion.*

Coded: *Black service before black health.*

CIVIL RIGHTS ACT (1866)

The Civil Rights Act of 1866 provided a foundation to ensure equal protections for Blacks throughout the south and nationally. The Freedmen's Bureau was intended to create a pathway to help the formerly enslaved become active citizens. States were passing laws restricting rights of freedmen, and questions arose over whether Congress had the right to protect and enforce the life, liberty and property of the freedmen (Hackney, 1969). The Civil Rights Act (1866) attempted to ensure equal rights and protections to all its citizens and charged the government in the funding and enforcement of these efforts (United States Congress, 1866).

Be it enacted by the Senate and House of Representatives of the United States of America in Congress assembled, That all persons born in the United States and not subject to any foreign power, excluding Indians not taxed, are hereby declared to be citizens of the United States; and such citizens, of every race and color, without regard to any previous condition of slavery or involuntary servitude, except as a punishment for crime whereof the party shall have been duly convicted, shall have the same right, in every State and Territory in the United States, to make and enforce contracts, to sue, be parties, and give evidence, to inherit, purchase, lease, sell, hold, and convey real and personal property, and to full and equal benefit of all laws and proceedings for the security of person and property, as is enjoyed by white citizens, and shall be subject to like punishment, pains, and penalties, and to none other, any law, statute, ordinance, regulation, or custom, to the contrary notwithstanding.

Although initially vetoed by President Andrew Johnson, the vice president who succeeded President Lincoln following his assassination, the Civil Rights Act was passed with a two-thirds override.

The law protected basic civil rights including the ability to engage in commerce, make and enforce contracts, and gain and sell personal property. Other "political rights" were not protected.

The Civil Rights Act of 1866 was intended to establish citizenship for "all persons born in the United States" and define rights of citizenship. Finally, there was a goal to make denial of rights based on race illegal. Iowa Representative Wilson (United States House of Representatives, 1866), citing Kant, summarized the intent when he introduced the bill to the House:

> It provides for the equality of citizens of the United States in the enjoyment of "civil rights and immunities." What do these terms mean? Do they mean that in all things civil, social, political, all citizens, without distinction of race or color, shall be equal? By no means can they be so construed. Do they mean that all citizens shall vote in the several States? No; for suffrage is a political right which has been left under the control of the several States, subject to the action of Congress only when it becomes necessary to enforce the guarantee of a republican form of government. Nor do they mean that all citizens shall sit on the juries, or that their children shall attend the same schools. These are not civil rights and immunities. Well what are the meanings? What are civil rights? I see civil rights to be the absolute rights of individuals, such as-

Citing the words of Kant from Kant's Commentaries, Wilson (United States House of Representatives, 1866) continued with the following definition of civil rights for citizens according to the House Debates:

> "The right to personal security, the rights to liberty and the rights to acquire and enjoy property. Rights itself, in a civil society, is that which any man is entitled to have or to do, or required from others, within the limits of the prescribed law."

To use the language of Attorney General Bates, in the opinion already cited, Wilson (United States House of Representatives, 1866) also described the following: "the word rights is generic, common, embracing whatever may be lawfully claimed."

In his speech, Wilson (United States House of Representatives, 1866) also clarified his understanding of civil rights as natural rights that are distinct from the operations of government:

> The definition given to the term "civil rights" in *Bouvier's Law Dictionary* is very concise and is supported by the best authority. It is the following:

> Civil rights are those which have no relation to the establishment, support, or management of government.

> From this, it is easy to gather an understanding that civil rights are the natural rights of man; and those are the rights which this bill proposes to protect every citizen in the enjoyment of the Republic.

The bill would protect many civil rights but would selectively exclude important civic rights such as education, voting, and jury representation.

Coded: *Black have some civil rights.*

Coded: *Black as secondary citizens.*

FOURTEENTH AMENDMENT (1868)

Although the bill was passed and did protect civil rights of individuals, there was concern the Thirteenth Amendment was not sufficient in protecting and providing appropriate authority for the law. To protect from a potential future Congressional repeal or Supreme Court action, the protections would be embedded in a Fourteenth Amendment to the Constitution, among other rights (Newman & Gass, 2004). As violence increased, including that of the Ku Klux Klan, creating domestic terror, threatening Freedmen Bureau administration and election proceedings, Congress instituted "military Reconstruction." In order to be readmitted into the Union, former Confederate states would need to allow Blacks to vote and ratify the Fourteenth Amendment (Newman & Gass, 2004) The civil rights of citizens would be described as "privileges or immunities," as the Fourteenth Amendment would be ratified in July of 1868 (National Archives, 2024b).

> "All persons born or naturalized in the United States, and subject to the jurisdiction thereof, are citizens of the United States and of

the State wherein they reside. No State shall make or enforce any law which shall abridge the privileges or immunities of citizens of the United States; nor shall any State deprive any person of life, liberty, or property, without due process of law; nor deny to any person within its jurisdiction the equal protection of the laws."

Although the Fourteenth Amendment did grant the ability to enforce the protection of civil rights for all its citizens, including freedmen, through legislation, like the Civil Rights Act of 1866, the political rights of Blacks were left unaddressed and unsecured.

FIFTEENTH AMENDMENT (1870)

The glaring absence of the right to vote continued to grow, along with other suffrage movements. As abolitionist Douglas (1892) noted, the right to vote was "the one great power by which all civil rights are obtained, enjoyed, and maintained."

In February 1869, Congress passed the compromised proposal with the final necessary states ratifying the Fifteenth Amendment nearly a year later in February 1870 (National Archives, 2024a).

Article XV.

Section 1. The right of citizens of the United States to vote shall not be denied or abridged by the United States or by any State on account of race, color, or previous condition of servitude—

Section 2. The Congress shall have the power to enforce this article by appropriate legislation.

While the right to vote was a meaningful gain for Black men, all women were notably absent from the newly enshrined right. Additionally, there were many political rights not addressed in any of the civil rights acts and Amendments.

CIVIL RIGHTS CASES OF (1883)

The legal and political tensions through Reconstruction, Black Codes, and the Civil Rights Act of 1866 culminated in a series of five legal cases being heard by the Supreme Court in 1880 with a final ruling in 1883. Four of the cases were criminal cases focused on the denial of Blacks to enter theaters or hotels; the fifth was a civil case regarding the refusal to admit Mrs. Sallie Robertson to the "Ladies Car" of a train as she was a woman "of African descent." First argued in March 1883, the court issued a ruling the following October (Lado, 1995).

In an eight-to-one ruling, the court ruled that the Fourteenth Amendment only applied to "state action" and not to "public accommodations" which were privately owned (restaurant, hotels, theaters, etc). Writing for the majority, Justice Bradley (National Constitution Center, n.d.) wrote the following:

> The first section of the Fourteenth Amendment,—which is the one relied on,—after declaring who shall be citizens of the United States, and of the several States, is prohibitory in its character, and prohibitory upon the States. It declares that: "no State shall make or enforce any law which shall abridge the privileges or immunities of citizens of the United States; nor shall any State deprive any person of life, liberty, or property without due process of law; nor deny to any person within its jurisdiction the equal protection of the laws.

> It is State action of a particular character that is prohibited. Individual invasion of individual rights is not the subject-matter of the amendment. It has a deeper and broader scope. It nullifies and makes void all State legislation, and State action of every kind, which impairs the privileges and immunities of citizens of the United States, or which injures them in life, liberty, or property without due process of law, or which denies to any of them the equal protection of the laws. . . .

> It does not invest Congress with power to legislate upon subjects which are within the domain of State legislation; but to provide modes of relief against State legislation, or State action, of the kind referred to. . . .

> . . . When a man has emerged from slavery, and by the aid of beneficent legislation has shaken off the inseparable concomitants of that state, there must be some stage in the progress of his elevation when he takes the rank of a mere citizen, and ceases to be the special favorite of the laws, and when his rights as a citizen, or a man, are to be protected in the ordinary modes by which other men's rights are protected."

Writing the lone dissent, Justice Harlan (National Constitution Center, n.d.) again highlighted that slavery was not merely about servitude but a series of codes and laws directed at Black people and "other races" and that public spaces, invested or supported by public moneys, would be accessible to all citizens.

> The terms of the Thirteenth Amendment are absolute and universal. . . . [T]he Thirteenth Amendment may be exerted by legislation of a direct and primary character, for the eradication, not simply of the institution, but of its badges and incidents, are propositions which

ought to be deemed indisputable. . . . [T]heir freedom necessarily involved immunity from, and protection against, all discrimination against them, because of their race, in respect of such civil rights as belong to freemen of other races. . . . It remains now to inquire what are the legal rights of colored persons in respect of the accommodations, privileges, and facilities of public conveyances, inns, and places of public amusement. . . .

[R]ailroads are public highways, established, by authority of the State, for the public use; that they are none the less public highways because controlled and owned by private corporations. . . . [T]he right of a colored person to use an improved public highway, upon the terms accorded to freemen of other races, is as fundamental in the state of freedom, established in this country. . . . [W]hat value is [the] right of locomotion, if it may be clogged by such burdens as Congress intended by the act of 1875 to remove? They are burdens which lay at the very foundation of the institution of slavery as it once existed. . . .

The court had ignored the restrictive structures of the cases presented state laws and claimed that the "beneficent legislation" of the Thirteenth, Fourteenth, and Fifteenth amendments were sufficient to both shake off and undo slavery. The court stated plainly (and erroneously) in their ruling that any further legal protections for the formerly enslaved made them a "special favorite" under the law. Following the ruling, Alabama, Arkansas, Florida, Georgia, Kentucky, Louisiana, Mississippi, and Texas all passed new state laws of separation or segregation in public spaces for Black and whites in the years to follow (1887–1891) (Weaver, 1969). The Civil Rights cases would shift Black Code to "Jim Crow." The ruling also laid the foundation for *Plessy v. Ferguson* in the years that followed.

Coded: *Black people are secondary citizens in states.*

Coded: *Whites have full access to public accommodations.*

Coded: *Black accessibility is secondary to white comfort.*

PLESSY V. FERGUSON (1896)

Following the Civil War and through reconstruction there was noted Black progress. Over two hundred towns and communities would be established for Black Americans during this time (D. L. Brown, 2015). Sixteen Black politicians would serve in the US Congress, along with approximately 1,500 other Blacks elected to state positions (Foner, 1996). There would be a rise in skilled employment and, as noted before, a rise in schools for Black youth, as well.

FIGURE 10 THE FIRST COLORED SENATOR AND REPRESENTATIVES – IN THE FORTY-FIRST AND FORTY-SECOND CONGRESS OF THE UNITED STATES

SOURCE: Currier & Ives. (1872). Retrieved from the Library of Congress.

The rise of domestic terror, violence and lynching, Black Codes and Jim Crow laws, and the Civil Rights Cases of 1883 slowed and stymied much of the pronounced progress of Black Americans following the end of the Civil War. *Plessy v. Ferguson* (1896) would have profound impact institutionalizing separation (segregation), solidifying the legal framework for racial segregation in the US.

Following his arrest for sitting in the "whites-only" car of a segregated train and violating the recently passed Separate Car Act (1890) of Louisiana, Homer Plessy was arrested.

> Section 1. Be it enacted by the General Assembly of the State of Louisiana, That all railway companies carrying passengers in their coaches in this State, shall provide equal but separate accommodations for the white and colored races. . . . No person

or persons shall be permitted to occupy seats in coaches other than the ones assigned to them on account of the race they belong to.

Plessy's lawyers argued that Louisiana Judge John Ferguson should have dismissed the charges as unconstitutional, as the law was in violation of the Fourteenth Amendment. The Louisiana Supreme Court upheld Judge Ferguson's original ruling, and Plessy appealed all the way to the Supreme Court. The Supreme Court in a seven-to-one ruling upheld the ruling and established the "separate but equal doctrine." Justice Henry Billings Brown wrote for the majority:

> "The object of the [Fourteenth] amendment was undoubtedly to enforce the absolute equality of the two races before the law, but, in the nature of things, it could not have been intended to abolish distinctions based upon color, or to enforce social, as distinguished from political, equality, or a commingling of the two races upon terms unsatisfactory to either. Laws permitting, and even requiring, their separation in places where they are liable to be brought into contact do not necessarily imply the inferiority of either race to the other, and have been generally, if not universally, recognized as within the competency of the state legislatures in the exercise of their police power. The most common instance of this is connected with the establishment of separate schools for white and colored children, which have been held to be a valid exercise of the legislative power even by courts of States where the political rights of the colored race have been longest and most earnestly enforced. . . ."

> ". . . We think the enforced separation of the races, as applied to the internal commerce of the state, neither abridges the privileges or immunities of the colored man, deprives him of his property without due process of law, nor denies him the equal protection of the laws, within the meaning of the Fourteenth Amendment."

The majority opinion wrote that commingling was unnatural and required states to police at those times races are "brought into contact with each other." Education separation was both the example and rationale for the "separate but equal" doctrine. Separation by race was asserted as a right of states, and the states had the authority to empower others to enforce the separation (conductors). The case did not truly address a question of the filing—whether the government had the authority to legally recognize race as a category. Nor did the case identify what individuals or traits the state was recognizing when it recognized race.

FIGURE 11 EAST LOUISIANA RAILROAD COMPANY

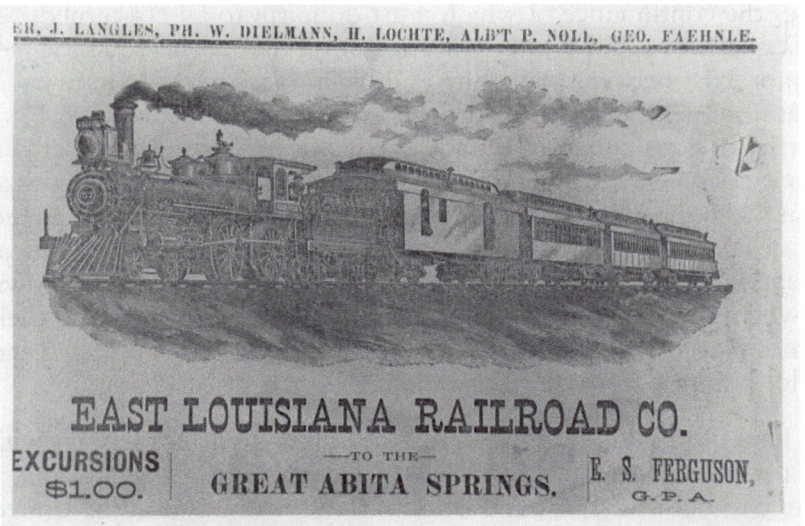

ER, J. LANGLES, PH. W. DIELMANS, H. LOCHTE, ALB'T P. NOLL, GEO. FAEHNLE.

EAST LOUISIANA RAILROAD CO.

EXCURSIONS $1.00. | —TO THE— GREAT ABITA SPRINGS. | E. S. FERGUSON, G. P. A.

SOURCE: Retrieved from the Historic New Orleans Collection.

Writing the lone dissent, Justice John Marshall Harlan, the Justice from a slave-holding family in Kentucky (Inskeep, 2021), noted:

> "In respect of civil rights common to all citizens, the Constitution of the United States does not, I think, permit any public authority to know the race of those entitled to be protected in the enjoyment of such rights. Every true man has pride of race, and, under appropriate circumstances, when the rights of others, his equals before the law, are not to be affected, it is his privilege to express such pride and to take such action based upon it as to him seems proper. But I deny that any legislative body or judicial tribunal may have regard to the race of citizens when the civil rights of those citizens are involved. Indeed, such legislation as that here in question is inconsistent not only with that equality of rights which pertains to citizenship, National and State, but with the personal liberty enjoyed by everyone within the United States.
>
> . . . The sure guarantee of the peace and security of each race is the clear, distinct, unconditional recognition by our governments, National and State, of every right that inheres in civil freedom, and of the equality before the law of all citizens of the United States, without regard to race. State enactments regulating the enjoyment of civil rights upon the basis of race, and cunningly devised to defeat legitimate results of the war under the pretence of

recognizing equality of rights, can have no other result than to render permanent peace impossible and to keep alive a conflict of races the continuance of which must do harm to all concerned. This question is not met by the suggestion that social equality cannot exist between the white and black races in this country. That argument, if it can be properly regarded as one, is scarcely worthy of consideration, for social equality no more exists between two races when traveling in a passenger coach or a public highway than when members of the same races sit by each other in a street car or in the jury box, or stand or sit with each other in a political assembly, or when they use in common the street of a city or town, or when they are in the same room for the purpose of having their names placed on the registry of voters, or when they approach the ballot box in order to exercise the high privilege of voting.

. . . I am of opinion that the statute of Louisiana is inconsistent with the personal liberty of citizens, white and black, in that State, and hostile to both the spirit and letter of the Constitution of the United States. If laws of like character should be enacted in the several States of the Union, the effect would be in the highest degree mischievous. Slavery, as an institution tolerated by law would, it is true, have disappeared from our country, but there would remain a power in the States, by sinister legislation, to interfere with the full enjoyment of the blessings of freedom to regulate civil rights, common to all citizens, upon the basis of race, and to place in a condition of legal inferiority a large body of American citizens now constituting a part of the political community called the People of the United States, for whom and by whom, through representatives, our government is administered. Such a system is inconsistent with the guarantee given by the Constitution to each State of a republican form of government, and may be stricken down by Congressional action, or by the courts in the discharge of their solemn duty to maintain the supreme law of the land, anything in the constitution or laws of any State to the contrary notwithstanding."

The ruling also enforced that the state would codify and enforce the identity onto individuals rather than allowing individuals to decide for themselves. Through the ruling, people acting under the belief of racialized separation laws, could also assign race to other individuals.

Coded: *Black means separate citizen.*

Coded: *The Government imposes race.*

Coded: *White can assign race to people.*

THE ONE DROP RULE AND JIM CROW

The Civil Rights Cases of 1883 and *Plessy v. Ferguson* put the control of discrimination and the protection of civil rights on individual states. Segregation and separation doctrines were drafted in the constitutions of readmitted former Confederate state, and in response to the Supreme Court rulings. The race laws that were formed following the Civil Rights cases and Plessy were commonly referred to as Jim Crow laws, from the minstrel era shows with caricatures of Black people. Restrictive states would attempt different ways to measure race, with "blood quantum" or the "one drop rule" being the prevailing principle.

Earliest version of the one drop rule would appear in Tennessee's Black Codes (1865) (Trammell, 2022).

> Sec. 1 Be it enacted by the General Assembly of the State of Tennessee.,That all Negroes, Mullattoes, Mestizos, and their descendants, having any African blood in their veins, shall be known in this State as "persons of color."

Ultimately, Jim Crow and other race laws centered around blood-defined African ancestry would include the following: housing, health care, adoption, sex, marriage, public accommodations, and transportation (trains, boats, and street cars). The federal government, as noted before, would include blood (blood quantum) definitions into the US Census with racial categories such as quadroon and octoroon. States could employ different calculations for different settings, but the result was to stratify access to various social systems, with one definition that would remain unconstrained, white (Hochschild & Weaver, 2007).

Twenty-one states would adopt separation policies, using *Plessy v. Ferguson* as a model. Each would implement separation statutes or laws focusing on school segregation, with Tennessee and three other states (Oklahoma, Georgia, and Florida) also enacting statutes focusing on private schools, too. North Carolina and Florida required not only separate schools but also separate textbooks (Murray, 1997).

K-12 public schools weren't the only focus of separation of learning spaces. Texas, Missouri, and North Carolina also required separate public libraries. Seventeen states had separate teacher training schools and colleges (Murray, 1997). The separation of education and the separation of public access was the segregation of employment and training.

SOURCE: Vachon, John, 1938. Retrieved from the Library of Congress.

Statutes during this era also limited Indigenous peoples, as comparable regressive laws would restrict their access to firearms, alcohol, housing, and education.

These laws were used as a framework to the Indian Reorganization Act of 1934, using blood quantum as a criteria for tribal membership to calculate the amount of federal benefits per population a tribe would receive. This was a shift from more historic traditions of concepts like lineage and kinship to understand tribal membership and citizenship. The result probably restricted tribal relationships and associations and the limited federal tribal benefits associated with membership (Schmidt, 2011).

These laws also served as a eugenic framework that inspired other twentieth century nationalistic movements, including the Nazi Party (Parry, 2017). The scope of laws, policies, and systems influenced by scientific racism would permeate not just the workplaces and courthouses but the walls of school-houses in an education system just being built.

Coded: *Black is any perceived African ancestry.*

Coded: *Black and Indian are separate housing.*

Coded: *Black and Indian have limited access to firearms.*

Coded: *White unrestrained access to society.*

Coded: *Black and Indian are ancillary education.*

Coded: *Black is ancillary employment.*

Coded: *Black is limited mobility.*

Coded: *Indian is genetically pure tribal membership, not ancestral.*

THE COMMITTEE OF TEN (1892)

By the end of the 1800s, public education was growing. There continued to be a wide range of learning experiences. In 1891, at the National Council for Education meeting, there was concern that the instructions and subjects being taught weren't preparing students for the requirements of admission to college. The summary of the proceedings, findings, and recommendations were summarized in the *Report of the Committee of Ten on Secondary School Studies (1894)* (National Education Association of the United States, 1894). A committee of ten men, headmasters and university presidents, was authorized to write a report on "uniformity." Information would be gathered through a series of conferences between secondary school teachers and college teachers focusing on the three principal subjects needed for college admissions: American history, geometry, and Latin. Teaching methods, the extent of the curriculum, and duration of each subject would be discussed. The subjects increased after an initial meeting to include English, Greek, Latin, "Other Modern Languages," mathematics, natural history (biology, botany, physiology, and zoology), geography (physical geography, geology and meteorology), civic government, history and political economy, astronomy, chemistry and physics.

**FIGURE 13   REPORT OF THE COMMITTEE OF TEN ON SECONDARY
SCHOOL STUDIES**

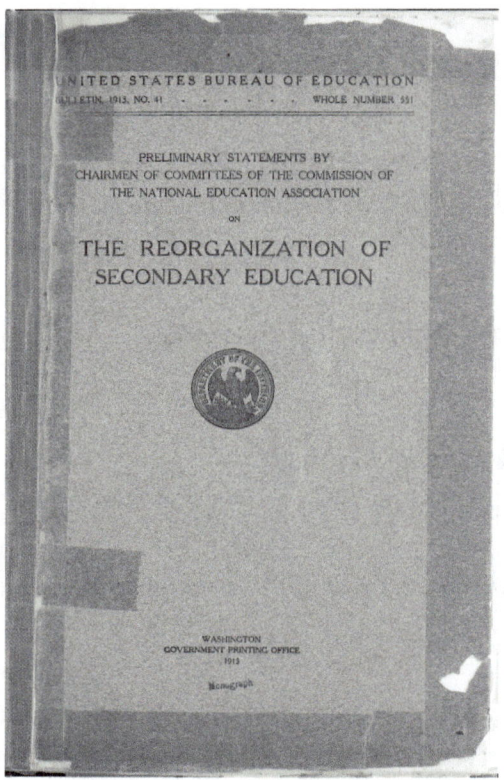

Through the work, the Committee had recommendations. Education should be taught across twelve years (or grades), elementary grades (one through eight) and secondary schools (nine through twelve). The number of days in a week a subject would be taught, ranging from twice to five times a week, was also recommended. The recommended number of subjects taught at each school was contingent on how much money the school had.

There was a tension in the report, as it was specifically founded on developing students that met requirements for college admission; however, there was also a desire to prepare students for the duties of life and make college and scientific schools accessible to all students. Many of the elements found by the Committee of Ten and their report are the same structures and elements found in education today. It is clear the model was focused on European culture, as noted by the initial languages and how centrally located the languages were in the initial and overarching recommendation. There should be pause in reflecting on the direct benefit that the presidents and headmasters that formed the committee would have in creating a national school system centered on college admissions. There were problematic implications by those selected for the committee, as well.

William Torrey Harris, Commissioner of Education, had recently written the introduction to the Commission's *Report on Indian Education*. This would lead to the forcible removal of children from their homes to boarding schools. Harris (1889) wrote the following:

> We owe it to ourselves and to the enlightened public opinion of the world to save the Indian, and not destroy him. We cannot save him and his patriarchal or tribal institution both together. To save him we must take him up into our form of civilization.

Charles Eliot, chairman of the Committee of Ten and president of Harvard, would not just support eugenics through faculty research but also toured and spoke publicly about eugenics and the support for segregation (Bacow, 2022).

The Committee of Ten's report would be widely distributed, shaping education policy and practice across the United States, and interwoven into later educational reforms. Still, the underlying influence of nationalism, scientific racism, and eugenics would be invisible systems as education continued to evolve.

CHAPTER 2 DISCUSSION QUESTIONS

- How did the inclusion of clauses like the three-fifths compromise and fugitive slave clause in the Constitution of 1787 contradict the ideals of liberty and equality proclaimed in the Declaration of Independence? What were the implications of these clauses on the development of racial hierarchies and the institution of slavery in early America?

- How did the categorization of race in the first census of 1790 and the Naturalization Act of 1790 shape the legal definitions of citizenship and personhood in the United States? Discuss how early legal definitions perpetuate racial hierarchies and reinforce systems of inequality.

- In what ways have the principles and practices established in the early public school systems of the nineteenth century shaped the trajectory of education policy and social mobility in America today? How did the transition from private and exclusive education systems to publicly funded schools reflect broader movements for social reform and equity in mid-nineteenth century America and onward?

- In what ways do the themes of citizenship, race, and constitutional rights raised by the Dred Scott case continue to resonate in debates over

(Continued)

(Continued)

civil rights and social justice in modern American society? What alternative interpretations of constitutional principles could have led to a different outcome for Dred Scott and other enslaved individuals seeking freedom?

- How does the legacy of slavery and the Civil War continue to influence understanding of race, citizenship, and the role of government in ensuring equality under the law? In what ways do understanding the events leading up to and following the Civil War inform efforts to address systemic racism and promote equity in the present day?

- What lasting impacts did the Freedmen's Bureau have in the South and beyond? How did its initiatives contribute to the evolution of public education? How did this opposition faced by the Freedmen's Bureau resonate with current struggles for educational equity and access?

- How did the southern states' implementation of Black Codes after the Civil War reflect a desire to maintain control over the formerly enslaved population? What were the intended outcomes, and how did these laws perpetuate systemic oppression?

- How did the Black Codes serve as a precursor to the Jim Crow laws that followed? What similarities and differences can be identified? How were these legal frameworks for racial segregation in the United States into and throughout the twentieth century?

- Evaluate the effectiveness of the Civil Rights Act of 1866, the Fourteenth Amendment, and subsequent legal challenges such as the Civil Rights Cases (1883) and *Plessy v. Ferguson* (1896) in addressing the oppression of the Black Codes. To what extent did these legal measures succeed or fail in protecting the rights of Black Americans during Reconstruction and beyond?

- How did figures like Charles Eliot, who supported eugenics and segregation, contribute to the underlying biases in educational policies shaped by the Committee of Ten? What are the lasting systemic impacts of such ideologies on educational systems, equity, and inclusion?

- In what ways do the recommendations of the Committee of Ten still resonate in today's educational practices? How can awareness of their historical context help educators and policymakers address current challenges in education?

CHAPTER 3

....

THE EVOLVING AMERICA

Systems and Scientific Racism

EUGENICS

As Reconstruction gave way to Jim Crow, eugenics was seen as the scientific explanation to a racialized hierarchy, written and developed in laws, policies, and systems to shape society. Eugenics also served to frame a hierarchy rapidly strained and changing as the United States immigration population grew from approximately seven million around 1880 to nearly fourteen million by the 1920s (Hirschman & Mogford, 2009). Sir Francis Galton, half-cousin to Charles Darwin, built an approximation of his cousin's evolutionary theories, to improve the "stock" of humanity. The deterministic view of humanity was blind to environmental or educational conditions, believing genes and gene purity were most important. While Darwin would not expand his work into areas such as population breeding and break with his cousin in this and other areas, Galton's work increased in popularity and the eugenics movement had widespread influence in politics, public policy, and education in Britain, the United States, and Germany (Paul, 2003).

> Eugenics is the science which deals with all the influences that improve the inborn qualities of a race; also with those that develop them to the utmost advantage. The improvement of the inborn qualities, or stock, of some one human population. . . .
>
> . . . . It must be introduced into the national conscience, like a new religion. It has, indeed, strong claims, to become an orthodox religious tenet of the future, for eugenics co-operates with the workings of nature by securing that humanity shall be represented by the fittest of races. - Galton (1904)

Not only preferred physical traits, but intelligence was also seen as a eugenic priority, with "feeble-minded" individuals seen separate from the preferred "stock." Ability, moral character, nervousness, and criminality were also seen as inherited traits.

Henry Goddard was the director of the Vineland Training Center for Feebleminded Boys and Girls (1906–1918). He wanted to use eugenics to explain why some children were "slow learners" and translated the IQ tests from the French psychologist Alfred Binet. First testing the children of Vineland, Goddard expanded to Ellis Island, using the test to state that the diverse populations of immigrants to the United States were representative of their various ethnic groups and nations of origin but were all "below the 12 year-old limit and therefore feeble-minded." The Vineland Center would train more than one thousand teachers, applying directly many of the testing practices (Stoskopf, 2002).

Lewis Terman, an educational psychologist from Stanford, built off the work of Goddard. Testing and tracking his high IQ students across their lifetimes, Terman partnered with Goddard, and American Psychological Association President, Robert Yerkes, tested over 1.7 million army recruits. Not only would educational testing become more entrenched in the evolving education reform movement but the research would also be instrumental in the passing of the Immigration Restriction Act of 1924 (Stoskopf, 2002).

The Immigration Restriction Act of 1924 banned immigration from Asia and Africa and created quotas to limit immigration from southern and eastern Europe. The highest quotas were for individuals and families from northern or western Europe where people were found to be more "desirable" (Garver, 1991). White would be the center for defining racial and ethnic categories; assigning otherness or permanent foreign status (illegality) to those entering the country, with further imposed rules based on race or national origin to follow (Ngai, 2017).

States also were passing laws to ban "aliens" from property ownership and various types of government employment. Written into their constitutions during this time, Idaho (1890) & Arizona (1912) barred employment in government, while Washington (1889), South Carolina (1895), and Oklahoma (1907) constitutions barred land ownership. States would expand through various statutes to limit immigrants in society in the years following the Great Depression and through World War I and World War II. Arizona, New Mexico, Texas, Washington and California laws had clear racist origins, targeting people from Asia, specifically China and Japan. California's law, the Alien Property Initiative Act of 1920 (California Alien Land Law of 1920), would later be found by the US Supreme Court as unconstitutional, as it was discriminatorily targeting Japanese and other people of Asian descent barred from naturalization due to the Immigration Restriction Act of 1924. Descendants of those barred from naturalization would have their land taken by the US government as if the persons didn't exist. This was found to be a violation of the Fourteenth Amendment (Murray, 1997).

Practices were not just focused on land and jobs. By 1935, thirty-seven states had existing or pending laws for the forced sterilization of citizens. As noted before, the "breeding of the stock" was one of the primary foci of eugenics and eugenicists. This could be done through "positive" eugenics (social policies) to promote selective breeding or "negative" eugenics, which was the prevention of reproduction like sterilization. Targeted were immigrants, people of color, disabled people, unmarried mothers, those with mental illness and poor people, all with the eugenic goal of protecting the "stock." The coercive sterilizations were done with the authority of state laws under the supervision of state medical superintendents, legislators, and other "medical reformers" with some states still having the same laws in existence and continuing to perform forced sterilizations in some states in the present day (Ko, 2016).

Schools became centers for the nationalistic push of both policy and politics of the era. There was a clear eugenics influence also impacting education reform in the early twentieth century (Reisner, 1922). The convergence of creating a cohesive national identity following Reconstruction, fears of a rise of a Black republic with the freedoms of the formerly enslaved, and concerns of diluting racial purity through an intermingling of national identities and languages (seen as the same through the lens of eugenics), and a range of daily practices were built into the evolving school system (Reisner, 1922). Eugenicists saw schools as "a sieve through which all children in the country are passed" (Popenoe & Johnson, 1918). Prolific public education architects such as John Franklin Bobbit, G. Stanley Hall, and E. L. Thorndike developed various school programs through the eugenics lens, including intelligence testing, curriculum development, teacher training on ability, gifted education, vocational training, and school organizations (Winfield, 2007).

Best reflecting the national tone and ambitions for public education of the era was the Smith-Towner Bill (Beman, 1924) later re-introduced as the Sterling-Towner Bill (Beman, 1924). The bill was informed by the National Education Association's Commission on the Emergency of Education, summarizing the democratic and educational issues that existed both before and during World War I. The bill would have created the Department of Education. The other aspects of the bill would reflect the nationalistic and eugenic undertones of the time. The Smith-Towner Bill would provide states with $100 million (with states required to match the funds) for the purpose of Americanizing immigrants. The focus was on teacher preparation, removal of illiteracy, and physical education (Reisner, 1922). The contents of the bill are noted in the *Handbook for the National Department of Education* (1926):

> Sec 5 That it shall be the duty of the Department of Education to conduct studies and investigations in the field of education and to report thereon Research shall be undertaken in a.) illiteracy b.) immigrant education c.) public school education and especially

rural education d.) physical education including health education recreation and sanitation e.) preparation and supply of competent teachers for the public schools and f.) in such other fields as in the judgment of the Secretary of Education may require attention and study.

SEC. 9. That in order to encourage the States in the Americanization of immigrants, three-fortieths of the sum authorized to be appropriated by section 7 of this Act shall be used to teach immigrants ten years of age and over to speak and read the English language and to understand and appreciate the spirit and purpose of the American Government and the duties of citizenship in a free country.

The National Education Association's Commission on the Emergency of Education noted that the rising immigration population was physically unfit to serve, unable to understand English military commands, and didn't appreciate the American issues that brought the country to war (Reisner, 1922). The language had nationalist and eugenic themes, and the bill was drafted to ensure that the population was battle ready should the need for a draft arise again. The bill had the support of the National Education Association (who drafted some of the bill's earliest language), and, notably, the Ku Klux Klan. Expanding from local and domestic terrorism, the Klan supported the bill as they felt it would promote national purity. National Klan leader, Hiram Evans, stated regarding public education, "We will be a homogeneous people. We will grind out Americans like meat out of a grinder" (Slade, 2023) Both versions would not come to a vote in either house of Congress despite favorable committee reports. The opposition was focused mostly on concerns of loss of local control and support of the private Catholic schools emerging at the start of the twentieth century (Mitchell, 1949).

Supporting the nationalist role of education, states passed laws requiring students stand and recite a pledge to the American flag. "The Pledge of Allegiance" published in *The Youth's Companion* magazine by Francis Bellamy was written with explicit editorial goals: Americanizing the flood of European immigrants, healing continued divisions between north and south, enlisting students in the four hundredth anniversary of Columbus's voyage, and selling an overstock of American flags held by the magazine. The pledge to the flag would be recited with children giving a straight armed salute, known as the Bellamy Salute, named after the pledge's author (Roberts, 2022).

**FIGURE 14   SCHOOL CHILDREN PLEDGING ALLEGIANCE TO THE
              FLAG IN 1908**

SOURCE: Retrieved from the Library of Congress.

American educators, policymakers, and education researchers were known to frequently visit Germany through the late 1800s and early 1900s to observe their nationalized model of education. The German (Prussian) system was noted not just as a national model but also for folding nationalism—portraying the German race as superior to any other race—into the educational framework (Reisner, 1922). The hierarchical nature of the German school system with its standardized curriculum and teaching training and personnel was seen as an extension of nationalistic social control (Reisner, 1922); although noted as distinctly unAmerican at the time, these elements are present in every school in America today.

National education influenced by eugenics would take hold and expand during this time not just in the United States but also in Germany. Hitler praised the United States in *Mein Kampf*, noting the progress the US made toward a racial hierarchy, serving as a model for the Nuremberg Laws (Whitman, 2017). There seemed striking parallels in German education to the American model as much as there was in policy and law. Ziemer (1941) would write about his direct interactions and observations of the Nazi-German era education system. There was a heavy focus on German language instruction and physical education, so students would be "ready for action." Boys would receive instruction on biology, science, mathematics, and history, while girls would receive additional lessons on home economics and eugenics (Ziemer, 1941).

The German national educational manual, *Education and Instruction, Official Publication of the Reich and Prussian Ministry of Knowledge, Education and National Culture,* noted the following: "The German school in the Third Reich is integral part of the National Socialistic order of living. It has the mission, in collaboration with the phases of the party, to fashion, and mold the National Socialistic Being according to Party orders." Teachers and students, reflecting other members of the Party, exclaimed, "Heil Hitler, Seig Heil!" while raising their right hand to the sky, palm down (Ziemer, 1941). The movement was an eerie reflection of the Bellamy Salute children in the United States would do during "The Pledge of Allegiance."

In the fall of 1935, in Minersville Pennsylvania, a ten-year-old boy refused to stand along with his fifth grade class for "The Pledge of Allegiance." A Jehovah's Witness, William Gobitis, felt that the act would be a ritual, worshiping images other than God and forbidden by Scripture. The teacher tried to force William's hand to the saluting position, unable to do so, William faced other discipline. William would be expelled from school for his "insubordination," despite stating his religious (First Amendment protected) beliefs (Driver, 2018).

> "I do not salute the flag not because I do not love my country, but I love God more and I must obey His commandments."

Both William and his older sister Lillian were expelled; the family placed their children in private school to continue their education and sued Minersville School District for financial relief. The case was ruled and upheld by lower courts for the Gobitis family and found that requiring students to stand and salute was a constitutional violation. The case would be appealed and make it to the Supreme Court in April 1940 and be decided the following June. Ruling eight to one the court ruled in favor of the district and upheld the salute.

Justice Frankfurter (*Minersville School Dist. v. Gobitis*, 1940) wrote the majority opinion:

> The case before us must be viewed as though the legislature of Pennsylvania had itself formally directed the flag salute for the children of Minersville; had made no exemption for children whose parents were possessed of conscientious scruples like those of the Gobitis family, and had indicated its belief in the desirable ends to

be secured by having its public school children share a common experience at those periods of development when their minds are supposedly receptive to its assimilation, by an exercise appropriate in time and place and setting, and one designed to evoke in them appreciation of the nation's hopes and dreams, its sufferings and sacrifices. The precise issue, then, for us to decide is whether the legislatures of the various states and the authorities in a thousand counties and school districts of this country are barred from determining the appropriateness of various means to evoke that unifying sentiment without which there can ultimately be no liberties, civil or religious. To stigmatize legislative judgment in providing for this universal gesture of respect for the symbol of our national life in the setting of the common school as a lawless inroad on that freedom of conscience which the Constitution protects, would amount to no less than the pronouncement of pedagogical and psychological dogma in a field where courts possess no marked and certainly no controlling competence.

. . . The preciousness of the family relation, the authority and independence which give dignity to parenthood, indeed the enjoyment of all freedom, presuppose the kind of ordered society which is summarized by our flag. A society which is dedicated to the preservation of these ultimate values of civilization may, in self-protection, utilize the educational process for inculcating those almost unconscious feelings which bind men together in a comprehending loyalty, whatever may be their lesser differences and difficulties.

Writing the dissenting opinion, Justice Stone (*Minersville School Dist. v. Gobitis,* 1940) wrote the following:

The very fact that we have constitutional guaranties of civil liberties and the specificity of their command where freedom of speech and of religion are concerned require some accommodation of the powers which government normally exercises, when no question of civil liberty is involved, to the constitutional demand that those liberties be protected against the action of government itself.

. . . So here, even if we believe that such compulsions will contribute to national unity, there are other ways to teach loyalty and patriotism, which are the sources of national unity, than by compelling the pupil to affirm that which he does not believe, and by commanding a form of affirmance which violates his religious convictions. Without recourse to such compulsion, the state is free to compel attendance at school and require teaching by instruction and study of all in our history and in the structure and organization of our government, including the guaranties of civil liberty which tend to inspire patriotism and love of country. I cannot say that government here is deprived of any interest or function which it is entitled to maintain at the expense of the protection of civil liberties by requiring it to resort to the alternatives which do not coerce an affirmation of belief.

The guaranties of civil liberty are but guaranties of freedom of the human mind and spirit and of reasonable freedom and opportunity to express them. They presuppose the right of the individual to hold such opinions as he will and to give them reasonably free expression, and his freedom, and that of the state as well, to teach and persuade others by the communication of ideas. The very essence of the liberty which they guaranty is the freedom of the individual from compulsion as to what he shall think and what he shall say, at least where the compulsion is to bear false witness to his religion. If these guaranties are to have any meaning, they must, I think, be deemed to withhold from the state any authority to compel belief or the expression of it where that expression violates religious convictions, whatever may be the legislative view of the desirability of such compulsion.

Following the ruling, the Gobitis children would face hurls of stones and jeers as children would yell, "Here comes Jehovah!" The children would be sent away and a state police cruiser would park outside the family business amid threats that the family business would be burnt down by a mob (Driver, 2018). In response to the ruling in days that followed, more Jehovah Witness children were expelled, a place of worship was burned down in Maine, and sixty Jehovah witnesses were attacked while preaching in Illinois (Gobitis, 1993). While the nationalistic and eugenic influences would shape education, policy, and politics, Americans were bracing themselves. Despite the interwoven nature of German and American politics, policies and education in the previous decades, by the year of the Gobitis ruling, 65 percent of Americans prepared for an anticipated German attack on the United States (Driver, 2018).

Coded: *White is the desired citizen.*

Coded: *White has the right to lineage.*

Coded: *White right to employment.*

Coded: *White right to own land.*

WORLD WAR II AND THE GI BILL (1944)

As the United States fell into World War II, American soldiers, including large numbers of Black soldiers, supported the war efforts both domestically and abroad. Harrowing stories of sacrifice and heroism would be present throughout the war, despite the armed services remaining segregated.

As the Great War continued in both Europe and the Pacific, a bill was introduced into Congress in January 1944. The Servicemen's Readjustment Act of 1944 would provide extended benefits for both men and women veterans and would support President Roosevelt's goals for expanding the middle class and improving economic recovery from the war. The benefits would apply to the nearly sixteen million American soldiers supporting the war efforts.

The bill provided a range of benefits for the servicemen, including unemployment allowances, government-backed loans for homes and businesses, education funding, and job-searching assistance. The government-backed loans rapidly increased home ownership across the country, supporting the purchase, improvement, or new construction of property. Over four million home loans for over $30 billion would be approved and guaranteed by the Veterans Administration by 1955 (U.S. Department of Defense, 2020), which were responsible for over one-third of all new homes built after the war.

Education funds would also transform higher education and the American workforce. College had previously been a more narrow educational experience for the affluent and elite, but with the support of government funds, college enrollment expanded to a wide range of working-class veterans from rural and inner city regions. The increased enrollment also saw an increase in the number and types of course offerings, as well as the overall number of schools and programs. Nearly eight million soldiers utilized the education benefits in the first seven years of the bill, raising the number of advanced degrees in the US by 20 percent (U.S. DoD, 2020).

As over 1.2 million Black soldiers returned to US soils, they faced racism and discrimination domestically after fighting for freedom abroad. Serving in a segregated armed forces, Black service members were disproportionately dishonorably discharged compared with their white counterparts, leading to many servicemen being ineligible for veterans' benefits (McCallister, 2023).

The Department of Veterans Administration was noted for discriminatory practices. As southern practices of offering labor jobs with extremely low wages for Black laborers continued, the VA would cut benefits for veterans if they were notified the soldiers refused the jobs. In southern states, various VA branches failed to employ Black veterans in the same manner as white soldiers. The VA staffing was predominantly white, leading to outright discrimination in the dropping and denial of benefits. This racially unbalanced staffing also resulted in denial of accreditation of support systems to help veterans of color like the United Negro and Allied Veterans of America. Five states were granted permission to create Black American Legion posts, but this was in order to promote and maintain segregation (Herbold, 1994).

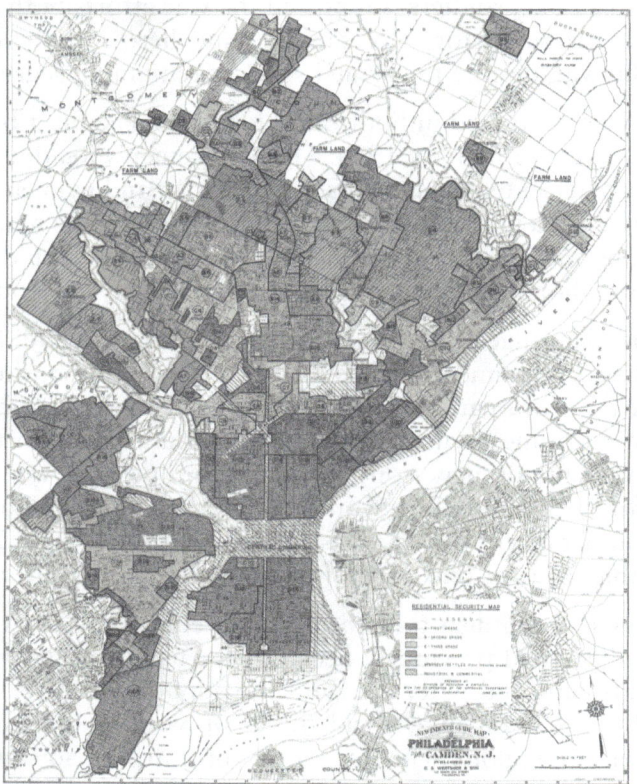

SOURCE: Mapping Inequality.

While the federal government provided subsidized loans for housing, the federal government was also promoting housing segregations (in both north and south) through the Home Owners' Loan Corporation (HOLC). HOLC was designed for homeowners at risk of foreclosure, providing them with new, more affordable low-interest loans to enable them to make new payments and stay in their homes. The refinancing decisions and administration of loans were made through a system of appraisals and value assessments. HOLC created color-coded maps of areas across the nation with green showing "safe" neighborhoods and redlined regions meaning high risk. One of the conditions for appraisal was the racial composition of the neighborhoods. The communities with people of color would have "little to no value" and would be colored red. The appraisal systems would be driven by both the federal guidelines and appraisers' (real estate agents) code of ethics, which required them to maintain segregation (Rothstein, 2017).

In 1934, the Federal Housing Administration (FHA) was created to insure mortgage lenders for not just new home mortgages but also rehabilitation and maintenance loans as well. The FHA developed their own maps and appraisal standards and added the HOLC data and standards to the FHA appraisals and practices. Black neighborhoods were not the only ones deemed at risk—racially mixed neighborhoods and white ones in proximity to Black neighborhoods were designated as high risk properties and communities. In addition, school desegregation was also a noted risk factor as the *Federal Housing Administration' Underwriting Manual* (1938) observed:

> The social class of the parents of children at the school will in many instances have a direct bearing. Thus, physical surroundings of a neighborhood area may be favorable and conducive to enjoyable, pleasant living in its location. However, if the children of people living in such an area are compelled to attend school where the majority or a considerable number of the pupils represent a far lower level of society or an incompatible racial element, the neighborhood under consideration will prove far less stable and desirable than if this condition did not exist.

The *FHA Underwriting Manual* was illustrative of the federal government's role in not just drafting and maintaining segregated neighborhoods and communities but also building a segregated school system. This system extended beyond the school wall to across the "colorlined" borders of the community.

At the local level, specific deeds to homes, in both the north and south, have race-specific language barring sale to individuals based on their race or country of origin. The clauses in deeds were referred to as "restrictive covenants." Restrictive covenants were dependent on the previous homeowner and not the future owners of the home. As new housing developments grew across the United States, community associations (or homeowner associations) were used as a tool to ensure all new owners were of one race. Membership into the community associations could be a requirement for home purchase, with a "whites only" clause part of the bylaws of the various associations. The contracts and associations were used to sue and evict many Black families from their homes, with the defense of the discrimination often pointing to the FHA existing rules and guides. Conversely, the FHA often demanded new builders and developers include racial covenants as part of their financing agreements (Rothstein, 2017).

HOLC and the FHA played a significant part in the New Deal rise of the white middle class. The GI Bill would directly partner with the FHA in the appraisal and administration of its low-interest housing loans, expanding on the racialized effects of the federal housing rules.

In addition to housing, the GI Bill also provided servicemen a range of educational opportunities. Nearly eight million soldiers took advantage of the educational opportunities at two- and four-year colleges and universities, vocational training schools, on-the-job training programs, and farm training. Most of the US colleges and universities remained segregated following

WWII and Black veterans would not be considered for admission (Herbold, 1994). To limit access and demand for white institutions and universities, fourteen states entered into the Southern Regional Compact (Murray, 1997). Florida, Maryland, Georgia, Louisiana, Alabama, Mississippi and Tennessee, Arkansas, Virginia, North Carolina, South Carolina, Texas, Oklahoma, and West Virginia stated that their combined states were a *region* that delivered higher education services (Murray, 1997). This allowed for the expansion of the "separate but equal" doctrine regarding higher education, as Black students could be denied admission in their home state of Maryland since a Black institution could be located within the same region, even if that was several states away (Klibaner, 1983).

Following the war, only 5 percent enrolled under the GI educational benefits in any course of programs (Woods, 2013). Historically Black Colleges and Universities (HBCUs) suffered an incredible demand and strain during this period, as applicants skyrocketed, but endowments and federal aid plummeted (Herbold, 1994). The majority of HBCUs were located in the south, where nearly 80 percent of the Black population lived in the US. Total enrollment in HBCUs would grow from 43,000 in 1940 to over 75,000 by 1950. In 1947, when the VA surveyed leading HBCUs, it found that over half of the applicants that year were turned away due to lack of space (Woods, 2013). Those admitted to Black colleges and universities of the era faced challenging educational conditions. The schools received roughly 25 percent of the funding that white schools obtained. The Black veterans were still motivated to take advantage of the educational credits (Herbold, 1994). The education and training credits included a stipend that was a comparable amount to the generally lower wages Black workers could earn at the time (Meschede et al., 2022). Many Black veterans sought out trade schools and vocational training programs as their best, if not only, option.

Both the housing and education benefits would create lasting benefits in wealth generation for all veterans, but notably not equally. The differences in equitable distribution of the soldiers created notable and significant differences in outcomes. An analysis for the Institute for Economic and Racial Equity (Meschede et al., 2022) found Black veterans would share over $12,000 in wealth generated from housing and education benefits with their children, while white veterans would generate over $390,000 in wealth from the benefits for their children. White nonveterans would generate over $283,000 of wealth to pass onto their children, benefiting in all likelihood from the structural changes in accessibility in both the housing market and education system for working class whites. Black nonveterans would have $15,462 of wealth to share with their descendants when compared to veterans' descendants; simply the GI Bill did not create any structural ways for nonveteran Blacks during the early twentieth century to accrue generational wealth through either education or housing.

Systems of housing and education would shape both systems over the years to come. The ripple effects from the restrictive housing rules would have a lasting outcome on emerging neighborhoods, school districts, and even classroom desks.

Coded: *White the focus of government assistance.*

Coded: *Black separate communities.*

BROWN V. BOARD OF EDUCATION (1954)

As the landscape of the communities and schools grew throughout the United States, the strain of the unequal education system grew, as well. In 1954, seventeen states and the District of Columbia required school segregation and an additional four made school segregation optional (Arizona, Kansas, New Mexico, and Wyoming) (Murray, 1997). In December 1952, the Supreme Court began hearing a case that was a combination from five states that required or supported school segregation. *Gebhart v. Belton* (from Delaware), *Briggs v. Elliot* (from South Carolina), *Davis v. the County Board of Prince Edward County* (from Virginia), *Bolling v. Sharpe* (from Washington D.C.), and most notably *Brown v. the Board of Education of Topeka* (from Kansas) would be heard jointly before court and be known as *Brown v. the Board of Education*. The grouping notably reflected segregation as a national and not a state or local issue.

The Brown case specifically was a class action lawsuit against the Board of Education in Topeka. Plaintiff Oliver Brown attempted to enroll his daughter, Linda, at the school closest to their home, which was all white, rather than have Linda ride the bus to the all Black school farther away. They were joined by twelve other local Black families facing similar circumstances.

The National Association for the Advancement of Colored People (NAACP) sponsored all five cases with the case led by chief counsel (and future justice) Thurgood Marshall. The legal strategy included research from historians and social scientists, including the Doll Experiment, which showed how children would adopt racial biases from systemic structures like school segregation (NAACP Legal Defense Fund, 2020).

The court deliberated until the following June 1953, and then asked to rehear arguments for all five cases to determine whether Congress had considered public school segregation as a factor in drafting the Fourteenth Amendment. During the hearings, US Assistant Attorney General J. Lee Rankin filed an amicus curiae or "friend of the court" brief (1954) on behalf of Attorney General James McGranery, expressing support for the desegregation of schools. The brief is summarized as follows:

> The subordinate position occupied by Negroes in this country as a result of governmental discriminations ("second-class citizenship," as it is sometimes called) presents an unsolved problem for American democracy, an inescapable challenge to the sincerity of our espousal of the democratic faith.

> In these days, when the free world must conserve and fortify the moral as well as the material sources of its strength, it is especially important to affirm that the Constitution of the United States places no limitation, express or implied, [*32] on the principle of the equality of all men before the law. Mr. Justice Harlan said in his dissent in the Plessy case (163 U. S. at 562):

> We boast of the freedom enjoyed by our people above all other peoples. But it is difficult to reconcile that boast with a state of the law which, practically, puts the brand of servitude and degradation upon a large class of our fellow–citizens, our equals before the law.

> The Government and people of the United States must prove by their actions that the ideals expressed in the Bill of Rights are living realities, not literary abstractions. As the President has stated:

> If we wish to inspire the people of the world whose freedom is in jeopardy, if we wish to restore hope to those who have already lost their civil liberties, if we wish to fulfill the promise that is ours, we must correct the remaining imperfections in our practice of democracy.

> We know the way. We need only the will.

The court ruled unanimously, nine to zero, in favor of Brown and the other plaintiffs. Chief Justice Warren (*Brown v. Board of Education*, 1954) wrote the opinion for the court:

> "Today, education is perhaps the most important function of state and local governments. Compulsory school attendance laws and the great expenditures for education both demonstrate our recognition of the importance of education to our democratic society. It is required in the performance of our most basic public responsibilities, even service in the armed forces. It is the very foundation of good citizenship. Today it is a principal instrument in awakening the child to cultural values, in preparing him for later professional training, and in helping him to adjust normally to his environment. In these days, it is doubtful that any child may

reasonably be expected to succeed in life if he is denied the opportunity of an education. Such an opportunity, where the state has undertaken to provide it, is a right which must be made available to all on equal terms. We come then to the question presented: Does segregation of children in public schools solely on the basis of race, even though the physical facilities and other "tangible" factors may be equal, deprive the children of the minority group of equal educational opportunities? We believe that it does.

. . . We conclude that in the field of public education the doctrine of "separate but equal" has no place. Separate educational facilities are inherently unequal." "Therefore, we hold that the plaintiffs and others similarly situated for whom the actions have been brought are, by reason of the segregation complained of, deprived of the equal protection of the laws guaranteed by the Fourteenth Amendment."

The court in its opinion and ruling gave no clear directions or timetable on the implementation of desegregation, leading to schools and states to ask the court for "relief" to guide (or delay) desegregation efforts. In April 1955, the Supreme Court heard arguments, which would be known as Brown II. In May 1955, the court upheld its unanimous vote in the unconstitutional nature of school desegregation but reversed its decision regarding desegregation for all cases but Delaware (as the case was ruled for immediate integration due to the clear evidence of qualitative differences between the Black and white schools). Justice Warren (*Brown v. Board of Education*, 1955), again wrote the opinion for the court:

The judgments below, except that, in the Delaware case, are accordingly reversed, and the cases are remanded to the District Courts to take such proceedings and enter such orders and decrees consistent with this opinion as are necessary and proper to admit to public schools on a racially nondiscriminatory basis with all deliberate speed the parties to these cases.

The lower courts and states were responsible for the implementation plan for school desegregation. No clear timetable would be established besides, "all deliberate speed," halting most desegregation progress following the ruling.

Mounting resistance would come in many different forms (Sutherland, 1955): States would use gradual integration plans (grade-per-year); gerrymander attendance zones and district lines; close white schools; create transfer plans; publicly fund/support private schools or privatize public schools; or outright deny desegregation orders. Federally, led by Virginia's US Senator Harry Bryd, a coordinated effort of legislators was formed, as over one hundred signed the "Southern Manifesto," in response to Brown. Byrd also led on the state-level for Virginia a plan called "Massive Resistance," a series of legislative actions passed in response to Brown: These removed state funding for any integrated school and allowed the governor to close such schools; created a racially motivated three-member Pupil Placement Board for assigning students to schools; and implemented a grant program to support private (white) schools (Hershman, 2020).

The Supreme Court was not seeking to become more involved in school administration and gave much latitude to lower courts and legislature, as long as the law was not explicitly race focused. Scholars at the time of the Brown II ruling noted the on-going practice of residential segregation or educational gerrymandering as a means of perpetuating school segregation and this would continue to be an acceptable practice before the courts. Nationally between 1954 to 1960, Black students would move from nearly no integration, at 0 percent to 0.1 percent of students in majority-white schools (Orfield et al., 2014).

Ultimately, Brown would never design a plan for school desegregation; the court would simply ask states and local entities to create plans using any standard other than race. The court still didn't identify or challenge how states determine race. The court did not challenge the notion that race was not the primary factory preceding separate and unequal systems of education. The lack of challenge perpetuated many states' oppressive systems based on preferred biological traits and perpetuated the unequal systems found in housing, employment, and protection under the law, which the education system was dependent upon "to be equal and fair."

> **Coded:** *Black education is separate but equal.*

> **Coded:** *Black education is in housing.*

> **Coded:** *Black education is in funding.*

> **Coded:** *Black education is in state policy.*

CIVIL RIGHTS ACT (1964)

As Brown v. Board of Education spurred opposition and resistance, it also served as a spark to further inspire and drive other efforts across the United States against the discrimination of the second class citizenship system it continued to perpetuate. School integration would continue to move forward gradually. In 1957, nine students in Little Rock Arkansas would be challenged by widespread threats, intimidation, and bigotry. This included the governor of Arkansas who initially mobilized the Arkansas National Guard to prevent the Little Rock Nine from entering the schools, only to have President Eisenhower issue an executive order federalizing the Arkansas National Guard and protect the students as they integrated into Little Rock's Central High School (Branton, 1983).

The Civil Rights Act of 1957 would be passed shortly after the Little Rock Nine Incident. Proposed by President Eisenhower, the legislation was the first civil rights legislation since the Civil Rights Acts of 1875. The Act created the Civil Rights Commission in the Department of Justice and an independent agency with ability to do fact finding to inform policy and civil rights legislative development, the Civil Rights Commission. The Act created the President's Civil Rights Commission, an independent agency with the ability to do fact finding to inform policy and civil rights legislation development. The Act also led to the establishment of the Civil Rights Division within the Department of Justice, creating a new assistant attorney general position within the department. (Mayer, 1989). The Civil Rights Commission was a six-person commission that could investigate racial discrimination and civil rights violations. Despite its passage, the bill faced strong opposition in the Senate, including the longest filibuster in Senate history to block the legislation (Mayer, 1989). As a result, the federal government had no enforcement mechanisms for protecting voting rights and desegregating schools. The research and reports from the Civil Rights Commission would be instrumental for later legislation (Sturkey, 2018).

Congress would pass the Civil Rights Act of 1960 in an attempt to close the loopholes or outright holes in the legislation. Then Senator, Lyndon Johnson, was instrumental in passing the Act. Although it may have been at the expense of stripping the bill of any meaningful impact (Sturkey, 2018), the Act did provide voting rights protections including a "voting referee." However, applying for support for voting discrimination was seen as too complicated to be effective. Title II of the Act focused on the use of explosives and fleeing after using explosives to destroy a building; this was likely in response to the wide range of terrorism. The terrorism included widespread bombings of homes, places of worship, and even Clinton High School in Tennessee in 1958 to prevent integration (West, 2017). The Act did criminalize the obstruction of federal court orders, including desegregation orders in school. Still, the Civil Rights Act, while offering additional protections, did not have many practical enforcement efforts (Sturkey, 2018).

Civil unrest, activism, and advocacy continued to drive for changes. The work of the Congress of Racial Equality (CORE) to desegregate interstate transit on the Freedom Rides and the integration of the campus of the University of Mississippi, Alabama, and the Birmingham campaign continued to draw attention to desegregation and antidiscrimination efforts (Levy, 2019).

The Birmingham Campaign, led by Dr. Martin Luther King, Jr. and Reverend Fred Shuttlesworth, was a series of nonviolent protests, including sit-ins, marches, boycotts, negotiations, and other direct actions by members of the community, the Southern Christian Leadership Conference and Alabama Christian Movement for Human Rights, and school-aged children (Brown-Nagin, 2022). The continued acts of state-sponsored violence in response to the protest and the continued deployment of federal guards to counter the violence prompted President Kennedy in June 1963 (Kotlowski, 2005), in his broadcasted *Report to the American People on Civil Rights*, to propose legislation that would become the Civil Rights Act of 1964. Kennedy (1963) noted the following in the address:

> "Next week I shall ask the Congress of the United States to act, to make a commitment it has not fully made in this century to the proposition that race has no place in American life or law. The Federal judiciary has upheld that proposition in the conduct of its affairs, including the employment of Federal personnel, the use of Federal facilities, and the sale of federally financed housing.
>
> But there are other necessary measures which only the Congress can provide, and they must be provided at this session. The old code of equity law under which we live commands for every wrong a remedy, but in too many communities, in too many parts of the country, wrongs are inflicted on Negro citizens and there are no remedies at law. Unless the Congress acts, their only remedy is in the street.
>
> I am, therefore, asking the Congress to enact legislation giving all Americans the right to be served in facilities which are open to the public--hotels, restaurants, theaters, retail stores, and similar establishments.
>
> This seems to me to be an elementary right. Its denial is an arbitrary indignity that no American in 1963 should have to endure, but many do.
>
> I have recently met with scores of business leaders urging them to take voluntary action to end this discrimination and I have been encouraged by their response, and in the last 2 weeks over 75 cities have seen progress made in desegregating these kinds of facilities. But many are unwilling to act alone, and for this reason, nationwide legislation is needed if we are to move this problem from the streets to the courts.
>
> I am also asking the Congress to authorize the Federal Government to participate more fully in lawsuits designed to end segregation in public education. We have succeeded in persuading many districts to desegregate voluntarily. Dozens have admitted Negroes without

violence. Today a Negro is attending a State-supported institution in every one of our 50 States, but the pace is very slow.

Too many Negro children entering segregated grade schools at the time of the Supreme Court's decision 9 years ago will enter segregated high schools this fall, having suffered a loss which can never be restored. The lack of an adequate education denies the Negro a chance to get a decent job.

The orderly implementation of the Supreme Court decision, therefore, cannot be left solely to those who may not have the economic resources to carry the legal action or who may be subject to harassment.

Other features will also be requested, including greater protection for the right to vote. But legislation, I repeat, cannot solve this problem alone. It must be solved in the homes of every American in every community across our country.

In this respect I want to pay tribute to those citizens North and South who have been working in their communities to make life better for all. They are acting not out of a sense of legal duty but out of a sense of human decency.

Like our soldiers and sailors in all parts of the world they are meeting freedom's challenge on the firing line, and I salute them for their honor and their courage.

My fellow Americans, this is a problem which faces us all—in every city of the North as well as the South. Today there are Negroes unemployed, two or three times as many compared to whites, inadequate in education, moving into the large cities, unable to find work, young people particularly out of work without hope, denied equal rights, denied the opportunity to eat at a restaurant or lunch counter or go to a movie theater, denied the right to a decent education, denied almost today the right to attend a State university even though qualified. It seems to me that these are matters which concern us all, not merely Presidents or Congressmen or Governors, but every citizen of the United States.

This is one country. It has become one country because all of us and all the people who came here had an equal chance to develop their talents.

We cannot say to 10 percent of the population that you can't have that right; that your children cannot have the chance to develop whatever talents they have; that the only way that they are going to get their rights is to go into the streets and demonstrate. I think we owe them and we owe ourselves a better country than that.

Therefore, I am asking for your help in making it easier for us to move ahead and to provide the kind of equality of treatment which we would want ourselves; to give a chance for every child to be educated to the limit of his talents.

As I have said before, not every child has an equal talent or an equal ability or an equal motivation, but they should have an equal right to develop their talent and their ability and their motivation, to make something of themselves."

Draft legislation was sent from the Kennedy administration to the House of Representatives. The proposed legislation would ban discrimination in public places, support desegregation efforts in schools, and protect voting rights. The House added language to protect employment, expanded desegregation orders to all publicly owned spaces (beyond just schools), and authorized the US attorney general to bring suits on behalf of Black plaintiffs or those whose civil rights were violated (a component that had been stripped from the previous Civil Rights Acts) (Fox, 2022).

FIGURE 16   THE MARCH ON WASHINGTON FOR JOBS AND FREEDOM, AUGUST 28, 1963

SOURCE: Leffler, W. K., photographer. (1963). Retrieved from the Library of Congress.

The bill gained momentum following the March on Washington. In August 1963, the March on Washington for Jobs and Freedom brought together 250,000 gathered at the Lincoln Memorial seeking equal opportunities, fair treatment and the passage of the Civil Rights Act. Civil Rights leaders and musicians led the day culminating in King's famous "I Have a Dream" speech. Following the March, civil rights leaders, including King, met with President Kennedy and Vice-President Johnson (Gilbert, 1982). A few weeks later, in September 1963, four girls died and twenty-two more people were injured in a bombing at the 16th Street Baptist Church in Birmingham, Alabama. Their deaths sparked more outrage and calls for the signing of the Civil Rights Act (English-Reif, 2020). The following November, President Kennedy was assassinated; President Johnson pressured Congress to pass the legislation in his first speech as president. Johnson would sign the Civil Rights Act into Law the following July (1964).

The Civil Rights Act of 1964 would provide broader protections, prohibiting discrimination for not just race and "color" but also national origin, religion, and sex. Discrimination against the hiring, promoting or firing of individuals on the basis of race, color, national origin, religion, and sex was also included. Discrimination in public places, accommodations, and federally funded programs was banned. There were now enforcement and protections for voting rights and school desegregation. The US attorney general was authorized to bring suit to schools on behalf of Black plaintiffs to support desegregation; and the secretary of education was authorized to collect data, which could be used to support plaintiff suits, on desegregation efforts and provide funding to support desegregation efforts.

There would be key areas of the Civil Rights Act of 1864 that would focus on systemic change in education. Title VI (1964) would provide protections against discrimination, using federal funding as the incentive and deterrent (National Archives, 2022):

> No person in the United States shall, on the ground of race, color, or national origin, be excluded from participation in, be denied the benefits of, or be subjected to discrimination under any program or activity receiving Federal financial assistance.

To support the efforts of the US attorney general, the courts were identified as the mechanism for deliberating and identifying remedies for districts found to continue to be segregated in Title IV (1964):

> The Attorney General is authorized, after giving notice of such complaint to the appropriate school board or college authority and after certifying that he is satisfied that such board or authority has had a reasonable time to adjust the conditions alleged in such complaint, to institute for or in the name of the United States a civil action in any appropriate district court of the United States against such parties and for such relief as may be appropriate, and such court shall have and shall exercise jurisdiction of proceedings instituted pursuant to this section, provided that nothing herein shall empower any official or court of the United States to issue any order seeking to achieve a racial balance in any school by requiring the transportation of pupils or students from one school to another or one school district to another in order to achieve

such racial balance, or otherwise enlarge the existing power of the court to insure compliance with constitutional standards. The Attorney General may implead as defendants such additional parties as are or become necessary to the grant of effective relief hereunder.

The range of remedies available to be used by the courts would be tested as resistance to the Civil Rights Act and desegregation efforts grew. The following year, the Voting Right Act would be passed along with the Elementary and Secondary Education Act.

Hundreds of thousands of people would be needed to be deployed as military or as civil activists to ensure basic human rights would be enshrined and codified into legislation.

ELEMENTARY AND SECONDARY EDUCATION ACT (1965)

Following the Civil Rights Act of 1964, the Johnson administration proposed and advocated for a range of educational acts in partnership with Congress. President Johnson, a child of two teachers and a former teacher at every educational level himself, made education the key component of his signature "War on Poverty" (Casalaspi, 2017).

The federal government had been minimally involved in K–12 education and the broader education system. Johnson at the start of his presidency signed into law the Higher Education Facilities Act of 1963 and the Vocational Education Act of 1963. These laws increase the involvement of the federal government in education by expanding funding for new building construction and renovation at high education institutions, as well as supporting vocational training in secondary schools, vocational schools, and communities, respectively (Casalaspi, 2017).

Progressing from the bills, in 1964, Johnson also signed the reauthorization of the National Defense Education Act (1958). The bill provided loans and scholarships for teacher preparation in science and modern foreign language, grants for math and science state programs, and modern language programs in schools. In addition, it established guidance counseling services and provided funds for research into media and technology use for educational purposes. The 1964 amendments expanded the list of subjects to include civics, history, geography, English, and reading as well as support for those who were in teacher preparation programs for "disadvantaged youth" (Hunt, 2023).

In January 1965, Johnson introduced to Congress a legislative package focused on education titled, "Towards Full Educational Opportunity" (Casalaspi, 2017). The plan, which became the Elementary and Secondary

Education Act (ESEA), contained five parts or Titles. Title I had several design components. Unlike previous federal investments, the focus of the program was both to decrease political resistance and to be employed as a tool for social change with "disadvantaged children." Local school districts with high concentrations of children from low-income households would receive additional funding to close the skills gap in math, reading, and writing. Title II supported the purchase of library books and textbooks; over two-thirds of schools in 1965 had no libraries at all. Title III supported "Supplemental Educational Centers and Services." These funds were applied to a wide range of categories: guidance counseling, school health, psychological services, and social work as well as the construction or leasing of buildings to house physical education, recreational activities, or instructional materials. Title IV supported the development of educational research facilities. Title V supported state education departments and their administration.

The bill was signed into law the following April, releasing the largest amount of federal funds ever into K–12 education. The use of Title I funds did lead to a decrease of drop outs, failures, suspensions, and expulsions in the years that followed. The increase of federal funds to education and the constraints of the Civil Rights Act to bar administering federal funds to institutions that discriminate based on race spurred more desegregation efforts in order to have access to the funds. Southern states, which received the majority of Title I funds, saw Black student attendance to predominantly white schools increase from 6 percent to nearly 32 percent two years following the passage of the Elementary and Secondary Education Act (ESEA) (Gamson et al., 2015). The law would undergo several revisions in the subsequent years, shifting its focus and impact with each revision.

The bill would be the foundational design for the subsequent systems for public education. Drafted as a parallel system to the Civil Rights Act and Voting Rights Act, there would be continued challenges and changes to the ESEA system of K–12 education in the years to come.

GREEN V. SCHOOL BOARD OF NEW KENT COUNTY (1968)

Virginia's "Massive Resistance" continued to perpetuate a segregated system of education. Students would need to apply to the State Pupil Placement Board to be reassigned to a new school, or the students would automatically be reassigned to the school they previously attended, under the schools "freedom of choice plan" (Allen & Daugherity, 2020). In 1964, New Kent County's schools, the all-white New Kent School and the all-Black George W. Watkins schools, had a few Black students apply for admission to the Black or white school, respectively. In the years that followed, few Black students applied and transferred to New Kent, and no white students applied to Watkins. Calvin Green, president of the New Kent NAACP and school teacher, filed a petition with other residents of New Kent and the Virginia

State Conference NAACP on behalf of his youngest son, Charles Green, the namesake of the case that would be brought before the Supreme Court in April 1968, *Charles C. Green et al. v. County School Board of New Kent County.*

The Court ruled swiftly in the following May 1968. Justice Brennan delivered the opinion (*Green v. County School Board, 1968*).

> The pattern of separate "white" and "Negro" schools in the New Kent County school system established under compulsion of state laws is precisely the pattern of segregation to which Brown I and Brown II were particularly addressed, and which Brown I declared unconstitutionally denied Negro school children equal protection of the laws. Racial identification of the system's schools was complete, extending not just to the composition of student bodies at the two schools but to every facet of school operations—faculty, staff, transportation, extracurricular activities and facilities. In short, the State, acting through the local school board and school officials, organized and operated a dual system, part "white" and part "Negro."

> . . . We do not hold that "freedom of choice" can have no place in such a plan. We do not hold that a "freedom-of-choice" plan might of itself be unconstitutional, although that argument has been urged upon us. Rather, all we decide today is that in desegregating a dual system a plan utilizing "freedom of choice" is not an end in itself. As Judge Sobeloff has put it,

> Freedom of choice is not a sacred talisman; it is only a means to a constitutionally required end—the abolition of the system of segregation and its effects. If the means prove effective, it is acceptable, but if it fails to undo segregation, other means must be used to achieve this end. The school officials have the continuing duty to take whatever action may be necessary to create a "unitary, nonracial system."

The Green case gave renewed focus on targeting the "dual school systems" found throughout not just the south but also the north. The court made more clear its direction for school authorities and leaders:

> School boards such as the respondent then operating state-compelled dual systems were nevertheless clearly charged with the affirmative duty to take whatever steps might be necessary to convert to a unitary system in which racial discrimination would be eliminated root and branch. The constitutional rights of Negro school children articulated in Brown I permit no less than this, and it was to this end that Brown II commanded school boards to bend their efforts.

The case highlighted the weight of historic oppression such as systemic issues of housing and segregation and also pointed to a unitary school system as a means of repair or justice. The thrust of the case accomplished this while pointing to the factors to identify segregated school systems: faculty, staff, transportation, extracurricular activities, and facilities.

These, while not exhaustive, would be the best attempt of deeper analysis by the court in understanding the systemic factors driving racism in education. The country's struggle over desegregation would continue to strain both the nation and the court.

SWANN V. CHARLOTTE-MECKLENBURG (1971)

Challenges to school integration continued, with more fights landing in front of the Supreme Court. In collaboration with the NAACP Legal Defense fund and nine other black families, Darius Swann, a professor at a university in Charlotte, sued the Charlotte-Mecklenburg Schools (CMS) Board of Education after the Board denied their request to have his child, James, be assigned to the predominately white school closer to their home. The Swanns' case initially lost, as the board was "pursuing clear progress toward integration." The board's plans "towards progress" relied on zoning districts for educational gerrymandering and school choice options (Farinde et al., 2014). The Swanns refiled with the US District Court and won, requiring CMS to submit a new desegregation plan. As the CMS was found unsatisfactory by the court, the court ordered CMS to institute a new expert-designed plan, which included rezoning school attendance zones, busing, and grade-level grouping at the elementary grades (first to fourth, fifth to sixth) (Swann et al., 1971). The Board of Education appealed, believing the plan was unreasonable, which led to the case being heard before the Supreme Court in October 1970.

The Supreme Court heard *Swann v. Charlotte-Mecklenburg Schools Board of Education* in October 1970. Through the arguments, it explored distinct problems.

The use of racial quotas one area explored. The court clearly communicated that limited uses of racial composition quotas could be used as a starting point but not as a rigid requirement.

The overall racial composition of a school or "one-race school(s)" was argued. Schools of a single (or virtually single) racial composition would not in itself indicate segregation practices; but there should be a high level of scrutiny with school authorities able to demonstrate that the racial composition does not result from their present or past discriminatory practice. One area the court highlighted was students and families' voluntary desegregation from "majority-to-minority" schools with transportation provided.

The appropriate use of attendance zones was noted. The court highlighted that the objective of desegregation needs to be the lens from which attendance and zoning plans are written. Attendance zones not designed in this manner may be insufficient, while pairing and grouping plans are helpful tools to consider.

Finally, the court found that school assignment to the schools closest to their home may not be enough to dismantle the dual school system. Busing was highlighted as an effective "remedial" tool. The court summarized the following opinion (1971):

> Desegregation means the assignment of students to public schools and within such schools without regard to their race, color, religion, or national origin, but "desegregation" shall not mean the assignment of students to public schools in order to overcome racial imbalance.

> In the past, choices in this respect have been used as a potent weapon for creating or maintaining a state-segregated school system. In addition to the classic pattern of building schools specifically intended for Negro or white students, school authorities have sometimes, since Brown, closed schools which appeared likely to become racially mixed through changes in neighborhood residential patterns. This was sometimes accompanied by building new schools in the areas of white suburban expansion farthest from Negro population centers in order to maintain the separation of the races with a minimum departure from the formal principles of "neighborhood zoning." Such a policy does more than simply influence the short-run composition of the student body of a new school. It may well promote segregated residential patterns which, when combined with "neighborhood zoning," further lock the school system into the mold of separation of the races. Upon a proper showing, a district court may consider this in fashioning a remedy.

> The central issue in this case is that of student assignment, and there are essentially four problem areas:

> 1. to what extent racial balance or racial quotas may be used as an implement in a remedial order to correct a previously segregated system;

> 2. whether every all-Negro and all-white school must be eliminated as an indispensable part of a remedial process of desegregation;

> 3. what the limits are, if any, on the rearrangement of school districts and attendance zones, as a remedial measure; and

> 4. what the limits are, if any, on the use of transportation facilities to correct state-enforced racial school segregation.

The Supreme Court ruled unanimously in favor of the Swanns and the NAACP. Justice Burger (*Swann, J. E., et al. v. Charlotte-Mecklenburg Board of Education*, 1971) wrote the opinion for the court. He pointed to previous practices highlighted by the Green case as the initial standard for school equity:

> When a system has been dual in these respects, the first remedial responsibility of school authorities is to eliminate invidious racial distinctions. With respect to such matters as transportation, supporting personnel, and extracurricular activities, no more than this may be necessary. Similar corrective action must be taken with regard to the maintenance of buildings and the distribution of equipment. In these areas, normal administrative practice should produce schools of like quality, facilities, and staffs.

The court's affirming of busing practices had the most lasting and broad impact on both Charlotte-Mecklenburg Schools and national desegregation practices. Notably, Burger wrote that the goal of considering race as a tool of integration rather than segregation had some value, reversing the design and intention of segregation practices. CMS became the standard for desegregation practices nationally for nearly two decades. The plan directly challenged the systemic structures such as residential redlining, which impacted subsequent systems like school composition and quality (Graff, 2021), by using one of the factors, racial identification as a means to create a counteractive process. The school system would be celebrated for the model practice, and economic progress in the region would grow (Graff, 2021).

MILLIKEN V. BRADLEY (1974)

Despite some gains in desegregation efforts, school segregation remained prominent. Resistance to desegregation efforts continued to be present in both the south and north.

In 1970, on behalf of her two children, Ronald and Richard Bradley, as well as Black children throughout Detroit, Verda Bradley and the NAACP sued then-Governor Robert Milliken and other state officials, asserting that the state of Michigan had intentionally segregated the Detroit public school system through practices such as housing segregation (Meinke, 2011). Federal District Court Judge Stephen Roth heard testimony on redlining practices, exclusionary zoning, housing discrimination, and police-sanctioned violence in a coordinated plan to create not just housing segregation but also educational segregation (Runyan et al., 2022).

Prior to the initial federal testimony for *Milliken v. Bradley*, Detroit had gained national attention regarding race and integration. Detroit had become one of the most diverse and the most segregated cities in the

US (Runyan et al., 2022). Growing pressures continued as segregation, racial injustice, and the decline of the car industry contracted leading to the Uprising of 1967 (Emeka, 2023). The aftermath left many dead but also supported reform efforts with a focus on addressing many systemic issues that lead to the upheaval, including the education system (Emeka, 2023).

The Detroit Board of Education developed a plan that addressed many of the educational calls for reform. Known as the April 7th Plan, it referred to a voluntary desegregation and decentralization plan that would integrate eleven racially identifiable high schools. The state legislature ultimately blocked the plan by passing a bill, Public Act 48 (Act 48), which placed school districts (and integration plans) under local neighborhood control. The bill also included an "open enrollment" policy permitting white students to transition out of Black schools, undoing the work of integration in the previous few years (Runyan et al., 2022).These actions led Verda Bradley and many Detroit families to join with the NAACP to sue Governor Milliken and others in federal court.

The federal case reviewed the history of discriminatory state-sanctioned segregation (de jure segregation) in the policies and practices of the Home Owners' Loan Corporation, the Federal Housing Administration, and the Veterans Affairs. New school construction in white neighborhoods, school boundaries drafted to promote the most racially segregated schools, and the open attendance zone policy, drafted and supported by the Detroit Board and state officials, were also scrutinized in the case. Federal Judge Roth found that the Detroit Board of Education, state, and government policy at all levels were responsible for racial discrimination and school (and housing) segregation. Judge Roth noted that an interdistrict remedy would be necessary, as the Detroit Public Schools and surrounding districts were designed to be segregated through de jure segregation. Judge Roth (*Bradley v. Milliken*, 1971) wrote the following:

> Governmental actions and inaction at all levels, federal, state and local, have combined, with those of private organizations, such as loaning institutions and real estate associations and brokerage firms, to establish and to maintain the pattern of residential segregation throughout the Detroit metropolitan area. It is no answer to say that restricted practices grew gradually (as the black population in the area increased between 1920 and 1970), or that since 1948 racial restrictions on the ownership of real property have been removed. The policies pursued by both government and private persons and agencies have a continuing and present effect upon the complexion of the community as we know, the choice of a residence is a relatively infrequent affair. For many years FHA and VA openly advised and advocated the maintenance of "harmonious" neighborhoods, i. e., racially and economically harmonious. The conditions created continue. While it would be unfair to charge the present defendants with what other

governmental officers or agencies have done, it can be said that the actions or the failure to act by the responsible school authorities, both city and state, were linked to that of these other governmental units. When we speak of governmental action we should not view the different agencies as a collection of unrelated units. Perhaps the most that can be said is that all of them, including the school authorities, are, in part, responsible for the segregated condition which exists. And we note that just as there is an interaction between residential patterns and the racial composition of the schools, so there is a corresponding effect on the residential pattern by the racial composition of the schools.

In conclusion, however, we find that both the State of Michigan and the Detroit Board of Education have committed acts which have been causal factors in the segregated condition of the public schools of the City of Detroit. As we assay the principles essential to a finding of de jure segregation, as outlined in rulings of the United States Supreme Court, they are:

1. The State, through its officers and agencies, and usually, the school administration, must have taken some action or actions with a purpose of segregation.

2. This action or these actions must have created or aggravated segregation in the schools in question.

3. A current condition of segregation exists.

We find these tests to have been met in this case. We recognize that causation in the case before us is both several and comparative. The principal causes undeniably have been population movement and housing patterns, but state and local governmental actions, including school board actions, have played a substantial role in promoting segregation. It is, the Court believes, unfortunate that we cannot deal with public school segregation on a no-fault basis, for if racial segregation in our public schools is an evil, then it should make no difference whether we classify it de jure or de facto. Our objective, logically, it seems to us, should be to remedy a condition which we believe needs correction. In the most realistic sense, if fault or blame must be found it is that of the community as a whole, including, of course, the black components. We need not minimize the effect of the actions of federal, state and local governmental officers and agencies, and the actions of loaning institutions and real estate firms, in the establishment and maintenance of segregated residential patterns which lead to school segregation to observe that blacks, like ethnic groups in the past, have tended to separate from the larger group and associate together. The ghetto is at once both a place of confinement and a refuge. There is enough blame for everyone to share.

In response to the ruling, the Detroit Board submitted a new integration plan which focused on cross-district busing across the fifty-three Detroit-area school districts. The ruling and appeal were upheld by the Court of Appeals, leading the case to be reviewed by the Supreme Court. The case was heard before the Supreme Court in February 1974.

In a narrow five to four decision, the court overturned the lower courts. Writing for the narrow majority, Chief Justice Burger (*Milliken v. Bradley,* 1974) wrote the following:

> Here, the District Court's approach to what constituted "actual desegregation" raises the fundamental question, not presented in *Swann,* as to the circumstances in which a federal court may order desegregation relief that embraces more than a single school district. The court's analytical starting point was its conclusion that school district lines are no more than arbitrary lines on a map drawn "for political convenience." Boundary lines may be bridged where there has been a constitutional violation calling for inter-district relief, but the notion that school district lines may be casually ignored or treated as a mere administrative convenience is contrary to the history of public education in our country. No single tradition in public education is more deeply rooted than local control over the operation of schools; local autonomy has long been thought essential both to the maintenance of community concern and support for public schools and to quality of the educational process.
>
> . . . We conclude that the relief ordered by the District Court and affirmed by the Court of Appeals was based upon an erroneous standard and was unsupported by record evidence that acts of the outlying districts effected the discrimination found to exist in the schools of Detroit.
>
> Accordingly, the judgment of the Court of Appeals is reversed and the case is remanded for further proceedings consistent with this opinion leading to prompt formulation of a decree directed to eliminating the segregation found to exist in Detroit city schools, a remedy which has been delayed since 1970.

The dissent by Justice Orville Douglas noted that the case was actually seen four times before the Court of Appeals and both issues of segregation and desegregation plans were reviewed. The Supreme Court focused exclusively on the question of the integration plan, but it provided no plan for Detroit after years of court battles. Douglas noted that the state of Michigan set and established the borders and the education system was not locally controlled but state controlled, "as a matter of Michigan law, the State itself has the final say as to where and how school district lines should be drawn."

Douglas (*Milliken v. Bradley,* 1974) wrote bluntly the court ruling echoed previous problematic rulings of the court:

> When we rule against the metropolitan area remedy, we take a step that will likely put the problems of the blacks and our society back to the period that antedated the "separate but equal" regime of Plessy v. Ferguson.
>
> The reason is simple. The inner core of Detroit is now rather solidly black; and the blacks, we know, in many instances are likely to be poorer, just as were the Chicanos in San Antonio School District v. Rodriguez. By that decision, the poorer school districts must pay their own way. It is therefore a foregone conclusion that we have now given the States a formula whereby the poor must pay their own way.
>
> Today's decision, given Rodriguez, means that there is no violation of the Equal Protection Clause though the schools are segregated by race and though the black schools are not only "separate" but "inferior."
>
> So far as equal protection is concerned, we are now in a dramatic retreat from the 7-to-1 decision in 1896 that blacks could be segregated in public facilities, provided they received equal treatment.
>
> ... The creation of the school districts in Metropolitan Detroit either maintained existing segregation or caused additional segregation. Restrictive covenants maintained by state action or inaction build black ghettos. It is state action when public funds are dispensed by housing agencies to build racial ghettos. Where a community is racially mixed and school authorities segregate schools, or assign black teachers to black schools or close schools in fringe areas and build new schools in black areas and in more distant white areas, the State creates and nurtures a segregated school system just as surely as did those States involved in *Brown v. Board of Education* when they maintained dual school systems.
>
> All these conditions and more were found by the District Court to exist. The issue is not whether there should be racial balance, but whether the State's use of various devices that end up with black schools and white schools brought the Equal Protection Clause into effect. Given the State's control over the educational system in Michigan, the fact that the black schools are in one district and the white schools are in another is not controlling—either constitutionally or equitably. No specific plan has yet been adopted. We are still at an interlocutory stage of a long drawn-out judicial effort at school desegregation. It is conceivable that ghettos develop

on their own, without any hint of state action. But since Michigan, by one device or another, has, over the years, created black school districts and white school districts, the task of equity is to provide a unitary system for the affected area where, as here, the State washes its hands of its own creations.

Douglas noted that the court applied a still developing standard to the *new* and ongoing process of upholding the law and school desegregation. The *Milliken v Bradely* decision also made the court appear to retreat from the work before it had fully begun.

Justice Marshall (*Milliken v. Bradley,* 1974) added to the dissent:

> The flaw of a Detroit-only decree is not that it does not reach some ideal degree of racial balance or mixing. It simply does not promise to achieve actual desegregation at all. It is one thing to have a system where a small number of students remain in racially identifiable schools. It is something else entirely to have a system where all students continue to attend such schools.

> . . . Desegregation is not and was never expected to be an easy task. Racial attitudes ingrained in our Nation's childhood and adolescence are not quickly thrown aside in its middle years. But just as the inconvenience of some cannot be allowed to stand in the way of the rights of others, so public opposition, no matter how strident, cannot be permitted to divert this Court from the enforcement of the constitutional principles at issue in this case. Today's holding, I fear, is more a reflection of a perceived public mood that we have gone far enough in enforcing the Constitution's guarantee of equal justice than it is a product of neutral principles of law. In the short run, it may seem to be the easier course to allow our great metropolitan areas to be divided up each into two cities one white, the other black-but it is a course, I predict, our people will ultimately regret.

Ultimately, Justice Marshall's dissent would seem prophetic. Prior to *Milliken v. Bradley* in 1965, the Detroit public schools were nearly 55 percent Black, a year after the ruling the DPS was now 65 percent Black. The Detroit Public Schools were 82 percent Black by 2020. In the decades that followed, DPS would struggle not just with student enrollment but financial instability, falling under state control for years. School desegregation would be halted, if not reversed in the following years (Orfield et al., 2014). The ruling would signal that school district boundaries would become castle walls of defense to support white flight. The ruling also was veiled in racism, as the white suburban schools were implied to be damaged by a more diverse student body rather than that the greater school community and community at large would benefit from a more integrated school system.

The Supreme Court ruling (1974) did remand the federal district courts for a new plan. Federal Judge DeMascio (who replaced the late Judge Roth) worked with experts to design a new plan with significant educational components: reading programs, parental involvement, school-community relations, students' rights and responsibilities, curriculum design, bilingual education, multiethnic education, accountability, cocurricular activities, teacher and administrator in-service training, guidance and counseling programs, and revised testing procedures (Marcus, 1992). The state was ordered to pay half of the additional costs of the educational components. Michigan appealed the ruling, which was upheld and again *Milliken v. Bradley* (*Milliken II*) was before the Supreme Court.

Milliken II was heard before the court in March 1977 with a ruling the following June (1977). Chief Justice Burger wrote the unanimous opinion affirming the district courts (*Milliken v. Bradley*, 1977):

> The decree requires state officials, held responsible for unconstitutional conduct, in findings which are not challenged, to eliminate a *de jure* segregated school system. More precisely, the burden of state officials is that set forth in *Swann*—to take the necessary steps "to eliminate from the public schools all vestiges of state-imposed segregation."

> The educational components, which the District Court ordered into effect *prospectively,* are plainly designed to wipe out continuing conditions of inequality produced by the inherently unequal dual school system long maintained by Detroit.

> These programs were not, and, as a practical matter, could not be, intended to wipe the slate clean by one bold stroke, as could a retroactive award of money in *Edelman.* Rather, by the nature of the antecedent violation, which, on this record, caused significant deficiencies in communications skills—reading and speaking—the victims of Detroit's *de jure* segregated system will continue to experience the effects of segregation until such future time as the remedial programs can help dissipate the continuing effects of past misconduct. Reading and speech deficiencies cannot be eliminated by judicial fiat; they will require time, patience, and the skills of specially trained teachers. That the programs are also "compensatory" in nature does not change the fact that they are part of a plan that operates *prospectively* to bring about the delayed benefits of a unitary school system.

In his concurring opinion Justice Marshall wrote the following:

> I write to emphasize its uniqueness, and the consequent limited precedential effect of much of the Court's opinion.

Normally, the plaintiffs in this type of litigation are students, parents, and supporting organizations that desire to desegregate a school system alleged to be the product, in whole or in part, of *de jure* segregative action by the public school authorities.

The principal defendant is usually the local board of education or school board. Occasionally, the state board of education and state officials are joined as defendants. This protracted litigation commenced in 1970 in this conventional mold. In the intervening years, however, the posture of the litigation has changed so drastically as to leave it largely a friendly suit between the plaintiffs (respondents Bradley et al.) and the original principal defendant, the Detroit School Board. These parties, antagonistic for years, have now joined forces, apparently for the purpose of extracting funds from the state treasury.

As between the original principal parties—the plaintiffs and the Detroit School Board—no case or controversy remains on the issues now before us. The Board enthusiastically supports the entire desegregation decree even though the decree intrudes deeply on the Board's own decision making powers. Indeed, the present School Board proposed most of the educational components included in the District Court's decree. The plaintiffs originally favored a desegregation plan that would have required more extensive transportation of pupils, and they did not initially propose or endorse the educational components. In this Court, however, the plaintiffs also support the decree of the District Court as affirmed by the Court of Appeals.

Thus the only complaining party is the State of Michigan (acting through state officials), and its basic complaint concerns money, not desegregation. It has been ordered to pay about $5,800,000 to the Detroit School Board. . . .

Although the court upheld the district court's ruling, the new remedy was not to change the racist education system but to mitigate the effects done by the system. The largest message taken from *Milliken* was that busing would no longer be a viable tool in desegregation efforts, nationally halting many desegregation efforts. Other lessons from *Milliken II* were that the state and other educational entities may be responsible for compensatory educational programs and fees for historic and present segregation that seemed lost in the briefest passing of time. Most notably, the Supreme Court departed from seeking "a unitary system in which racial discrimination would be eliminated root and branch" to simply compensating families and children damaged by a racist dual system that would be indefinitely delayed.

Coded: *Mitigating racial trauma is preferred over preventing racial trauma.*

Coded: *Black means separate and still unequal in school systems.*

Coded: *White has preference of schools.*

Coded: *White has preference of systemic remedies.*

NO CHILD LEFT BEHIND (2001)

While the Supreme Court struggled over the desegregation of schools, the Elementary and Secondary Education Act would have several revisions. Most notably at this time, the Educational Amendments of 1972, which amended ESEA, introduced Title IX (which the acts would be generally referred to). Title IX would be added to prohibit sex discrimination in federally funded education programs. Subsequent reauthorizations included the Education Consolidation and Improvement Act (ECIA) (1981) and Improving America's Schools Act (IASA) (1994), which progressively increased the standard used to evaluate students and accountability measures of school districts (Gamson et al., 2015). The ECIA revisions notably withdrew federal funding, support, and **intervention** for "domestic social endeavors," which included desegregation, education, civil rights investigations, and enforcement (Darling-Hammond & Marks, 1983).

These reauthorizations and revisions would lay the foundation for the most notable reauthorization known as No Child Left Behind (NCLB). NCLB was a bipartisan bill seen initially as a tool for educational equity with the focus on educationally underserved students, including English-language learners, special education students, economically disadvantaged students, and minoritized students. For the different student populations ("subgroups"), equity would be achieved with "100 proficiency" on annual achievement tests published in an annual "report card" or district-level summarizing report (Klein, 2015). In theory, the report would demonstrate the national schools each closing the achievement gap, or "closing the gap." The achievement gap was the noted disparity in average performance between Black students (and other minoritized students) and their white peers. The act was right in collecting data, defining disparity between schools and districts, and making that data public. The transparency of school demographic data and performance was likely one of the most helpful tools of the act. Teachers working in Title I schools were required to be "highly qualified," meeting established standards in specific subject areas or developmental areas (Klein, 2015).

Most significant in NCLB were the accountability measures of the reauthorization. States risked losing federal funding for not complying with the new requirements. Schools published annual report cards, showing their Adequate Yearly Progress (AYP), on the annual achievement tests. Schools that didn't demonstrate progress (AYP) risked a range of penalties. After two years, the school would be given technical assistance and students could transfer to another public school. Students could use Title 1 (T1) funds to pay for compensatory educational supports like supplemental school or tutoring after a third year of not meeting AYP. A fourth year would require staffing changes, and a fifth year would require structural changes including a change to a charter school or allowing takeover by the state or a private management company (Lawrence, 2006).

In a report released by the Council of Chief State School Officers (Blank, 2011), it's evident that the goal of NCLB to close the achievement gap, failed. As the gap continued to widen in more than half the states in both reading and math in the subsequent years, NCLB amounted to a perversion of ESEA. Students who suffered from lack of access to higher quality schools due to segregation at the start of ESEA were penalized under NCLB through reduced funding and state takeovers because their schools lacked the systemic supports to help them thrive.

Student transfers were permitted after two years but only in the same district; the impermeable walls of *Milliken v. Bradley* still existed (Krieg, 2011). Student growth in hard-working districts could easily be outpaced by the rising standards of AYP toward 100 percent, leading districts to be penalized regardless of innovations, reforms, or incremental student progress constrained by conditions outside the walls of their buildings.

NCLB was notably underfunded. Title I was notably funded more than $10 million less by 2015 than the anticipated allocation for 2007 of $25 million (Klein, 2015). The federal allocation funds for schools still only amounted to approximately 10 percent of the operating costs; simply, districts with more local funds would continue to have more investment funds then those districts targeted in the NCLB funding (Darling-Hammond et al., 2007). School entities with few students identified in a subgroup automatically made AYP under NCLB, providing disproportionate advantage both financially and regarding interventions and progress with racially segregated school systems (Reardon et al., 2013).

The funding wasn't just noted in domestic policy analysis. Compared to other developed countries, centralized (federal) funding for education is and remains one of the lowest among industrialized nations (OECD, 2019).

NCLB served as a distraction from actual systemic change. The standard focused resources on test administration and test-taking rather than teacher recruitment/preparation, enriching curriculum, and other educational material like library resources. The focus on test performance was also separate and not directly related to the development of other deeper learning skills like critical thinking, metacognition, or other performance skills (Darling-Hammond et al., 2007). Rather than narrowly focus on assessment performance policy investments in high quality preschool and child healthcare would have been better approaches, as both have been demonstrated both domestically and internationally to support student achievement (Fiscella & Kitzman, 2009).

Ultimately, No Child Left Behind used the same definitions of race that had evolved to support racist systems without attempting to change or challenge the systems. The policy created lofty goals for students but did not invest in the lofty goals of changing the system. The systems of school segregation were perpetuated with tools to address these injustices dismantled decades before. Most importantly, valuative judgements of students' ability, mirroring the racist and language of the past, continued through the lens of achievement testing.

Coded: *Black means underfunded and underscored.*

Coded: *White system reforms benefit white systems.*

STUDENTS FOR FAIR ADMISSIONS, INC. (SFFA) V. PRESIDENT & FELLOWS OF HARVARD COLLEGE (HARVARD) (2022)

The shifting scales of changing systems and the impact on education was demonstrated during *Students for Fair Admissions, Inc. (SFFA) v. President & Fellows of Harvard College (Harvard)*. The plaintiff, SFFA, was founded by Edward Blum, a former financial advisor and congressional candidate turned legal strategist who focused on removing civil rights protections (or in his words, "racial preferences") in America (Liptak, 2017). He led *Shelby County v. Holder* (2013), the narrowly decided Supreme Court case that undermined the Voting Rights Act, struck down the process, including the formula that states and regions with the deepest darkest histories of voter suppression would require federal approval prior to making changes to voting policies to ensure they were nondiscriminatory (Liptak, 2017). The case led to a rise in voter suppression laws and voter disenfranchisement (Chang et al., 2021). Next, Blum challenged, unsuccessfully, the University of Texas's race-conscious admissions policies in *Fisher v. University of Texas* (Hannah-Jones, 2013).

Abigail Fisher, the plaintiff in *Fisher v. University of Texas*, and her father Richard Fisher joined Blum on the board of directors for SFFA (Hinger, 2018). Blum actively sought Asian plaintiffs and then filed the suit on their behalf against both Harvard University under Title VI of the Civil Rights Act, stating that the practices discriminated against Asian candidates in preference of white candidates (and other races) (Hinger, 2018). The case was later consolidated with a case filed by SFFA against the University of North Carolina under the equal protection clause of the Fourteenth amendment. The number of plaintiffs and their identities were sealed.

The initial suit was filed in November 2014, eventually leading to a court hearing and ruling from the federal court in October 2019. Expert witnesses and current and former Harvard employees and students testified over the course of three weeks to inform Judge Burroughs's ruling.

The judge found no evidence of conscious prejudice or discriminatory motivations, as she noted that "Harvard has demonstrated that no workable and available race-neutral alternatives would allow it to achieve a diverse student body while still maintaining its standards for academic excellence." (Caldera et al., 2019) The ruling was affirmed by the First Circuit Court of Appeals that found the ruling consistent with decades of Supreme Court precedent and that Harvard's use of race was narrow in efforts of diversifying the student population (Bolotnikova, 2020). SFFA appealed the ruling to the Supreme Court; the case was argued in October 2022, with a ruling the following June 2023.

During oral arguments, the justices had some concerns inconsistent with presenting arguments. Justice Thomas (*Students for Fair Admissions, Inc. v. President and Fellows of Harvard College,* 2022) said, "The word diversity [appears] quite a few times, and I don't have a clue what it means. It seems to mean everything for everyone" (Seddiq & Epstein, 2022). *The Guardian* (Kirchgaessner, 2023) would report a month after the ruling that Thomas's staff had received seven payments in 2019 from SFFA attorney William Consovoy, who was a former clerk to Thomas, as well.

The court would rule six to two, with Justice Jackson, a Harvard alumni, abstaining. Writing for the majority, Justice Roberts (*Students for Fair Admissions, Inc. v. President and Fellows of Harvard College,* 2022) wrote the opinion:

> Respondents nonetheless contend that an individual's race is never a negative factor in their admissions programs, but that assertion cannot withstand scrutiny. Harvard, for example, draws an analogy between race and other factors it considers in admission. "[W]hile admissions officers may give a preference to applicants likely to excel in the Harvard-Radcliffe Orchestra," Harvard explains, "that does not mean it is a 'negative' not to excel at a musical instrument." But on Harvard's logic, while it gives preferences to applicants with high grades and test scores, "that does not mean it

is a 'negative'" to be a student with lower grades and lower test scores. This understanding of the admissions process is hard to take seriously. College admissions are zero-sum. A benefit provided to some applicants but not to others necessarily advantages the former group at the expense of the latter.

We have time and again forcefully rejected the notion that government actors may intentionally allocate preference to those "who may have little in common with one another but the color of their skin." The entire point of the Equal Protection Clause is that treating someone differently because of their skin color is *not* like treating them differently because they are from a city or from a suburb, or because they play the violin poorly or well.

The court seemed to rest much of its efforts in writing the majority opinion attacking dissent. The fifth section focused on the dissent, with half the section stating that dissenting opinion's misunderstanding of the legal components of the Fisher cases. The court concludes with the excerpt from the dissent of Justice Harlan from *Plessy v Ferguson* (1896):

But in view of the Constitution, in the eye of the law, there is in this country no superior, dominant, ruling class of citizens. There is no caste here. Our Constitution is color-blind, and neither knows nor tolerates classes among citizens. In respect of civil rights, all citizens are equal before the law. The humblest is the peer of the most powerful. The law regards man as man, and takes no account of his surroundings or of his color when his civil rights as guaranteed by the supreme law of the land are involved.

The conclusion of the majority opinion held, absent the meaning of the clear words of Harlan and the present in the evidence and rulings of the lower courts. The civil rights for individuals regarding higher education and many other aspects of modern America simply continue to not be guaranteed. Practices like race conscious admissions help to support efforts to ensure that constitutional guarantee, until the guarantee can be fully realized. While Justice Roberts included an excerpt out of context to validate the ruling opinion, Justice Harlan concluded the following in his dissent (1896).

The sure guarantee of the peace and security of each race is the clear, distinct, unconditional recognition by our governments, National and State, of every right that inheres in civil freedom, and of the equality before the law of all citizens of the United States, without regard to race. State enactments regulating the enjoyment of civil rights upon the basis of race, and cunningly devised to defeat the legitimate results of the [Civil War] under the pretence of recognizing equality of rights, can have no other result than to render permanent peace impossible and to keep alive a conflict of races the continuance of which must do harm to all concerned. . . .

The claim of race neutrality in college admissions equated to a color-blind approach. The race neutral policies take away the language of discrimination and oppression but do not acknowledge or remove the ongoing oppressive practices, systemic factors, or lasting impacts. In the court's recommendation of remedies to the ruling, it asked students to speak to courage, motivation, or determination. The call for students to voice their character was done while silencing years of legal precedence, civil action, and educational practices that were developed to address very real and present racist practices and systems. Writing the dissenting opinion, Justice Sotomayor (*Students for Fair Admissions, Inc. v. President and Fellows of Harvard College*, 2022) said the following:

> Brown was a race-conscious decision that emphasized the importance of education in our society. Central to the Court's holding was the recognition that, as Justice Harlan emphasized in Plessy, segregation perpetuates a caste system wherein Black children receive inferior educational opportunities "solely because of their race," denoting "inferiority as to their status in the community." Moreover, because education is "the very foundation of good citizenship," segregation in public education harms "our democratic society" more broadly as well. In light of the harmful effects of entrenched racial subordination on racial minorities and American democracy, Brown recognized the constitutional necessity of a racially integrated system of schools where education is "available to all on equal terms."

> . . . Those rejected arguments mirror the Court's opinion today. The Court claims that Brown requires that students be admitted " 'on a racially nondiscriminatory basis.' It distorts the dissent in Plessy to advance a colorblindness theory. Today's decision wakes the echoes of Justice John Marshall Harlan [in Plessy]"); The Court also invokes the Brown litigators, relying on what the Brown "plaintiffs had argued."

> If there was a Member of this Court who understood the Brown litigation, it was Justice Thurgood Marshall, who "led the litigation campaign" to dismantle segregation as a civil rights lawyer and "rejected the hollow, race-ignorant conception of equal protection" endorsed by the Court's ruling today. Justice Marshall joined the Bakke plurality and "applaud[ed] the judgment of the Court that a university may consider race in its admissions process." In fact, Justice Marshall's view was that Bakke's holding should have been even more protective of race-conscious college admissions programs in light of the remedial purpose of the Fourteenth Amendment and the legacy of racial inequality in our society. The Court's recharacterization of Brown is nothing but revisionist history and an affront to the legendary life of Justice Marshall, a

great jurist who was a champion of true equal opportunity, not rhetorical flourishes about colorblindness.

. . . Today, the Court concludes that indifference to race is the only constitutionally permissible means to achieve racial equality in college admissions. That interpretation of the Fourteenth Amendment is not only contrary to precedent and the entire teachings of our history, but is also grounded in the illusion that racial inequality was a problem of a different generation. Entrenched racial inequality remains a reality today. That is true for society writ large and, more specifically, for Harvard and the University of North Carolina (UNC), two institutions with a long history of racial exclusion. Ignoring race will not equalize a society that is racially unequal. What was true in the 1860s, and again in 1954, is true today: Equality requires acknowledgment of inequality.

After more than a century of government policies enforcing racial segregation by law, society remains highly segregated. About half of all Latino and Black students attend a racially homogeneous school with at least 75% minority student enrollment. The share of intensely segregated minority schools (i.e., schools that enroll 90% to 100% racial minorities) has sharply increased. To this day, the U. S. Department of Justice continues to enter into desegregation decrees with schools that have failed to "eliminat[e] the vestiges of de jure segregation."

. . . Systemic inequities disadvantaging underrepresented racial minorities exist beyond school resources. Students of color, particularly Black students, are disproportionately disciplined or suspended, interrupting their academic progress and increasing their risk of involvement with the criminal justice system. Underrepresented minorities are less likely to have parents with a postsecondary education who may be familiar with the college application process. Further, low-income children of color are less likely to attend preschool and other early childhood education programs that increase educational attainment. All of these interlocked factors place underrepresented minorities multiple steps behind the starting line in the race for college admissions.

. . . Overruling decades of precedent, today's newly constituted Court singles out the limited use of race in holistic college admissions. It strikes at the heart of Bakke, Grutter, and Fisher by holding that racial diversity is an "inescapably imponderable" objective that cannot justify race-conscious affirmative action, ante, at 24, even though respondents' objectives simply "mirror the 'compelling interest' this Court has approved" many times in the past. At bottom, without any new factual or legal justification, the

Court overrides its longstanding holding that diversity in higher education is of compelling value.

To avoid public accountability for its choice, the Court seeks cover behind a unique measurability requirement of its own creation. None of this Court's precedents, however, requires that a compelling interest meet some threshold level of precision to be deemed sufficiently compelling. In fact, this Court has recognized as compelling plenty of interests that are equally or more amorphous, including the "intangible" interest in preserving "public confidence in judicial integrity," an interest that "does not easily reduce to precise definition."

As noted above, this Court suggests that the use of race in college admissions is unworkable because respondents' objectives are not sufficiently "measurable," "focused," "concrete," and "coherent." How much more precision is required or how universities are supposed to meet the Court's measurability requirement, the Court's opinion does not say. That is exactly the point. The Court is not interested in crafting a workable framework that promotes racial diversity on college campuses. Instead, it announces a requirement designed to ensure all race-conscious plans fail. Any increased level of precision runs the risk of violating the Court's admonition that colleges and universities operate their race-conscious admissions policies with no "specified percentage[s]" and no "specific number[s] firmly in mind." Thus, the majority's holding puts schools in an untenable position. It creates a legal framework where race-conscious plans must be measured with precision but also must not be measured with precision. That holding is not meant to infuse clarity into the strict scrutiny framework; it is designed to render strict scrutiny "fatal in fact." Indeed, the Court gives the game away when it holds that, to the extent respondents are actually measuring their diversity objectives with any level of specificity (for example, with a "focus on numbers" or specific "numerical commitment"), their plans are unconstitutional.

True equality of educational opportunity in racially diverse schools is an essential component of the fabric of our democratic society. It is an interest of the highest order and a foundational requirement for the promotion of equal protection under the law. Brown recognized that passive race neutrality was inadequate to achieve the constitutional guarantee of racial equality in a Nation where the effects of segregation persist. In a society where race continues to matter, there is no constitutional requirement that institutions attempting to remedy their legacies of racial exclusion must operate with a blindfold.

Today, this Court overrules decades of precedent and imposes a superficial rule of race blindness on the Nation. The devastating impact of this decision cannot be overstated. The majority's vision of race neutrality will entrench racial segregation in higher education because racial inequality will persist so long as it is ignored.

As race was constructed and continually rewritten in US law, it will never be able to be sufficiently measured. Race was never based on precision but rather on practice. Historically, race was not simply associated with injustice but used as a tool to disadvantage and minoritize various groups. The court claims and reinforces that race is a static concept in the law, while undoing decades of civil rights precedence. The court illustrated this by defining college admissions as "zero-sum." Social inclusion programs like race-conscious admissions practices acknowledge both the lasting and far reaching impact of racist systems and actively work to mitigate them. As a result, the case evidence shows the race-conscious programs led to a five-fold increase in admissions since 1980 and a two-fold increase since 1990. Accounting for race is a way of using the language of systemic racism to dismantle the system.

In essence, the court's ruling ignores the complexity of higher education and replaces it with the simplicity of black and white. By ignoring the overarching goal and the multiple factors considered beyond race in admission, the court distilled college admission to a question about race, perpetuating the same policy mechanisms of housing, labor, education, and more found in previous race laws throughout history. There should be a clear acknowledgment of the Asian-American students' concern, racist policies, and systemic damage to everyone, but that damage, like opportunity, is not zero sum.

As noted in the case, the most probable result would be a decline in historically underserved groups, a reduction of "African American representation . . . from 14 percent to 6 percent and Hispanic representation from 14 percent to 9 percent." A greater impact beyond only college campuses will occur. Race-conscious programs in college admission and beyond would fall under scrutiny and be under attack, while race-conscious programs that offer advantages to those who prominently identify as white, such as legacy admissions, dean's interest lists, and children of donors, would remain intact (Cineas, 2023). The Supreme Court case was cited in cases over sixty times in the remaining months of 2023. The use of "zero sum" as a framing could have corporate applications and put both public and private diversity, equity and inclusion programs under pressure and scrutiny. Other federally funding application driven programs could face challenges, like housing. A wave of discrimination suits to upend civil rights will likely be filed under the Civil Rights Acts Title VII, possibly dismantling systems of equity and broadening inequality.

Coded: *Racist systems are "zero sum."*

There is much history that could be represented. The patterns of coding race and education can be seen as well illustrated in the laws, policies, and practices of the two systems. However, these aren't just historic systems that were designed, as they continue to play out in our present and our futures.

There is much history that could be represented in this book that is not highlighted, showing the coding of race, advantage, and oppression. The patterns of coding race and education can be seen as well illustrated in the laws, policies, and practices of the two systems. However, these designed historic systems don't just exist in the past—they continue to play out in our present and our futures.

CHAPTER 3 DISCUSSION QUESTIONS

- How did the integration of eugenics principles into educational reforms reflect broader nationalist agendas in early twentieth-century America? What were the implications of using schools to promote a unified national identity based on racial and ethnic purity ideals?

- In what ways can we see echoes of eugenics ideology in contemporary discussions or policies, such as debates over immigration, genetics, or even educational tracking? How has awareness (or lack thereof) of this historical context shaped current societal attitudes and policies?

- How did the implementation of the GI Bill reinforce existing racial disparities in housing and education, despite its intent to support veterans? What lasting impacts did these policies have on communities of color?

- Discuss the immediate and long-term impacts of the *Brown v. Board of Education* decision on public education in the United States. How did different states and localities interpret and implement the ruling, and what were the outcomes of these approaches? What parallels can be drawn between the challenges faced during the desegregation era and ongoing issues in education today? How can understanding historical struggles inform efforts to achieve educational equity today?

- How did the Civil Rights Act of 1964 and the Elementary and Secondary Education Act of 1965 intersect to address systemic inequalities in education and public accommodations? Discuss their combined impact and in what ways the legislation met or missed their intended ideals.

- In *Green v. School Board of New Kent County* (1968), *Swann v Charlotte Mecklenburg* (1971) and *Milliken v. Bradley* (1974), the Supreme Court addressed segregation in schools. Compare and contrast the court's approaches in these cases. How did the court's decisions and interpretations shift overtime and where are the lasting effects?

- Despite its intentions for equity, No Child Left Behind (2001) ultimately failed to close the achievement gap. What systemic and historic factors contributed to this outcome?

- *Brown v. Board of Education* (1954) is cited in both the majority and dissenting opinions; describe how each opinion uses the case and contrast that with original case rulings of *Brown v Board of Education*. How might the reduction of race-conscious admissions policies impact not only diversity on college campuses but also broader efforts toward racial equity?

PART II

·····················

UNEQUAL FUTURES

The Risk of Inequality in Systems

CHAPTER 4

....

PRESENT AND FUTURE INEQUALITY

The analysis of US history clearly illustrates a series of laws, policies, and practices that created, maintained, and expanded inequality. Most evident of these were those constructed around race. The review of the history of race and education showed how race was defined and redefined in efforts to perpetuate power, separation, wealth exploitation, and social status. Through the scan of history, we can see how from year to year, era to era, the social systems created influenced subsequent years in policies, laws, access, and opportunities. The laws and policies reviewed don't exist in a different past but serve as a legacy code, creating ripple effects in the living present and future. The historical and statistical review of what systemic inequality looks like will never fully capture the real and lived experiences of those directly impacted, for individuals, families and communities. A deeper review and analysis of inequality in the present and future paints a real and powerful picture of the urgent and current need for systemic change. While inequality exists across many systems, education has been shown as an effective lever toward creating broader systems of equity.

Specifically, while college degree completion has grown for Black American from roughly 56,000 to 200,000 from 1974–2022 (National Center for Education Statistics, 2023), there is continued disparity in both college access and degree attainment. Notably, college enrollment numbers more than doubled in the same time period, 1974–2022, while the number of white American degree attainment grew slightly over the same time from 807,000 to 1.1 million, continuing to be the vast majority of completed college degrees (National Center for Education Statistics, 2023). White American degree completion has been a constant even as Black Americans have experienced disparities in higher education with greater exposure to for-profit institutions, less access to selective schools, higher out-of-pocket expenses, and a disproportionate representation of conferred certificates and associate degrees instead of bachelor's degrees (Libassi, 2023). High school graduation rates have grown for both Blacks and whites, along with every racial group since 1992 (Office of Economic Policy, 2023).

The homeownership gap between Blacks and whites has also widened since 1976, with Black ownership falling slightly from 44 percent to 43 percent. White ownership, on the other hand, has risen during that same period from 69 percent to 72 percent. Housing contributes to the wealth gap. The Black–white racial wealth gap continues to remain the largest between groups, a wealth gap that appears to be growing, although income and wealth for both groups is on the decline (Derenoncourt et al., 2022).

FIGURE 17 A HEADLINE FROM *FORBES* REGARDING INEQUALITY AS A GLOBAL RISK

≡ **Forbes**

FORBES > BUSINESS > RETAIL

Rising Income Inequality Is Throwing The Future Of Capitalism Into Question, Says World Economic Forum

Lauren Debter Former Staff
I cover the retail industry.

Jan 11, 2017, 01:18pm EST

Inequality was highlighted as a global risk in 2017 by the World Economic Forum. The global risk reports identify high severity risks that may have worldwide impact in the next decade across industries, economies, and multiple different parties. The reports are developed from surveys of leaders in academia, business, government, nongovernmental, and international organizations. The 2017 report noted that inequality contributed to political polarization. Education was also mentioned in the report as contributing to a decrease in inequality. The lack of economic opportunity was viewed in 2024 as a continued leading global risk (World Economic Forum).

UNEQUAL FUTURES

The impact of inequality ripples in many different areas and is associated with a wide variety of outcomes.

Equity was shown to lead to safer communities. An analysis of US states and Canadian provinces showed that the greater inequality, the greater the homicide rate and risk for violent crime (Daly et al., 2001). Similarly, when economic inequality decreased, violent crime also declined (Fajnzylber et al., 2002).

Overall, inequality is associated with more negative health effects (Wilkinson & Pickett, 2006). Public health issues such as obesity and related conditions to the disease have been shown to have a similar connection with inequality as have other health issues (Wilkinson & Pickett, 2006). In addition to fewer instances of heart disease, reduced inequality rates increased overall life expectancy and decreased infant mortality (Schenkman & Bousquat, 2021).

Wealth inequality was associated with greater depressive symptoms in men and was shown to have a stronger link to mental health issues (Yu, 2018), such as psychological distress (Carter et al., 2009).

ANALYZING INEQUALITY

Inequality can be described in many different terms. Income inequality is the difference in earnings between two or more identified groups. Wealth inequality is the difference between two or more groups regarding their total assets. The term assets refers to the total amount of investments that have monetary value (homes, income, stocks, etc.) minus liabilities, which create debt (removing money or value). Wealth can be both generated over a lifetime and inherited, while income focuses on only money earned during a single individual's lifetime.

The United States has the highest income inequality of any G7 country and those differences are drawn in color lines (Schaeffer, 2020). The top fifth of the US earners account for over 53 percent of the national income. The wealth gap between the top 5 percent of US earners and the bottom 20 percent has doubled in recent years (1989 to 2016), while the Black/white income gap has persisted over the past fifty years. Specifically, Black income is $0.60 to $1.00 of white income, higher than the 1970s (Schaeffer, 2020).

The French economist Piketty (2014) noted the impact of inequality following an analysis of wealth and inequality of over twenty countries spanning centuries of data. His unprecedented research found that inequality expands faster than economic growth. Simply put, inequality compounds faster than the rate of growth. He also found that restructuring of capital distribution led to profound economic growth and technological development found in the early to mid-twentieth century. Piketty noted that rising inequality was in part due to reduced access to skills training and higher education at the end of the twentieth century and throughout the twenty-first century.

As evident throughout history, educational inequality is not just a difference in the quality of educational services and resources, leading to differences in educational outcomes, but also, as noted, results in fundamental differences in access and opportunities for individuals, as well.

FIGURE 18 **THE 14 EDUCATIONAL OPPORTUNITY INDICATORS FROM THE REPORT CALLED *UNEQUAL ACCESS TO EDUCATIONAL OPPORTUNITY IN THE UNITED STATES (2022)***

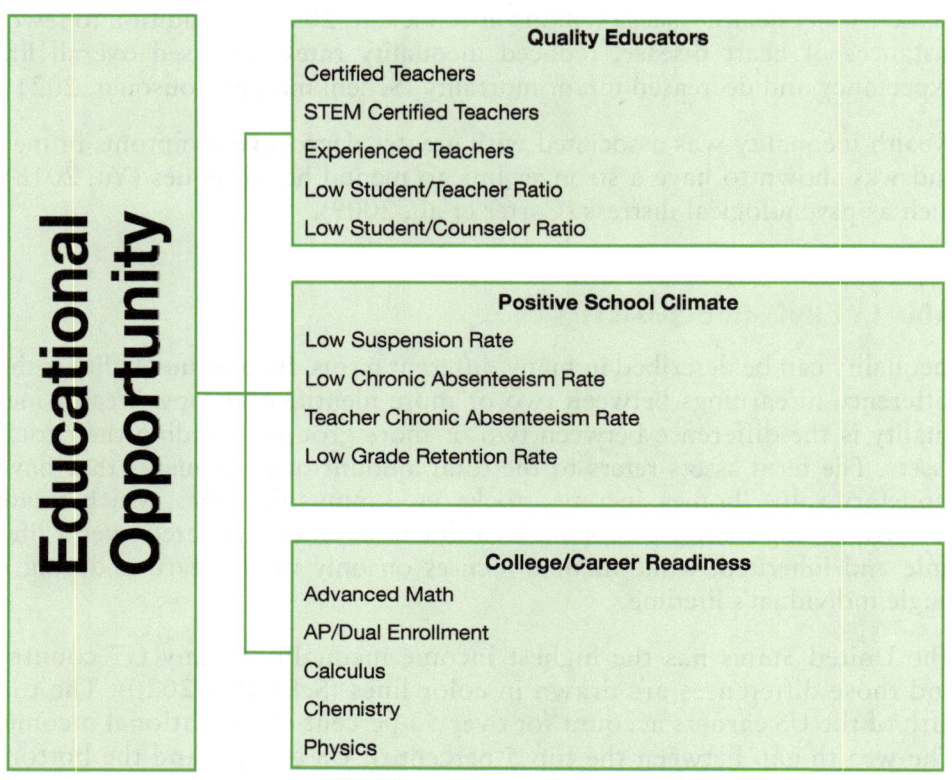

SOURCE: Shaw-Amoah & Lapp (2022). Unequal Access to Educational Opportunity in the United States. *Research for Action*.

The differences in access and opportunity can be analyzed. Analysis of the quality of educators can be done through examining several factors (Shaw-Amoah & Lapp, 2022; Fontana et al., 2020): the number of certified teachers (teachers who have met all of their state's certification requirements), STEM certified teachers (schools that have all science and math courses taught by teachers certified in the respective areas), experienced teachers (schools with 91 percent or more of teachers with two or more years of experience), a low student-to-teacher ratio (a ratio of one teacher to 14.9 students), and low student/counselor ratio (a ratio of one counselor to the recommended 250 students).

School climate can also be analyzed. Low suspensions, few student and teacher absences, and reduced grade-level retention rates can be indicators of a positive school climate. High school students having access to rigorous courses can reflect having access to broader college and career readiness skills and opportunities through the curriculum. Advanced math courses (trigonometry, statistics, precalculus), calculus, AP courses, chemistry, and physics can demonstrate a rich curriculum that provides students access to multiple pathways of opportunity.

Analysis of these areas (Shaw-Amoah & Lapp, 2022) shows that Black and Hispanic students were less likely to have access to quality educators or a positive school climate. Hispanic students had similar access as that of white students to a college and career readiness curriculum, while Black students were least likely to have access to rich curricular offerings. Black students are six times more likely to attend a high-poverty school compared to a low-poverty school, while white students are approximately five times more likely to attend a low-poverty school than a high-poverty school.

Income, wealth, and education show the contours of systems, their structures, and systemic behavior. Across the various systems, many different remedies and reforms were never fully realized.

SYSTEMS OF INEQUALITY

Through the analysis of history, there were clear patterns when the residents of the United States were denied their full citizenship. While inequality is pervasive in wealth distribution throughout the country and in present-day classrooms, it extends into areas such as labor, health, criminal justice, and more. As there are clear benefits across all groups when discussing programs, policies, and practices that reduce inequality, paradoxically many different initiatives have been stymied, blocked, or slowed once they've been reduced to a racialized issue of Black and white.

Health equity has shown to be a powerful tool to address inequality. Access to quality health care can serve to bridge divides, and the health care policy in the United States likely contributes to the low G7 inequality ranking. States that rejected Medicaid expansion noticeably have residents that now live approximately a month less on average than other states (Illing, 2019); and racialized attacks on the Affordable Care Act may also have limited the implementation and scope despite whites being the largest group (43 percent or 8.2 million) to gain coverage (Garrett & Gangopadhyaha, 2016).

Although the 1980s saw racialized attacks on "welfare queens," white people were the largest beneficiaries of government assistance programs (Foster & Rojas, 2018). In the present day, more than half of the millions of individuals participating and benefiting from poverty reduction programs are white, lifting approximately 40 percent of all participants out of poverty (Shapiro et al., 2017). Whites without a college degree were those who most benefited by these programs, pointing highlighting the broad value of such initiatives and the advantages of education programs, as well.

Other economic mobility programs, like access programs such as affirmative action, have been beneficial for all identifiable groups, but they have shown the most advantages for white women (Massie, 2023). Although areas such as housing, taxation, healthcare, criminal justice, and education have the potential to improve all citizens' lives, these sectors have historically faced and continue to face racial and classist hurdles.

The lasting impacts of stymied economic policies, anemic healthcare advances, and eroded environmental protections lead to repercussions for practices that treat communities as disposable rather than indispensable (Hopkins, 2020), reflecting a clear narrative seen throughout history. The applications of the definitions of race across history were most often used as tools of separation. The separation wasn't just based on public preference or American citizens' choices or traditions, but rather separation is interwoven into America's deepest and most fundamental binding documents. The racial codes birthed in the earliest days of the colonies to create distinctions between its people are the frames for modern language for concepts like identity, opportunity, safety, and worth. The racial identities as seen, maintained, and evolved from the earliest classifications the United States had for its citizens, leaves today's people (Black, white and beyond) feeling invisible or passed by in our modern country.

Historically, the exploitative or coercive practices are often done with a racialized narrative to follow, attributing fault or worthiness to character, intelligence, tradition, or merit as shown through skin tones. Short-term gains for some or zero-sum attitudes often outweigh mutually beneficial programs or policies, all undercutting long-term gains and the greater good. As shown, these occurrences continue to repeat, often expanding, in areas like education and beyond. Racist policies and practices confine some of our best human possibilities and collectively beneficial tools. Racism hurts everyone, just not evenly.

EDUCATION SOLUTIONS FOR UNEQUAL FUTURE

Refocusing on education, this can be a powerful equity and mobility tool. Local intervention to combat inequality was shown to reduce incidents like violent crime (Daly et al., 2001). There is a fundamental question: While the impact of inequality on education quality, access, and opportunity is clear, to what degree can education reform reduce or fight inequality?

Education is an intuitive tool for opportunity, and opportunity is one of the most precise tools for equity. Education was part of the earliest colonial designs in imagining a new society. Education was a precious resource for the enslaved and seen as a dangerous tool of the slavers to keep from the people. The Freedmen's vision for an emancipated America was through public education.

There is much power and potency of education as an equity tool. In comprehensive analysis, education is shown to have many effects. Intuitively understood, education is shown to increase income share for those economically disadvantaged. Surprisingly, income share for the extremely rich is reduced. The effects are most powerful for secondary education over both elementary and post-secondary education (Abdullah et al., 2015).

Universal access to early childhood education can be an equalizing force, as youth have the opportunity more broadly to gain access to skills and learning experiences not dependent on family resources. Students from high-earning homes have more opportunities for learning and skills acquisition not dependent on the education system (Raudenbush & Eschmann, 2015). Students who attend high-quality preschool will reap benefits many times over in fundamental areas that will shape their lives: They will increase their earning potential, lower their risk of committing violent crime, and improve their lifelong educational achievement. Going to a high-quality preschool will also enhance the overall quality of their education, reducing the need for them to receive special education services (Heckman et al., 2013).

Access to education, such as degree attainment, is not just associated with increased income but is also linked to a range of other outcomes. Net lifetime earnings for degree completion is approximately $500,000 for an associate degree and $1 million for a bachelor's degree. Currently, about 67 percent of jobs require a post-secondary degree, and this segment is over 80 percent of all earnings. This trend is expected to rise for both (Carnevale et al., 2024). Similar to the benefits of interventions focused strictly on bridging inequality, education attainment outcomes have similar advantages. Longer life expectancy, better nutrition, more good health behaviors, and better mental health are all associated with educational achievement. Degree attainment is linked to lower levels of crime, including violent crime and property crimes, and more positive civic engagement, such as voting, participation in community organizations, and volunteering. Lower and middle income groups report increased happiness resulting from earning a degree. (Carnevale et al., 2024).

Bridging inequality, education can be a tool for wealth generation. Those with higher degree attainment are shown to have high levels of wealth-generating skills and behaviors like stock and mutual fund investment (Castagno et al., 2023), and homeownership (Myers et al., 2019).

Education can be used as a tool of equity; unfortunately, education is often the target of divisive and oppressive policies and practices, leading to inequitable results. To be most effective, attention needs to be focused on the design of education systems, practices, and tools. Through the analysis of education systems, informed by the patterns of how inequality and oppression have been designed and implemented in the past, we can build more equitable futures. This can be done through a careful and detailed understanding of the structure, shape, and scope of education systems. Even with a knowledge of the systems of structures of historic and present systemic equality, we need to be equipped with the language and tools of systems design to build more equitable systems.

CHAPTER 4 DISCUSSION QUESTIONS

- Discuss the implications of the widening gap in bachelor's degree attainment between Black and white Americans despite overall increases in educational achievement. How might these disparities influence economic opportunities and social mobility across generations?

- Reflecting on Thomas Piketty's analysis of wealth and inequality, how does his observation that inequality compounds faster than economic growth resonate with the current economic landscape? What historical and systemic factors contribute to the acceleration of wealth disparities, and how can these insights inform policies aimed at promoting economic justice?

- Discuss the role of education as both a remedy for and a perpetuator of inequality. How do disparities in access to quality education, as described in the text, shape individual opportunities and broader societal outcomes? What policy changes could improve educational equity across different racial and socioeconomic groups?

PART III

·····················

SYSTEMIC CHANGE

CHAPTER 5

....

THE DYNAMICS AND COMPLEXITY OF SYSTEMS

The Supreme Court discussed dismantling "the dual systems" of the United States, but these systems has been shown to have a widespread negative impact in education and in other sectors. Clearly, efforts to create a more equitable and just world have continued, but the strategies for systemic change aren't broadly taught or known. Still, as noted earlier, even changes made locally have been shown to have significant benefits in addition to the positive outcomes resulting from broader systemic reforms.

When exploring the dual systems, clearly it's been demonstrated the evolving ways the coded systems of race changed over time. Systems of racism were defined as national origin, divine command, inherited servitude, and the blood-born citizenship class, with more clear identification of a social construction that still carry legacies from the past.

Education is a system evolving and changing over time. A **system** is a group of interconnected people (agents) or things (elements), working toward a goal. Practically, education is a system, a complex system, that has the goal of educating youth. Education is a complex system. Race and racism can also be described as a complex system, not just as solitary concepts in themselves but rather viewed as how each system was designed and applied in education, housing, employment, citizenship (and more). Increased understanding of race and education as complex systems, along with comprehending their composition, behavior, and shifts over time, can lead to more effective and equitable system designs and systemic change.

Systems work and interact with our lives, often invisibly. The tools to address these systems that actively impact our lives daily are accessible but not widely known. To make systemic change, clear ways need to be identified to help us understand the behavior of complex systems, such as education and race.

SYSTEMS CHARACTERISTICS

Fundamental to systemic change is thinking in systems. **Systems thinking** is seeing the world as a series of interconnected complex systems. A system is a description of the interaction of different interrelated or interconnected "agents" (people) or "elements" (parts or things). The interconnected elements work toward a function or purpose. The structure of a system is not just the elements but the interrelationships between agents and the elements. Often we're taught that systems are the "sum of their parts,"; instead, however, they are the sum of the relationships between the parts.

The relationships between parts can create different changes over time, as a small change in one part could lead to a larger or unpredicted effect in another part. Complex systems that aren't composed of uniform or static (unchanging) parts don't often have predictable changes. In a complex system, when one part is changed, it may impact another part this describes a characteristic called **nonlinearity**.

The nonlinear changes are normally described in two different types of behavior.: emergence and self-organization. Emergence refers to features or properties that arise when one element unpredictably interacts with another within the system. If the new feature or property creates a pattern of behavior, new systems, or structures (unintentionally or spontaneously), this is described as **self-organization**. Systems respond and adjust over time, showing that complex systems are often **adaptive systems**.

Systems are **dynamic**, meaning that systems change. Once consistent way all systems change is over time. Time is a constant as such systems are always changing, making change another constant. The changes can occur at many different scales or sizes over various time periods. The change over time in structure, behavior, and relationships is the dynamic nature of complex systems. The time frame of changes or the effects from different parts of the system are called **delays**. **Delays** are important: They can be shortened, improve effectiveness, extended to offer relief, or halt detrimental effects to the system. Delays are the windows of opportunity, the fuse to set things off, wait, anticipate, and lag behind.

Delays are the effects of time on the system. There are four common types of delays:

- Delays are the length of time it takes for changes in parts of a system to occur, or becoming aware that a change has occurred.

- Delays between being aware that a change has occurred and in deciding to act on that awareness

- Delays in taking action or implementing changes following awareness of a change

- Delays between the implementation of a change or action and the resulting effects of that change

SOURCE: Stroh (2015)

Using education as an example, a school is a complex system that has many different **agents** (parents, teachers, principals) and **elements** (classrooms, desks, funding, courses). Changing one element like funding could create a range of nonlinear results in class size, course offerings, teachers, and more. The loss of funding could reduce the number of quality teachers, which in turn could create some **emergent** effects. There could be the **emergence** of study groups to improve the learning of students, and those study groups could **self-organize** into a regular tutoring program, an **adaptation** of the funding cuts. There could be a **delay** in the dynamic action of limiting the number of teachers, as overall student academic performance or behavior would decline in the subsequent school years.

SYSTEMS BEHAVIOR

There are some key ways to understand the behavior of systems. A **stock** is the quantity, amount, or accumulation of an **element.** A **flow** is the change of the **stock** over time.

When systems interact and create a behavioral change in the systems or a change in the system's structure, that's called **feedback**. The continuous exchange of interactions is called a **feedback loop** (or feedback). Feedback is when a **stock flows** into or out of the same **stock**.

There are two types of feedback loops: **positive (self-reinforcing)** and **negative (self-correcting)** feedback. Self-reinforcing or positive feedback promotes growth, amplification, or increasing (or diminishing) returns. Self-correcting or negative feedback counteracts or opposes change. The terms positive and negative don't reflect good or bad in terms of quality, judgment, or outcomes and so forth. Positive and negative simply describe the dynamic behavior between a system and itself or between systems. One aspect of a complex system is that the system may have multiple positive and negative feedback occurring over time.

HUMAN HURDLES IN SYSTEMS THINKING

There are many real-world challenges when it comes to understanding, working with, and changing systems. Systemic change can often lead to unpredictable and also unintended or unwanted consequences. The consequences can be different types of resistance, including diluting the intervention, delaying it, or even being defeated by the responses to the systemic change.

LIMITED INFORMATION

The world we interact with is not uniform. There are different filters or lenses that often shift the information, creating bias. Often the information we receive, process, and act upon is one important feedback loop in systems' behavior. Similar to how a kindergarten child reacts, students may perceive their classroom as the entirety of how school exists. The kindergarten child might describe the school as follows:

"Where I learn my letters . . ."

"The place with a playground where I play with my friends"

"The place I go and sing songs"

None of those definitions would be wrong, but none would be accurate, either. Most individuals, regardless of age, only perceive or understand complex systems by the parts they interact with.

The thoughts and beliefs people consciously or unconsciously hold about systems are described in systems thinking as **mental models**. Mental models describe the generalizations, assumptions, and biases we all hold. The better we're able to understand our mental models, the better we can work to change systems that face fewer unintended consequences.

UNINTENDED AND COUNTERINTUITIVE CONSEQUENCES

When examining the results of systemic change, like interventions or policy change, we will note the effects that were planned, anticipated, or intended. The unintended effects or consequences, especially those that harm the system, our anticipated goals, or outcomes, are often described as side effects. Ultimately, there are only effects and no side effects. The effects, anticipated or not, create feedback shaping and influencing and drive complex systems.

Often people are led to understand their experiences as a series of events. The event-oriented approach leads to attributing and misattributing causality where it does not exist, particularly in complex (nonlinear) systems.

To effectively create systemic change, we need to understand and respond to the range of feedback in the system.

SYSTEMIC CHANGE CHALLENGES

Often the impact that the feedback, the loops, and that other interactions have on the system can resemble familiar behavioral patterns. Recognizing these patterns can help build more effective responses and reforms or lead to broader systemic change.

POLICY RESISTANCE

Policies are one of the most tangible representations of the structures and behaviors of systems. Often, energy can be invested in significant change or reform and produce little to no results. Often with complex systems, many agents (people or parties) push and pull the system in different ways with varying or contradictory goals for the system or the subsystems. In addition, strategies to address policy resistance are escalation or intensification between agents, a withdrawal from the system or goals, or interest convergence between the groups. A new system could also be drafted to better manage the escalation between parties.

TRAGEDY OF THE COMMONS

The tragedy of the commons refers to where there is a common shared resource that provides direct benefit to the agents (people or parties), but the resource could be ultimately overused, depleted, or eroded. Examples could be the impact of overfishing on wildlife populations or oceanic ecosystems, or the wasting and erosion of a pasture by the growing population of sheep added by a community's many herders. In education, examples could be overburdening teachers in multiple roles in larger classrooms or in locally funded public schools. Education. A financially strained district may face competition between schools within a district for qualified teachers, depleting the overall number of more qualified teachers available within the district as a whole. Strategies to address the tragedy of the commons can include education to help decision-makers better understand the consequences of consumption and values of restraint. Privatization is thought to be an effective strategy, as each individual will have high levels of responsibility for their divided portion of the common resource. Privatization is also used to mask or avoid other effective strategies like regulation. Regulation can be effective in creating mutually agreed upon behaviors to support or maintain the common resource(s).

INCREASING RETURNS

This feedback loop creates polarization in systems: The successful gain more success, the rich become richer, the powerful amass more power, and the poor become poorer. The inequitable distribution of resources has been shown to slow down economic systems, create instability, and vulnerability. Diversification strategies can help with increasing returns or balancing feedback strategies.

GOAL CALIBRATION

Goals describe both the function and the expected outcomes or outputs of a system. Goals help to identify areas that need to be targeted for corrective action and highlight the difference between success and failure. Badly defined goals can lead to mismeasurement or unmet goals. Competing goals, from multiple agents within a single system, can create delays, confusion on data and indicators, and ineffective interventions. Often, organizations and agents will confuse effort for goals and their subsequent results. The best way to calibrate goals is to have clear and specific goals and data that ties directly to the goals.

These common systemic behaviors can be used to increase awareness to build responses, to create common understanding, or employ as focal points to build collective action toward systemic change.

SYSTEMIC CHANGE

Understanding the **characteristics and behavior** of systems thinking can be applied to make systemic change. Taking steps to adopt a systems approach both individually and collectively can lead to more effective results. In applying systems thinking for systemic change, there are some basic steps.

As a problem is identified, understanding the problem as it is in a system or systems can be a different and effective approach. Defining the system is the first and fundamental step. Understanding the system as a whole and not just as a collection of parts helps to provide both focus and clarity. This can be done by defining the systems, the function, purpose, and goals.

Next, identifying, describing, and defining the different agents (people) and elements (things or parts) can help better understand the system. The process shouldn't stop at describing or **analyzing** the elements but should go further to **synthesize** the relationships between elements. Synthesizing is describing the relationship between elements and agents within the system's context and each other. This should also be explored at different **stages** or periods of time across the systems. Exploring different stages is to compare the system to see how it dynamically changes, responds, or adapts. The relationship between different agents and elements with a system may be described as **subsystems**. Exploring how the different relationships interact and influence the system's structure is describing the **feedback** of the system.

CONVENTIONAL PROBLEM-SOLVING TO SYSTEMIC CHANGE

The structure of the system gives rise to behavior. Often traditional or conventional problem-solving models will look for the "who" that caused the problem.

Understanding problems through a systems lens, as a pattern of behaviors, is highly effective despite occurring less often in conventional problem-solving methods. Structural explanations identify the behavior that can most change. Often narratives that drive behaviors in a system are just as likely to come *after* the system is established rather than before.

The shift from conventional problem-solving to systemic change occurs multiple layers. In a conventional model, the connection between a problem and the "cause" is traced and direct, while systemic change finds the relationship between problems and causes is often indirect and ambiguous.

People are the focus in a conventional process. There are individuals within and beyond an organization who will use people-focused language in conventional problem-solving models, seeking persons who are "responsible" for the problem/solution and/or feel that people rather than systems need to "change their behavior." They are individuals within or beyond the organization who are 'responsible for the problem, and need their behavior to change.' Agents (people) in systemic change models see themselves as part of the systems they are trying to change. The agents change their behavior to influence or control the system.

Conventional strategies will have a linear solution; successful short-term strategies will likely lead to long-term success. However, a systemic change framework recognizes that short-term strategies are unrelated to long-term success and that short-term changes will have unexpected long-term consequences that could be successful or detrimental.

To make changes or improvements, the conventional model will focus on enhancing the individual parts, while systemic change models will aim to further develop the whole system by strengthening the relationships with and between the parts. The same change model may mean conventional change will be done through making several individual changes at the same time, while a systemic change model will make a few targeted and coordinated changes over a period of time to impact the larger system rather than the parts.

The conventional focus that relies exclusively on people or specific situations or circumstances distracts from the higher **leverage points** that can create systemic change. Ultimately, while conventional problem-solving models will focus on the end point where the perceived problem occurs, systemic change models will focus upstream (earlier in the feedback loop or within the interactions of the system) to prevent the problem from occurring.

MENTAL MODELS

When applying problem-solving, our **mental models** are our only lens or view into systems. Just as we, as agents, are part of every system, our mental models are also directly influenced by the systems that we are also trying to change.

Mental models are the totality of how people understand systems, but mental models are not the systems themselves: they represent just one perception of the system. Mental models set priorities, make connections, and evaluate outcomes.

Mental models can become more detailed through time and experience. Mental models can be fluid or rigid; the level of detail that each agent's (person) mental model possesses doesn't reflect how much influence they have on the system directly. Agents could be in highly influential positions with little knowledge of systemic structure or elements.

There are several different common types of mental models to recognize in yourself and your teams when working toward systemic change.

Anchoring is the hyperfocus on a single piece of information or limited pieces of information.

Bikeshedding is the tendency to give disproportionate time, energy, and other resources to trivial, less important or easy matters, leaving important issues unaddressed. Also known as Parkinson's Law of Triviality, the bias will lead individuals or groups to avoid the complexity of systems, which are likely the most important parts of the system.

The Boiling Frog Syndrome is a particularly useful description of systems' approaches. Just as the slow raising of the water temperature would leave a frog unaware that it's being cooked, agents may be unaware or not effectively responding to the detrimental changes in systems as they may occur gradually over time.

Circle of Competence is an understanding of the knowledge and experiences of the various agents throughout the system. The more agents (people including oneself) that have an understanding of their skills and expertise and how that benefits the system, the more effective and efficient the system can become.

Confirmation Bias is a preconceived idea about a situation, concept, or system. New information that aligns with the initial notions are accepted, while new information that is contrary to the initial belief is ignored or rejected.

Dunning Kruger Effect is an overestimation of competence due to an individual's lack of knowledge or experience. This is an important model to be aware of in systems thinking, as true systemic change needs the knowledge of the system and not individuals.

First Principle is the breakdown of a process to its elements, basic concepts, and components. Systems are broken down into subsystems and elements. The deconstruction or decomposition of the system to its basic element helps to see not just how the components function but also explore the relationships between components.

Halo Effect or the "what is beautiful is also good effect" is when an individual assigns additional positive qualities to a person, situation, or systems that the individual already regards highly, or, conversely, attributes negative qualities to something which the individual already views negatively.

Hyperbolic Discounting is the preference for people to take lesser earnings sooner rather than larger payoffs in the future. The more distant the payoff, the less the payoff is valued. Delays in the system often are important to consider with this model. A tool to address this is second-order thinking, a two-tier thinking model where immediate consequences of actions and long-term outcomes are both considered.

Illusion of Control is the belief that an individual has influence or control of a system or its outcomes, even when there is not demonstrated influence.

Inversion is a backwards thinking strategy. Instead of thinking of the goal you or the system want to achieve, consider the inversion—what needs to happen in order to avoid failure. The reframing tool helps to provide perspective and insight and challenge the conventional framework of the systems and their relationships. The practice also helps to reduce risks and highlight new opportunities in systems.

Opportunity Cost is the real or perceived loss of value when an individual or group makes a decision and then misses out on the value of the other option. A choice between two objects has potential value in both, but in reality only one can be selected. Understanding the value between options, both in the short- and long-term, can be a key strategic action in systems work.

Optimism Bias is the belief the negative outcomes of the system will occur to others or not at all. The bias can lead to an overestimation of resources and a minimization of actual risk for individuals or the system.

Probabilistic Thinking is the ability to identify, evaluate, and prioritize the likeliness of outcomes from complex information. The Bayesian thinking approach to probabilistic thinking focuses on using the individual's past beliefs, knowledge, and experiences and actively incorporates new information and experiences to build more accurate predictions.

Scarcity Bias is the perception that a given resource is scarce, limited, or depleting. Scarcity is sometimes attributed to nondepletable resources in systems, like values, aspirations, or intentions of actors. Scarcity can be used to drive choice behaviors and actions.

Second-Order Thinking is a two-tier thinking model. The immediate consequences of actions are considered as are the long-term outcomes as well.

Social Proof is when individuals copy the actions of others when presented with ambiguous or uncertain situations. Often, the individuals will look to others' behavior as a cue to the "appropriate" behavior for a given situation.

Zero-sum Thinking is the perception that if one person succeeds, others lose. Also referred to as fixed-pie bias, there is a competitive belief that a direct connection exists between gains and losses, lending itself to feelings of scarcity or relative-deprivation.

SYSTEMIC STORYTELLING

Gathering information about systems can be produced through the story told about the systems. Through discussions with the many different agents throughout the system, their observations, insights, and experiences can give way to a range of different behaviors, patterns, functions and outcomes. The language can also identify shared or common elements in the system or other features as well.

The best systems stories will focus on a chronic problem. The repetition of an issue often indicates there are systemic issues. Understanding the scope of the issue is also beneficial. Those issues with a perceived limited scope would allow for more focus. Similar to repetition, the issues or problems with a known history will allow for a more meaningful shared, cocreated narrative or story.

The statement of the issue should be as accurate as possible. The problem statement should be nonjudgmental. There are traps in problems stating where the conclusion is reached in the problem statement. The traps could include blaming others, stating a solution rather than a problem, or minimizing the problem (due to bias or political reasons).

LISTENING LANGUAGES

In analyzing stories, the nouns and adjectives used can describe different elements or parts of the system (Stroh, 2015). The language may also reflect the inputs (causes) or outputs (results) of the system. Language used to describe people's roles in the system may describe key elements or functions of the system or subsystem. Language describing values may communicate the system's goals or expectations. The words used to express needs or pressure felt identify demands on the systems, feedback inputs, or resources (stocks). Results language can shape understanding on systems effectiveness, feedback output or flow, or performance. Quantitative data is helpful in measuring the language and information gathered, but using questions to have qualitative data scaled and compared over time can also be effective.

The action words that are being listened for are the verbs that show actions that change a system variable (A) to that which affects a second variable (B).

As an example, students (A) would be taught (->) changing (improving) their learning (B).

$$A->B$$

What also would be true as an example is that students (A) suspension (->) would result in learning (B) loss.

$$A->B$$

The action language can reveal types of changes over time, delays, or null (no change) effects (Stroh, 2015). Using the language can help to identify different mental models being applied or the systems change challenges, impacting the system.

The listening groups can reveal much about the shapes and contours of the system. The ability to gain multiple perspectives from the different agents of the system is essential for the best system map. The ability to list and compile thoughts on the key factors, root causes, and problems through the lens of all the agents help to build both scope and perspective.

One common trap is mistaking or confusing people (agents) with things (elements), or vice versa, where things (elements) are prioritized as people (agents). As such, it's essential to obtain every party's perspective in the listening process, or key parts of the system may remain invisible, creating unforeseen or unwanted results.

Example education questions:

- What does the issue look like for a principal or administrator? What factors or elements can be seen or experienced at this level?
- What does the issue look like for teachers, counselors, or other educators? What factors do they see or experience?
- What is the issue like for students and what factors do they experience?
- Who are the other agents (e.g. families and community members) and what key factors do they see or experience?
- Of the factors identified, can each agent-group identify which factors they either created or contributed to?

The shared and collective narratives can be instrumental tools not just to detect behaviors and patterns. The information can also be used to map or diagram the system or system behaviors, leading to broader systems knowledge, connectedness, and lending itself to systemic change.

SYSTEMS MAPPING

System maps are an excellent way to challenge and expand out mental models. When tackling problems, it's important to list all the key variables or elements. Once the elements have been identified, capturing the information or data to build a model is the next step. Graphs or diagrams can be visual models to understand systems and communicate ideas.

GRAPHING OVER TIME

When using graphs to indicate changes or dynamics, quantitative data such as money, attendance days, office referrals, and more can be used. Qualitative data like interviews, focus groups, or written information can be scaled or have magnitudes (or levels) ascribed to them. Applying the constant of time when graphing can help best capture and understand concepts like **flow** and **delays** when it is examining the dynamics of a system.

Examining student attendance rates across a school year may reveal patterns of absences at specific time intervals such as October and March. When compared with disciplinary referrals over the same time periods, one may find an increase in disciplinary referrals parallelling the absences. Nurse visits for generalized complaints of headache and stomach pain might also rise across the same periods. This might guide for interventions, not just ones focused on specific students, including fines for attendance or punishments like suspensions. Supportive strategies of student stress management, school connectedness, or adult mentoring may be successful in addressing all three concerns at once.

In addition to highlighting meaningful patterns of behavior, the illustrative nature of graphing over time can be used with teams to discuss and emphasize other variables, elements, patterns, and perceived causes.

STOCK AND FLOW MODELS

As sophisticated as systems thinking and modeling can be perceived, stock and flow models resemble household plumbing. The **stock** is thought of as a bathtub, a reservoir for the **elements** of the system that can be measured, counted, seen, or observed over time. Like the water, **flow** is the filling or draining of the bathtub (stock) overtime.

In education, the stock would be money in a student's lunch account being spent on meals and sweets, lowering the stock. More money would be added to the account, replenishing the stock. The student enrollment would also be a stock, with student attrition through moves, lowering the stock, and new enrollments raising the stock.

FIGURE 19   ENROLLMENT STOCK AND FLOW

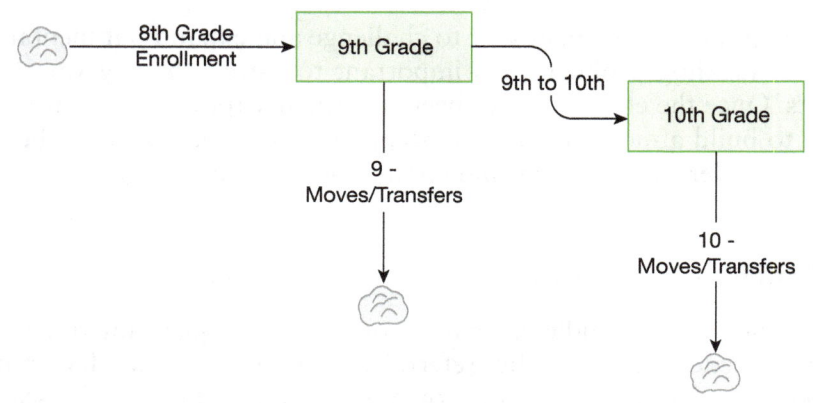

The changing of stocks over time due to their flow is called **dynamics**. If there is an equal flow of water in and out of the bathtub (stock) this is called **dynamic equilibrium** or equilibrium. The speed to fill the bathtub (stock) can be increased by increasing the water flow in or decreasing the water flow out.

Stock and flow models can help illustrate some of the strength or magnitude of some causal relationships. These models can be incredibly sophisticated, beyond simple diagrams using computer programs to create active and interactive simulations using tools such as Insight Maker or NetLogo. They can help to further measure, evaluate, and predict changes in the system over time. This can be used to create systems level interventions using time and distance to change the stock of the system to improve and optimize the outcomes of the system, intervention, or design.

CAUSAL LOOP DIAGRAM

Causal diagrams can be helpful tools as more information is gathered from partners and about the features of each system. The structure of the system can be revealed through the diagram to see the links between the multiple causes of the stated problem and the positive and negative loops that shape the problem. The diagram is a visual story, sharing how different behaviors occur over time.

The causal diagram shows the relationship with arrows that flow from one element or agent in systems to another. The causal diagram also displays known outside influences and depicts how they affect the system. Through looking at the interconnected parts of a causal diagram, areas of high influence and areas of high leverage are revealed. This process of impacting the target areas is called **feedback control.** Once the leverage points are identified, supports, interventions, or policies can be introduced and evaluated for their effectiveness.

Such diagrams are never done, and different parts of the system and its elements will continue to reveal themselves as understanding improves, which will further evolve the model.

A school could have the general concern with student motivation. Working with different partners and research, schools could reveal different elements of student motivation. The primary way students are motivated in school is through grades or academic performance. Fundamentally, good grades encourage students to continue to work hard and perform well, while bad grades encourage students to work harder and perform better. Green arrows indicate the growth in the feedback loop, in Figures 20, 21, and 22.

FIGURE 20   STUDENT MOTIVATION 1

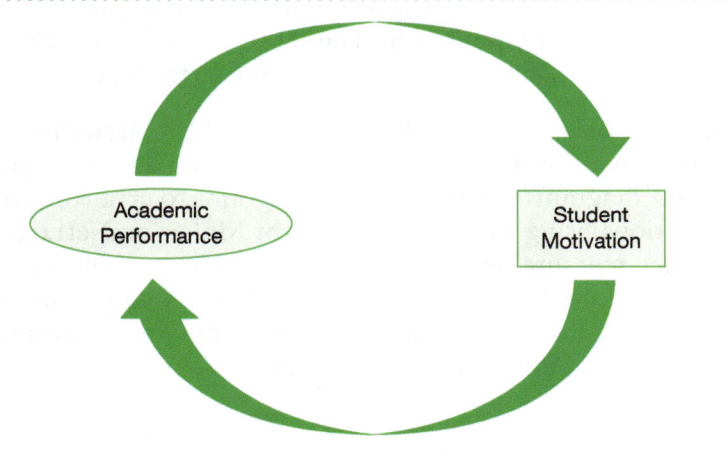

Nearly all partners provided feedback stating that there are different teaching strategies and approaches that motivate students more and help them to perform better in the classroom.

FIGURE 21   STUDENT MOTIVATION 2

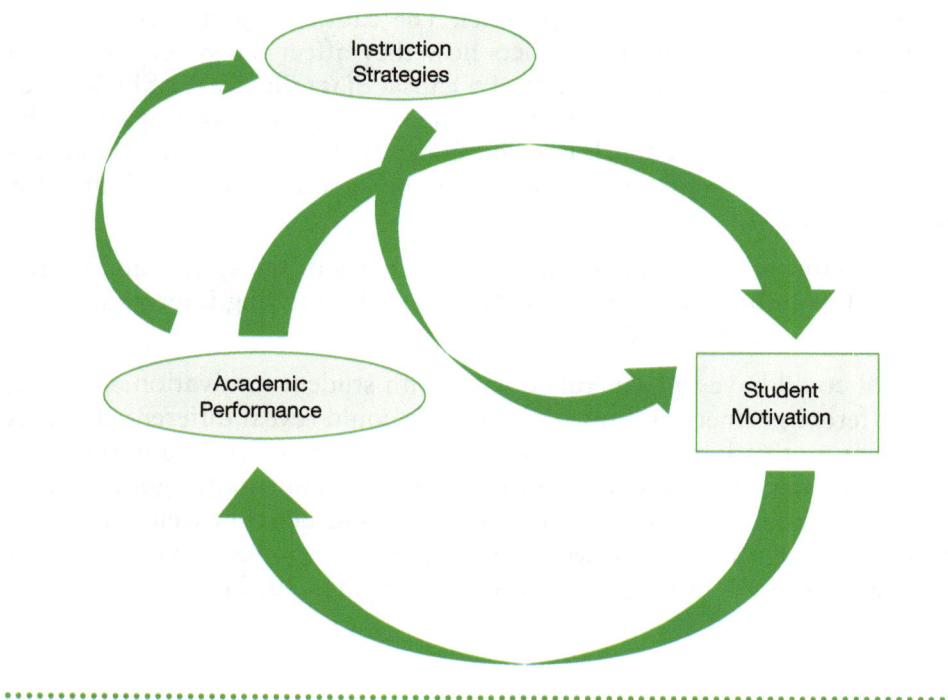

Some information reveals some students are more motivated than others. Further discussion reveals some students display different work habits and have various self-management strategies or other noncognitive skills compared to others.. It also appears that more students seem to demonstrate more noncognitive skills with certain teachers rather than others.

FIGURE 22   STUDENT MOTIVATION 3

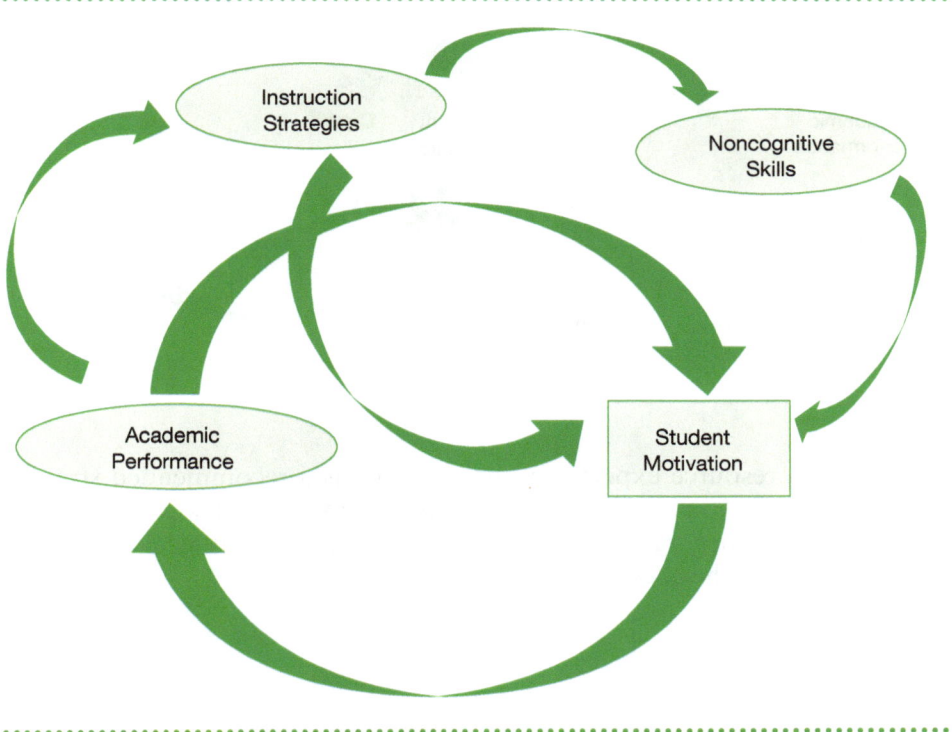

Some students are reporting feeling safe and accepted at school by both students and teachers, while other students are feeling less safe and supported. Those students seem to report less motivation to participate, engage, and even attend school. Separately, students report that grades also are a demotivator and that upon receiving a bad grade, students are less motivated to persist. The green arrows continue to point to positive growth, while white arrows point to a decline or negative impact in Figures 23, 24, and 25.

FIGURE 23 STUDENT MOTIVATION 4

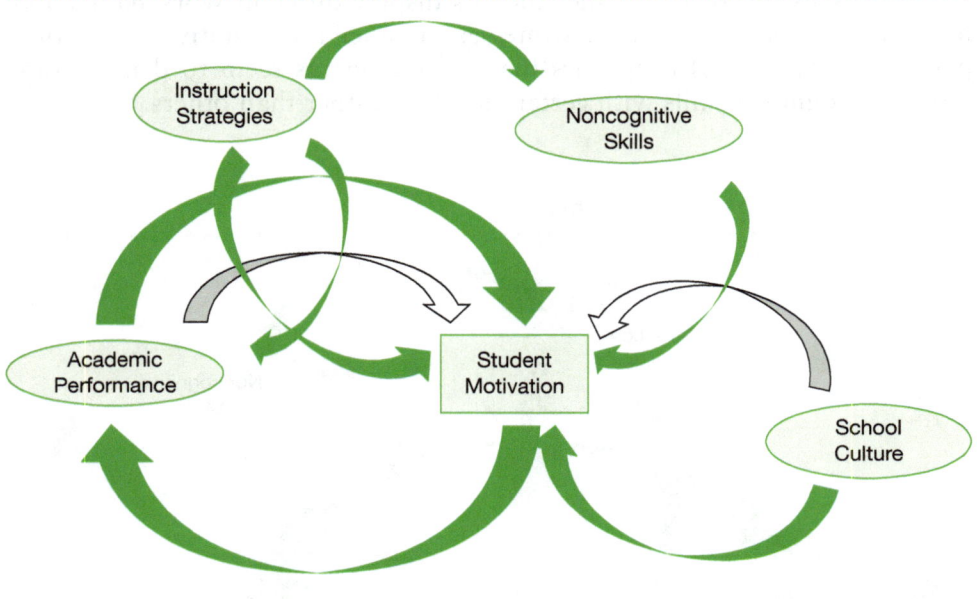

Working with resource experts, teacher training is a recommended strategy to increase the amount and quality of instructional strategies to support students. The teacher training also may include student connectedness strategies to improve school culture.

FIGURE 24 STUDENT MOTIVATION 5

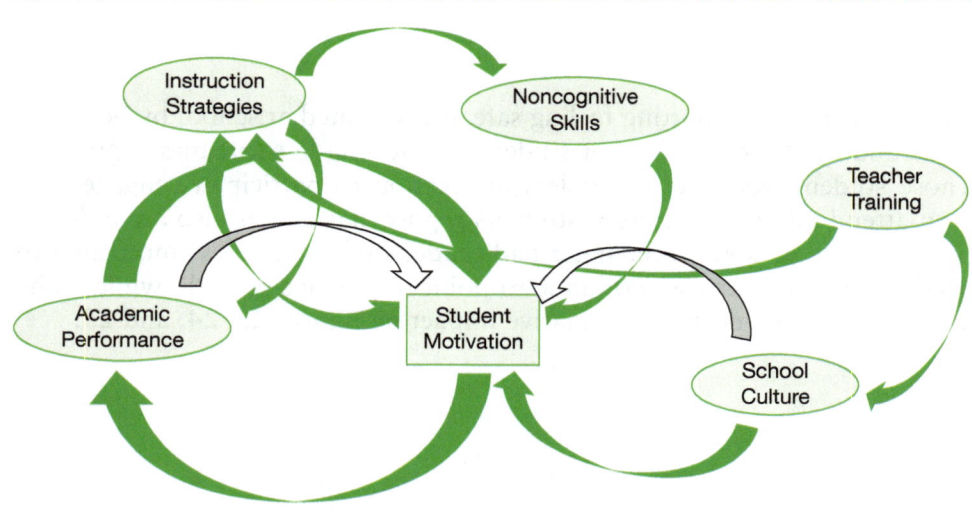

Support staff (like school counselors) with the appropriate training and background could also teach noncognitive skills directly to students and support teacher training. They could also lead in school-wide initiatives focused on school culture like safety and connectedness.

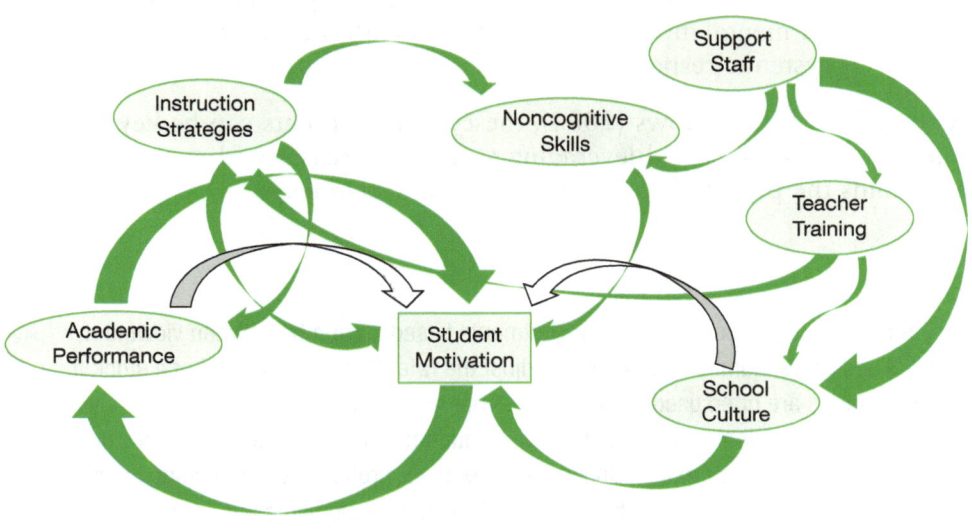

When examining the example **causal loop diagram** for student motivation, teacher training and the student support staff appear visually to have the most points of connection and most impact on downstream interventions on the system.

SYSTEM MODELING AND SIMULATION

The models can be used as education, communication, and strategy tools when understanding a system and implementing a strategy for systemic change. The same tools to build models can also be used to develop simulations for deeper understanding of the systems function and structure. The introduction of interventions and supports in systems produces a range of effects, and due to nonlinearity, the effects may be unpredictable or not immediately known. Experimentation and testing in real-world situations may not be practical or possible, but a simulation can be a tool to assist in understanding the complexity of a system.

The use of simulation tools are increasingly cost-effective and available. The simulation tools are also becoming more user friendly as technical capabilities advance requiring less technical expertise to use the simulation software. The most essential part in modeling is not simulation but continues to remain meaningfully connecting and engaging with people to identify the real needs and resources.

SYSTEMS LEVERAGE

Once there is an understanding of the structure and behavior of a system, different strategies can be applied for systemic change. The specific patterns, challenges, or mental models can be targeted with specific strategies to create a range of systemic responses.

As described by Meadows (2008), these leverage points can be key areas to intervene. Each described leveraging strategy increases with complexity but also holds the potential for the most systemic change.

Numbers is the use of specific parameters or adjustments based on numbers. When viewing a system as stocks and flows, numbers are used to adjust the rate (flow) or amount that a stock may receive or give. Numbers are often used regarding material resources (money, land, etc.). They could be used to describe spending limits or assign funding through taxes or air quality standards. In education, numbers were used to create standardized scores for proficiency and funding limits for schools. Numbers do not actually change the system or the primary elements but are commonly used as systems interventions.

Buffers are increased to the size of a stock. This can either directly increase the size of the stock itself or indirectly add spaces or reserves. In businesses, this is often additional inventory to deal with fluctuations in demand. Examples in education may be additional items, such as supplies like books for students who have lost or forgotten their materials. Buffers are useful in dealing with strains on the system but can be highly resource dependent, making the system less flexible.

Stock and Flow Structures are metaphors for real-life plumbing layouts. Similar to the real world, when the system gets backlogged, unpredictable or inefficient, there may need to be an overhaul of the plumbing systems. Routes, distribution, and flow can help to increase efficiency and output. The best strategies are to have sound design structures to begin with. Rebuilding and redesigning systems can meet with much resistance and may be resource dependent.

Delays are the amount of time to respond to the system. Delays in feedback can be too short or too long. To short of a delay means the response came before the system needed a response, which could lead to a loss of energy and resources prior to when the system would recalibrate or simply remained unaffected. Long delays may be the response occurs after the system met a critical moment and irreversible damage or change has occurred. Often in education, the delays regarding public communication about real or perceived matters of public interest create the biggest disruption to the system.

Balancing Feedback Loops are self-correcting feedback loops. These loops often work to correct or mitigate the amplifying or increasing returns effects found in the reinforcing loops of systems. These leverage points often arise in response to certain conditions or parameters being met within a system. The use is important to maintain stock, ensure system conditions, or continue to focus toward the system's goals. These practices are seen as emergency response mechanisms or insurance, functioning somewhere between correction, contingency, and recalibration.

Reinforcing Loops are amplifying in nature. They create increasing returns or "success for the successful." The value in such loops and structures is that they can increase values, resources, or returns for individuals, but often this creates disequilibrium or unbalances the system overtime.

The leverage tools to be mindful for balancing (negative) and reinforcing (positive) loops are that they can be used as systems interventions for each other. A system which is being slowed or stymied by a balancing loop might look where there are any reinforcing parts of the system to support or amplify. A system that exhibits characteristics like the tragedy of the commons—where individuals increasingly deplete a common shared resource to the detriment of the whole group—will benefit from the balancing (negative) interventions to slow the loop. The best leverage for feedback problems is feedback solutions.

The following are considered high leverage points.

Information Flow is a powerful leverage tool for systems change. All agents in the system do not have equal access to the information about the system. Unlike the other leverage strategies, information flow is creating a new feedback system that likely didn't exist before. In education, the rise of calls for diverse curriculum reflected new information flows in the education curriculum.

Rules are the language used to define the system. They define elements, roles, boundaries, authority, scope, and goals. Redefining and setting rules for the system creates new structures and behaviors for the system to follow. The fight for school boards in the 2020s was a reflection in education of the understood inherent power of rule-setting.

Self-organization is the development of systems or subsystems from the existing elements or components of a system. This can promote flexibility and allows adaptation to the challenges of the system; however, self-organization can give rise to a number of unforeseen outcomes or unexpected consequences. In education, the rise of charter schools to supplement "failing" schools gave birth to a wide range of educational institutions with exciting and new educational practices and resources. The increasing quantity of schools also created strain on the funding of school districts, and the quality of the schools varied widely.

Goals can be a powerful tool in systemic change. Clear and coherent goals can align the system and its agents in a collected fashion. As noted before, multiple goals can bring disequilibrium into a system and create competing subsystems or unintended consequences. Goals are high leverage as they can shift an entire system. A danger is that goals could stifle diversity, or a charismatic leader could shift an organization or system into unproductive directions. Having co-constructed goals help

(Continued)

(Continued)

to have a broader but focused goal for a system. In education, PBIS structures have been helpful to align systems for students' learning with clear goals and direction for the system to support students.

Paradigms are the shared mental models, norms, and beliefs both about the system and beyond. To challenge paradigms, careful and critical analysis of the old paradigms is essential, identifying the failures, inconsistencies, and anomalies. Creating a model of the new system and introducing it helps to shift from old paradigms. Collaborations to expand to communicate and share the paradigm shift can also lead to this system's change. Much of this book talked about the paradigm shift for fair and just public education; the Civil Rights Era was full of those calling for a new understanding of what public spaces like schools should be and what American citizenship entailed.

Transcending Paradigms is the highest level of leverage for systemic change. Understanding that paradigms are mental models and viewing more clearly systems and interactions among systems, agents, and elements allow individuals to more freely and directly interact and change systems. Specifically, the ability to transcend paradigms allows individuals to more readily see and apply all of the leverage tools available.

There are no magical tools when working with real-world systems. The ability to understand systems and their behavior allows for the ability to design more tools for systemic change.

LEADING FOR SYSTEMIC CHANGE

Through the understanding of systems through systems thinking, we are empowered to better influence and change systems. We can use the knowledge to connect with others and to use the connection to better identify our mental models and the actual underlying structure and behavior of systems. Seeing the structure and behaviors of systems allows us to use leverage to change the systems or design new systems. Systems thinking and design give us new lenses and tools to see and understand education and racism, how those systems work, and ways to build reform and systemic change. Applying systems thinking to equitable principles can create new systems of equity to shift from the constraints of oppressive systems.

CHAPTER 5 DISCUSSION QUESTIONS

- Reflecting on the description of education as a complex system, how does this perspective challenge traditional views of education and educational reform? Discuss how systems thinking can enhance our understanding of educational challenges and potential solutions, especially in addressing historic and present disparities.

- Considering the concepts of positive and negative feedback loops, how might these feedback mechanisms influence educational policies and practices? Give examples of how a feedback loop could amplify inequality in education, and propose strategies for implementing to counteract these effects.

- How do mental models influence decision-making and problem-solving? Discuss how different mental models among educators, administrators, families, and students can impact systems change efforts.

- What are common challenges faced when attempting to implement systemic changes in educational settings? How can an understanding of mental models and systems dynamics mitigate these challenges?

PART IV

DESIGNING EQUITABLE FUTURES

CHAPTER 6

....

REVERSE ENGINEERING RACISM AND EQUITABLE DESIGNS

THE SYSTEMS OF RACISM

Examining racism through a systems lens helps to understand the structures and behavior of racism as a complex and dynamic system.

Through the system's thinking, racist systems' resistance to change, unequal outcomes, and divergent experiences between individuals can be both explained and further explored. Understanding education as a complex system that is interwoven but separate from racist systems helps us to guide true systemic change.

Systemic change against racist systems is referred to as many different terms: social justice, equity work, DEI work, and more. The best framing is a simple one of antiracism. Antiracism is essentially the inversion principle of systems thinking. Through inversion, we critically analyze the system and the structures to actively avoid the system's outcomes that are racist in nature.

Many different models try to address countering racist structures and systems; few are rooted in a systems language in approach. Through some systems design principles, we can all be equipped to lead in systemic change.

IMPLEMENTING CHANGE

To make effective systemic change, there needs to be effective implementation of the new systems that might be introduced. Whether designed as interventions or supports, or new/novel systems, being mindful and intentional about the implementation is important when designing new systems. Implementation is the methodical integration of a strategy, intervention, system, or tool with an existing system.

Education, like other complex systems, can be thought of as a multilevel model. From the individual to the classroom to the building to the district, a multileveled framework can provide context for the implementation of systemic changes. Not all educational supports and interventions have been developed through a lens of equity or with a goal of equity, inclusion, or belonging (Shelton et al., 2021). Many training supports and interventions often are developed at the individual-level, which would not change the structures or systems driving inequality or disparity. A systemic change model is a mutlilevel implementation model, which provides both the focus and context for any designs to be delivered for change (Shortell, 2004).

The range of different ways equity can be conceptualized in any setting, let alone education, can vary widely. With a goal of equity, areas of connections, opportunity, and safety can provide focus for multileveled work. Disparity found in education can sometimes be measured as attendance issues, disciplinary outcomes, staffing, and post-secondary access. Through a lens of equity, attendance issues may indicate a lack of meaningful connections between students and their school or basic needs such as (psychological) safety, are not being met. Disproportionate discipline may be an opportunity issue, as there may be an imbalance of supportive staffing like school counselors or school psychologists, compared to other disciplinary or punitive measures. These basic frames of connectedness, opportunity, and safety can align with many of the outcomes sought when addressing issues of equity.

FIGURE 26   THE FOUR LEVELS OF CHANGE FOR IMPLEMENTATION

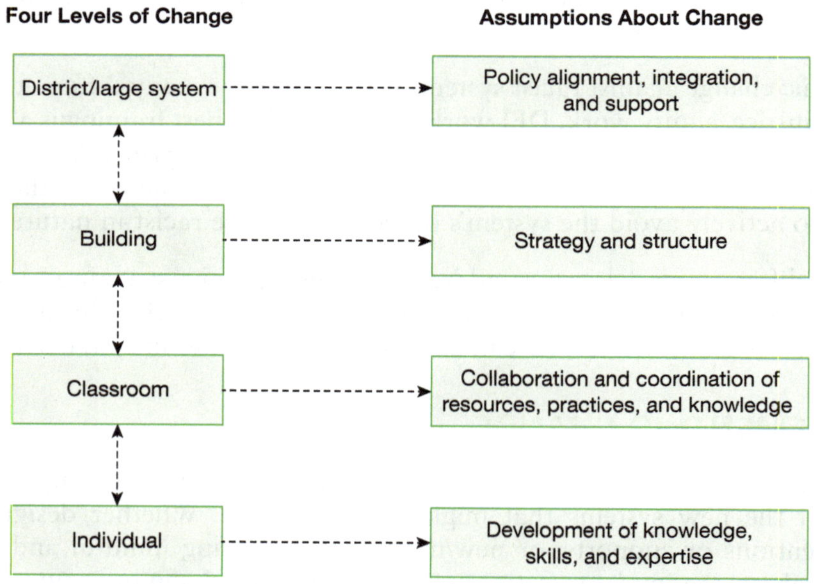

Four Levels of Change	Assumptions About Change
District/large system	Policy alignment, integration, and support
Building	Strategy and structure
Classroom	Collaboration and coordination of resources, practices, and knowledge
Individual	Development of knowledge, skills, and expertise

SOURCE: Adapted from Shortell, 2004.

Across the multilevels, there are implementation practices that can be applied for effective systemic change. Those practices include the following:

- **Foundational Practices**
  - ○ **Information practices**—rooting Grounding all practice in evidence-based or promising approaches that would support students or systemic change, while still relying on culturally relevant information that would provide a foundation for those practices designed to benefit humans, not the broader systemic structure. The understanding of promising and evidence-based practices helps to identify the practices with known outcomes and effects within the context (or constraints) of a system. The culturally relevant knowledge is the information ranging from the universal human characteristics to group-focused and individual-specific traits. This includes the collection of beliefs, norms, and values, as well as shared customs, definitions, traditions, and group standards. Building knowledge in information practices is essential in equitable implementation since it represents the balance of the fidelity of implementation and adaptability (Castro et al., 2010).
  - ○ **Date-informed practices**—the practices that gather the information, narratives, and experiences on the process and outcomes of systems.
  - ○ **Engagement practices**—the meaningful and active partnerships developed across a school system by those who participate, interact, or influence the system.

- **Development practices**
  - ○ **Fidelity and adaptability**—fidelity is the understanding and maintaining of the core elements. Adaptation is the deliberate alteration of the design or delivery of an intervention to improve its effectiveness for context, setting, or group (Castro et al., 2010).
  - ○ **Sustainability and scalability**—sustainability is the ability of support or intervention or support integrated into a systemic structure.

Across the multilevel implementation model, levels of focus would be from the lowest to highest levels: individual, classroom, school/building, and district level.

At the **individual level** participants focus most on reflecting and developing their information practices and expanding their knowledge of evidence-based practices and culturally relevant knowledge. At the individual level, people can make meaningful partnerships with others through engagement practices. Through data-informed practices, individuals can reflect on their roles and impact on the other levels and structures. For successful implementation of change at this level, it is crucial to develop skills and knowledge to achieve expertise.

At the **classroom level,** classroom level practices can further promote equity in a range of ways. To foster connections and build a sense of belonging, the use of media and curricula that represent students' many diverse lives and backgrounds is a reflection of high-level engagement and culturally relevant practices. These practices can complement the application of evidence-based and data practices to increase overall quality of pedagogy or teaching practice. The use of inclusive elements to promote connectedness and quality teaching practices will increase the aspects of safety for students. The range of research in classroom effectiveness can guide implementation at this level. Key at this level is the ability to build relationships and connections that promote collaboration, coordination, and the exchange of information and experiences.

At the **building-wide level,** policies and procedures can promote higher levels of student connectedness, opportunity, and safety. Analyzing the existing policies, procedures, and outcomes in ways that are creating opportunity, safety, or human connections for all students can be a high-level data practice that could yield more benefits than an "off the shelf" program. Developing and curating curricula and relevant teacher training and support can drive change at the lower levels in the classroom or for individuals. Engagement practices can expand to create direct partnerships with families and communities members to center policy creation on voices and experiences shared, as well as other collaborative efforts. Balancing fidelity and making adaptations can be achieved through a supportive network of coaching and consultation among trained staff. The use of specific data-information practices can evaluate both the outcomes and fidelity of program implementation, while the partnerships through engagement and culturally relevant information can guide necessary adaptations. The ability to build off the other practices to create consistent and coherent strategy and structure is essential at this level.

At the **district level,** policies and procedures, training and curriculum development can all be driven at this, the highest level of the multilevel framework. Hiring practices can also increase the quality and diversity of the staff; specifically, administrative hiring can be one of the essential tools in building sustainability and scalability for many of the fundamental and development practices across levels (Moir, 2018). Through careful evaluation of the impact of information and engagement strategies through data practices, the district level has the best ability to implement more effective strategies and policies to guide learning and promote connectedness, opportunity, and safety for students. The ability to translate macro state-level (or national) policies and legislation into practice on the building level or lower is guided by the balance of information and engagement practices. The understanding, design, and evaluation of policies and their outcomes is the most essential tool at this level.

This overarching framework can help to conceptualize and support systemic change in education systems. Implementation science is an immersive and expanding field that can guide sustainable change with the frame addressing some but not all of the many facets of the growing field. Having an implementation framework can help in the selection, design, and delivery of any number of equity-focused initiatives, leading to a more efficient and effective process and outcomes.

MODELING EQUITY

To understand how to make systemic change, it's helpful to take inventory of the different frameworks and models available that focus on addressing systems of racism and could be implemented. In reviewing the models, careful attention should be paid to the structure of each model and framework. Each model will outline different explicit or implied responsibilities for the agents, define the agents' relationship with the system, and will vary in how much they challenge or redesign systemic structures and behaviors.

Racial, Ethnic, Cultural Identity Framework (Sue, D. W. et al., 2022) was developed by psychologists Sue and Sue who discussed the developmental stages individuals pass through as they form a racial and cultural identity. The conceptual model serves as a guide to organizational group leaders to understand the attitudes, behaviors, and beliefs of their diverse members. In the first stage, the **Conformist Stage**, minoritized individuals may have a neutral or self-deprecating view of themselves and their racially identified group. During this stage, the dominant group is seen more favorably, while other minoritized groups perceive themselves as more neutral or negatively. In the **Dissonance Stage** minoritized individuals hold feelings of confusion or conflict about their racialized identity. The feelings of conflict and confusion extend to others in their identified racial group, including other minoritized groups and the dominant group. The **Resistance and Immersion Stage** is characterized by individuals holding an increased or strong self-appreciation for their own racial identity and for their identified racial group to which they belong. The views may be to the extent that the individual has racially or ethnocentric views about their racially or culturally identified group, believing the group is superior to other groups. There may be expressed empathy to other minoritized groups, while there is animus or negative view toward the dominant group. In the **Introspection Stage** individuals reflect on their own attitudes and beliefs toward themselves and other groups. They may have growing concern about their fundamental views of themselves and all of the other group attitudes or beliefs. **Integrative Awareness** is the final stage where individuals appreciate themselves, their racially identified group, and other minoritized groups, while maintaining selective appreciation of the dominant group. The Racial Ethnic and Cultural Identity Framework shares a range of perspectives but doesn't provide much regarding a framework to understand and evaluate the broader systemic structures at play and their impact on influencing individuals.

Courageous Conversations Compass is a conversational framework developed by Singleton (2014) for educators as a personal conversational dialogue tool when navigating discussions regarding race, the construction of race, and the multiple perspectives that arise when discussing issues of race. As demonstrated in this book, the construction of race in America was used as an evolving tool of separation; as such, it is understandable that dialogues on race and racism are difficult. The Compass can be a tool to navigate through difficult conversations regarding race and racism. The Courageous

Conversations Compass can be thought to have the similar layout of a more traditional compass, but rather than the cardinal points of north, south, east, and west, each corner is identified by four primary ways people engage in conversations about race: morally, intellectually, emotionally, and relationally. Those who respond and process information about race **morally** have deeply rooted *beliefs* which may prompt them to interpret information as "right/wrong" or have a gut or instinctual feeling about the matter or issue. Moral orientation may also identify this orientation as being centered in the *soul* or *spirit*. **Intellectually** is the detached search for more information or knowledge on the subject or issue. Processing through this orientation is often verbal and rooted in thinking or centered in the *head*. **Emotionally** is a response to information through *feelings*, whether they are physical sensations or intense emotional experiences, with the experience thought to be centered in the *heart*. **Relationally** is the response or connection to information about race or racism through our *actions*. Specific actions or behaviors are part of response with the orientation thought to be centered in the *hands and feet* section of the Compass. Like a real compass, the Courageous Conversations Compass is about orientation and movement. By first locating yourself on the Compass and reflecting on how you are oriented with the information or issue, you can then move toward the center to understand the perspectives of the information or issue from other three quadrants. In a shared conversation, the next step, once centered, is to take a step toward the other person. The centered approach allows for higher levels of engagement and connection. These tools can be helpful in sharing information and experiences but don't promote systemic change directly.

FIGURE 27   THE COURAGEOUS CONVERSATIONS COMPASS ADAPTED FROM SINGLETON (2014)

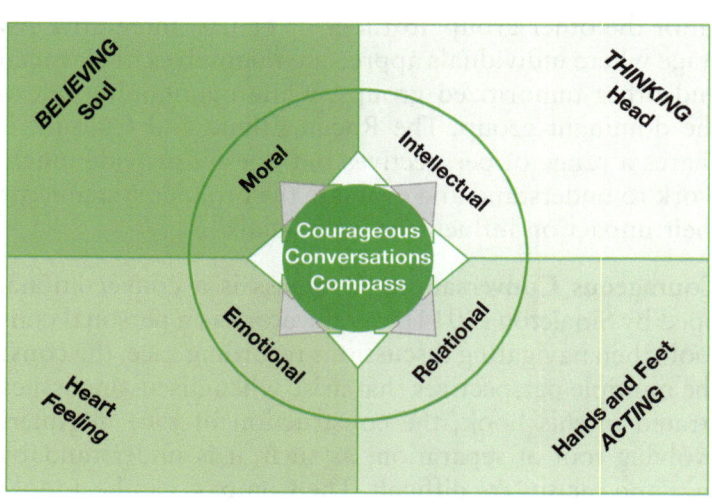

Courageous Conversations Compass
Singleton (2014)

The Learning for Justice Anti-Bias Framework (2022) is a conceptual teaching model which creates developmental learning standards across four domains: identity, diversity, justice, and action (IDJA). *Identity* is the set of characteristics or traits that distinguish an individual and which make an individual recognizable to a group. Identity includes both visual and invisible aspects of identity like skin tone and sexuality, respectively. Personal and social lenses of identity are also explored like values and race, respectively. *Diversity* is the collection of identities, experiences, and backgrounds that compose a group. Diversity is focused on the individual student differences and connections made through their experiences with a goal of fostering understanding and appreciation. *Justice* is a student's ability to identify and respond to unfairness, inequality, and injustice with individuals, institutions, or systems. *Action* is the celebration and honoring of both identities and diversity, while continuing to work toward justice. The Anti-Bias Framework expands on traditional equity-focused models, which focus almost exclusively on either prejudice reduction or motivating for collective action. The framework also is unique as it separates out individual understanding and group interaction and points toward systemic action. There is a high degree of focus on both self and group understanding with examinations into power structures and imbalances. The framework is tied to developmental standards to guide further exploration and implementation for both youth and educators.

DESIGNS FROM THE FIELD

▶ New teachers, ELA teachers and teachers of color actively use the Learning for Justice Anti-Bias Framework to guide discussion, complement instructional materials, and guide curriculum development.

"Using books such as Zaretta Hammond's [Culturally Responsive Teaching] and the Brain, Gholdy Muhammad's Cultivating Genius, and Joe Feldman's Grading for Equity, along with the Teaching Tolerance Anti-Bias framework, I have created critical discussions using novels to teach anti-bias topics." —High school ELA teacher (Woo et al., 2022)

YOUTH PARTICIPATORY ACTION RESEARCH (YPAR)

Youth Participatory Action Research is a collaborative community-based model. The model partners adults and youth, addressing social problems with inquiry and active participation to transform knowledge and practice in specific areas of young adults lives.

The inquiry is centered on and driven by the lived experiences, insights, and concerns held by youth. The youth participation is central where youth are seen as collaborators and co-researchers and not subjects of research, interventions, or programs. The transformative aspect is the active creation of outcomes to intervene or support the lives of young adults. This is done through collaboration, the sharing of power, applied research, shared agenda planning, and development of the methodology of educational practices, and much more. This results in diverse products, projects, and policy innovations. YPAR projects and programs have demonstrated effectiveness in areas of violence prevention, health, resource development, education and equity (Anyon et al., 2018). Youth partners have been shown to have a range of social and emotional gains following YPAR work.

YPAR work can help youth understand and analyze the systemic factors that influence and impact their daily lives (Cammarota & Fine, 2010). These projects can be instrumental in shifting perspectives, raising awareness, and effectively engaging other youth (Valdez et al., 2020).

Critical Race Theory (CRT) is an academic movement and framework that explores the perpetuation of social inequality through the lens of race. The collection of scholarly works examines how race has influenced the laws, policies, and practices leading to disparate outcomes. Although there is a range of diverse writing and scholarship, there are some tenets that have been ascribed to Critical Race Theory (Delgado & Stefancic, 2017). First to note is that **race is a social construct**—racism and race are the results of social thinking and relationships, not biology or genetics. **Racism is normalized** in the United States. Through the lens of CRT, racism is not individual acts of error or poor character, nor is racism accidental; rather, racism is interwoven into institutions and operates on both individual and systemic levels. Racism is difficult to address since it's not acknowledged. The impact of oppression is not limited to just race. Through *Intersectionality*, a range of social identities are explored, highlighting the compounding effect systemic oppression can have on individuals in the overlap of their multiple social identities, including race, gender, sexuality, religion, nationality, age, and ability. Everyone has overlapping identities that both support and are impacted by systemic factors. *Interest convergence* states that racial advancement has only met with significant progress when the goals of Blacks were consistent with the needs of whites. *Counter Storytelling* and unique voice is the sharing and amplification of experiences and voices from marginalized and minoritized groups that challenge the prevailing or dominant narratives, paradigms, or ideologies. The marginalized and minoritized voices are uniquely qualified to talk about the impacts of oppression from the system. The different theories and frameworks of CRT did create new tools to challenge and change systemic structures in law, education, and beyond.

There is a continuum of **Cultural** practices (Evans, 2021). *Culturally Sensitive Practices* promote an increased awareness of cultural similarities and differences between individuals in a nonjudgmental or valuative way. *Culturally Relevant Practices* are the attempt to link an individual's lived experiences, cultural heritage, and community cultural practices with another system like education. Students have their academic identity and their cultural identity and the two are bridged in a learning environment. **Culturally Responsive Practices** are bidirectional connections between the individual and the system. The system adapts to the individuals and sees their cultural background and experiences as assets to the system. In education, this would be an asset-driven strategy where students incorporate their culture into the learning experiences. **Culturally Sustaining Practices** are where an individual's heritage and culture are supported by the system and individuals both share, produce, and engage with the range of cultures interacting in the system. In education, a student's cultural practices would actively be incorporated into the broader institutional (systems) structures.

Antiracism is a broad term for a wide range of beliefs and practices. Noted antiracist author Ibram X. Kendi defines antiracism as the support of antiracist policy through action or the expression of antiracist ideas. In *How to Be an Antiracist*, Kendi (2019) summarized a Racial Equity model developed by his team:

- Admit racial inequity is a problem of bad policy, not bad people.

- Identify racial inequity in all its intersection and manifestations.

- Investigate and uncover the racist policies causing racial inequity.

- Invent or find antiracist policy that can eliminate racial inequity.

- Figure out who or what group has the power to instigate antiracist policy.

- Disseminate and educate about the uncovered racist policy and antiracist policy correction.

- Work with sympathetic antiracist policymakers to institute the antiracist policy.

- Deploy antiracist power to compel or drive from power the unsympathetic racist policymakers in order to institute the antiracism policy.

- Monitor closely to ensure the antiracist policy reduces and eliminates racial inequity.

- When policies fail, do not blame the people. Start over and seek out new and more effective antracist treatment until they work.

- Monitor closely to prevent new racist policies from being instituted.

The "How to Be Antiracist" approach does provide practical approach to address systemic issues through policy but doesn't expand on the design or implementation process for antiracist policy development.

► Boston-area youth used a Youth Participatory Action Research framework guided by the "How to Be Antiracist" framework to improve relationships and trust between youth of color and healthcare professionals while understanding the role intergenerational trauma plays between the two groups (Toraif et al., 2021).

In education, the Center for Antiracist Education (CARE, 2021) created a model focused on schools. First, the model Affirms the Dignity and Humanity of All People through centering instruction on the student. There is a school-wide approach to ensure that students feel heard, visible and safe, reflected in a curriculum that reflects the diversity and complexity of the human experience. The educators and the curriculum also Embrace Historical Truths. Students explore and challenge present-day injustice through a curriculum that counters dominant narratives with multiple perspective stories of resistance and perseverance. The goal of the rich curriculum is to Develop a Critical Consciousness in students. This is done through collaborative discussion and activities between educators and students to identify the invisible and observable ways racism is experienced by individuals and society. The learning aims to equip members to Recognize Race and Confront Racism through a demystification of stereotypes, and from the curriculum, students are able to see each other more fully and make deeper connections. They are taught how to directly address bias, privilege, power, racism and oppression. The curriculum focused on providing a critical examination of both policy and practice and how they support or impede human advance, equipping students with tools to work with the complexity of systems and Create a Just System.

These tools and frameworks are instrumental for their inherent value and serve as a foundation to expand equitable practices and design. Guided by implementation practices, these models and frameworks can be applied across a range of settings and contexts to promote more equitable outcomes. Still, using the tools of systems analysis and systems dynamics, tools can be created or adapted to addressing the specific challenges facing individuals across the many systems they may be confronted with.

REVERSE ENGINEERING RACISM

The models and frameworks listed are all valuable with an innumerable amount of other equity-focused frameworks, models, and theories not listed also highly valuable. The popular models listed mostly focused extensively on awareness and even analysis. Few discussed a framework for designing more equitable systems. There are design approaches that focus on equity and can promote systemic change.

Antiracist systems restructure existing racist systems, create new or parallel systems unattached to the racist systems, or devise systems to counteract or mitigate oppressive systems.

An antiracism approach is essentially reverse engineering racism. Famously black feminist author Audre Lorde wrote, "For the master's tools will never dismantle the master's house." Replicating racist systems would simply produce more racist systems. Still reverse engineering is not about simply recreating the same systems but about dismantling them to better understand the functions, measurements, performance, and parameters. Through reverse engineering (Otto & Wood, 1996), the initial hypothesis and investigation of the function (or goal is explored) while establishing a new design goal. Next, the system is deconstructed or dismantled to better understand the system through looking at its elements, subsystems, and interrelationships between the parts. After this phase, a new system or design is created with new stated goals. The new system or model is analyzed and then redesigned to optimal function.

Applying reverse engineering principles, practices, and design themes are elevated for antiracist work. First, this book performed a detailed analysis of racism through various systems. The coded language of race and racism were deconstructed. Patterns and themes about racist systems were highlighted through the process. Racist systems often are monolithic (focusing power or resources on specific individuals or small groups); conversely, antiracist systems would be distributive, sharing power and resources horizontally and not vertically. Racist systems are narrow, often trying to create social positions or policies on narrow criteria or conditions such as physical traits, income, or location; in contrast, antiracist systems would embrace complexity. Racist systems are also rigid, not changing when presented with new information or paradigms; conversely antiracist systems would be flexible and adaptable to meet the dynamic changes over time. Understanding the structures of racism helps to design more effective tools for equity. Comprehending the measurements and parameters used in racist systems helps to refocus on new equitable systems to measure progress, target areas most impacted by racists systems, and identify areas of leverage.

Reverse engineering racism is similar to the traditional engineering practice. First, you gather detailed information about the system. Through some of the analysis and synthesis strategies reviewed and an understanding of the elements, interrelationships and outcomes would be developed. Efforts should be made to understand and describe the disparity outcomes of the system. A clear outcome goal should be stated for the new system to be designed. Next, a design plan of the elements of the old system and the new design elements should be developed. The design should be implemented and then measured based on the goals. The design and model should be redesigned based on the data from the initial and subsequent designs.

- Investigate the racist system: Gather information about history and those impacted and the effects.

- Analyze and synthesize: Deconstruct the system to understand the components of the system and the agents or groups involved. Describe the disparity and causal effects and outcomes.

- Establish a clear and equitable goal: Define an actionable goal focused on equitable principles to the benefit of individuals.

- Design a new system: Design a system which uses elements of the old system for a redefined purpose. The elements may be focused areas previously targeted or extensively impacted by the old system or use the impacted group to focus broader systemic change.

- Evaluate and redesign: Measure and evaluate the results of the new system and identify areas for continued development or redesign.

In education, practices and policies that are punitive in nature, resulting in racial disparities, are racist systems that can be targeted by a reverse engineering approach to supplant therapeutic or restorative approaches. A broader educational example that reflects reverse engineering principles is the movement #CounselorsNotCops, a social justice and educational reform campaign aimed at divesting from law enforcement in schools and reinvesting in more school counselors and other support professionals. The movement is largely grounded in the American Civil Liberties Union report "Cops and No Counselors: How the Lack of School Mental Health is Harming Students." Through the analysis, the research team measured the presence of police officers in schools and the subsequent outcomes in arrests and law enforcement referrals. The new goal was to improve student mental health. Students were facing increased rates of trauma, depression and anxiety. The report drafted a framework to support the goal of the new system: It recommended increasing the number of school-based mental health professionals, including school counselors, psychologists, social workers, and nurses. The new framework included new systems designs such as legislative and policy priorities, data collection, and training and program recommendations at the federal, state, and local levels.

The new system, a Framework for Safe and Successful Schools (Cowan et al., 2013) makes the following policy recommendations.

1. Allow for blended, flexible use of funding streams in education and mental health services;

2. Improve staffing ratios to allow for the delivery of a full range of services and effective school-community partnerships;

3. Develop evidence-based standards for district-level policies to promote effective school discipline and positive behavior;

4. Fund continuous and sustainable crisis and emergency preparedness, response, and recovery planning and training that uses evidence-based models;

5. Provide incentives for intra- and interagency collaboration; and

6. Support multitiered systems of support (MTSS).

BEST PRACTICES FOR CREATING SAFE
AND SUCCESSFUL SCHOOLS

1. Fully integrate learning supports (e.g., behavioral, mental health, and social services), instruction, and school management within a comprehensive, cohesive approach that facilitates multidisciplinary collaboration.

2. Implement multitiered systems of support (MTSS) that encompass prevention, wellness promotion, and interventions that increase in intensity based on student need, and that also promote intimate school community collaboration.

3. Improve access to school-based mental health supports by ensuring adequate staffing levels, meaning school-employed mental health providers who are trained to infuse prevention and intervention services into the learning process and to help integrate services provided through school-community partnerships into existing school initiatives.

4. Integrate ongoing positive climate and safety efforts with crisis prevention, preparedness, response, and recovery to ensure that crisis training and plans: (a) are relevant to the school context, (b) reinforce learning, (c) make maximum use of existing staff resources, (d) facilitate effective threat assessment, and (e) are consistently reviewed and practiced.

(Continued)

(Continued)

5. Balance physical and psychological safety to avoid overly restrictive measures (e.g., armed guards, metal detectors) that can undermine the learning environment. Instead combine reasonable physical security measures (e.g., locked doors, monitored public spaces) with efforts to enhance school climate, build trusting relationships, and encourage students and adults to report potential threats.

6. Employ effective, positive school discipline that: (a) functions in concert with efforts to address school safety and climate; (b) is not simply punitive (e.g., zero tolerance); (c) is clear, consistent, and equitable; and (d) reinforces positive behaviors. Using security personnel or SROs primarily as a substitute for effective discipline policies does not contribute to school safety and can perpetuate the school-to-prison pipeline.

7. Consider the context of each school and its district and provide those services that are the most needed, appropriate, and culturally sensitive to that school's unique student population and learning community.

8. Acknowledge that sustainable and effective change takes time and that individual schools will vary in their readiness to implement improvements. These schools should be afforded the time and resources necessary to sustain such change over time.

STROH'S FOUR STAGES OF LEADING SYSTEMIC CHANGE

Another design model to build equitable systems is Stroh's (2015) Four-Stage Change Process. This is an effective model for an organization or groups and can help to facilitate collective action or change. The model is an activation model of change, building off of the "creative tension" between where a group wants to be and where they are. The model can facilitate change with either individuals or groups (collective level).

A group's shared vision, mission, and values help to state where the collective group "wants to be." If the group can have a clear idea of its current reality—"where that is" or "what they have"—the tension will lend itself to resolving in favor of the "wants." The shared endpoints of vision and reality create a higher level of alignment between individuals and a shared responsibility for the whole system. They identify, navigate, and bridge the creative tensions; four stages or steps are highlighted.

- **Stage 1 Readiness** - Building Foundation for Change

- **Stage 2 Understanding and Acceptance** - Facing Current Reality

- **Stage 3 Commitment** - Making an Explicit Choice

- **Stage 4 Focus, Momentum and Correction** - Bridging the Gap

FIGURE 28 FOUR STAGES OF LEADING SYSTEMIC CHANGE BY STROH

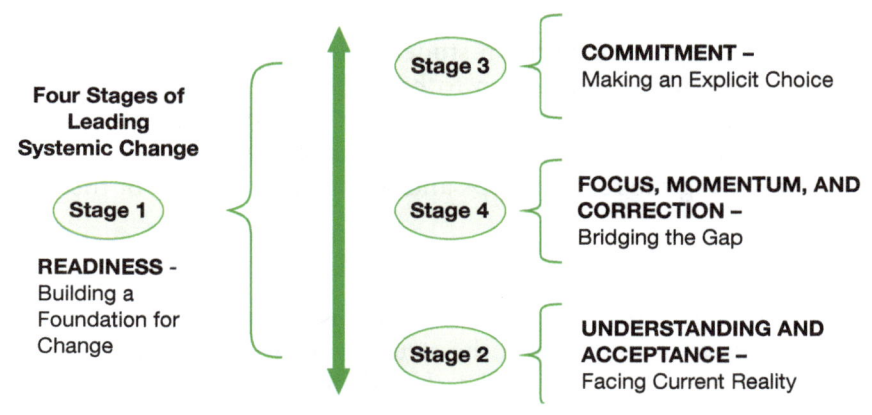

Stage 1 Readiness

In the first stage, the Readiness Stage, the foundation for systemic change is set. Leaders, designers or strategies Build the Foundation for Change. The foundation is built by engaging, activating, and equipping the various agents of the system into a partnership for change.

- The first step in the Readiness Stage is **identifying the agents or partners**. Depending on the project, there could be a wide range of diverse members to seek, identify, and consider. This will likely involve designing and developing strategies (subsystems) to engage with the partners both individually and collectively.

- Next, the **connections** between the partners need to be established or further enhanced. This can be done through creating a foundational or initial understanding of where individuals and the group feel they are now and what they want to achieve. The initial shared understanding of what's not working and what the ideal outcomes can be is instrumental as the group further develops more articulated understanding, goals, and action over time.

- Finally, **capacity building** to strengthen the connections between the agents or partners is necessary. This can be done by creating shared communication and educational tools and resources to help support the group's ability to think systemically. Additional capacity building strategies should focus on enhancing the groups productively to have conversations about complex or difficult topics, and building agency (action capacity) to take responsibility of the current reality (system structure).

The **Readiness Stage** should be noted as, for many groups or organizations, steps described in this stage may amount to the summation of their work, but really it's the first step. There are some key considerations to best enhance the practices. Specifically, in bringing together partners, special attention and effort should be to center the teaming around those most marginalized or impacted by the system. In education, this may include bringing in students or even black or brown students for specific race-related policy or initiatives and empowering them to have voice. Technology can be used to improve communication between partners ans share information and resources. The biggest tools are creating shared definitions, identifying clear roles, and exploring the relationships and outcomes (outputs) of the system.

Stage 2 Understanding and Acceptance

The Understanding and Acceptance Stage helps people and the group face the current reality (or understand the structure of the system). In addition, to further building and defining the shared understanding, there are two driving questions: What is happening, and why is it happening? The questions not only help to refine understanding but also facilitate communication with agents (group members), fostering their acceptance of responsibilities—whether unintentional or not—in creating the current reality. Building off the capacity building of the last stage, individual and group systemic capacity is the focus of the group to more deeply analyze and engage in the current system, the present reality.

The central tasks of Stage 2 include the following:

- **Identifying individuals and groups to interview** that have knowledge or insight to the history of the current situation or system. The individuals may not have history but instead possess unique knowledge or insight about the system, or they could help to further refine the questions driving interviews and analyses.
- As **information** is collected, it should be organized and then synthesized. This could include gathering deeper information, making connections or other efforts to improve the quality and clarity of information.
- A **preliminary system analysis** is then developed. The factors and feedback contributing toward the achievement, inhibition, or derailment of the vision or goals. An initial systems map can be used to guide and focus insights.
- Individuals and group members are engaged and supported in **developing their own analysis** of the system, relationships, and factors. Sharing the preliminary map (possibly with adjusted language for those still developing the systems thinking vocabulary may be helpful). Sharing systems archetypes and behavior may also help groups to see other patterns and behaviors.
- Mental models can be **identified and surfaced,** or made explicit. The models may then be analyzed and shared to better understand how the models influence the behavior of the various agents and affect other systems' patterns or structures.

- The insights from the systems map and mental model analysis leads to **systemic change conversations.** Seeing the system and the many interactions can build both awareness and acceptance and can also identify key leverage points that agents or group members may now see they influenced in ways not previously identified. The key is to use the group dialogue about the system to not just build acceptance and awareness but drive action to new alternatives for system or group behavior.

Stage 3 Commitment

The Commitment Stage is when an explicit choice is made by the group for "what they really want." The collective group makes a conscious commitment toward aspirations, vision, and goals with a fuller awareness of not just the perceived benefits but also the costs and trade-offs. Through the Understanding and Acceptance Stage, often the dissonance or differences between the expressed goals of the system and the actual goals the system is working toward are better elicited. The behavior and outcomes of a system are based on the design and structure of the system.

- Understanding the **Payoffs of Perpetuation** is important. What is the reinforcing feedback that allows the current system to remain? The payoffs to perpetuating the system's structure are often illustrated in the patterns of past interventions. These may be quick fixes that may provide some short-term relief or gratification but don't change the underlying structure or long-term results. There is a cost for systems change; sometimes it is material, money, time or resources; or the costs could be power, influence, or psychological gratification. What is the collective response to the benefits of the status quo versus the costs of change?

- **Comparing the Case for Change** is focused on the cost of not changing and the benefits of changing. Often, most energy in groups is focused on the benefits of not changing (maintaining a status quo) and the costs of change (resistance).

- A fundamental goal is to see if a **both/and solution** can be created where both the benefits of the existing and new system can both exist. Particularly when the cost of not changing and the benefits of change seem divergent, irreconcilable, or polarized, organizational design strategies like Polarity Management (Johnson, 1992), may be helpful. Going through the interviews and analysis of previous stages leads to identification of the elements between the two Change questions. The systems mapping and synthesis of the polarized elements can reveal points of interdependence. Simply, this approach can lend itself to create a new integrated goal. Traps of equitable design can be found here. There often will be a preference and tendency for "better-before-worse," prioritizing short-term gains or relief without focus or consideration of long-term outcomes or effectiveness. This contrasts with the contrary concept and tendency of "worse-before-better," that things get worse (or more difficult) before they get better. The perceived or anticipated discomfort or security of groups may be prioritized over benefits of the whole group; or in contrast, the same prioritization may be against the present realities of discomfort or insecurity of other group members.

- The group is asked to make an **explicit choice** or commitment. The case for change is bolstered by the systems design process itself. The group design process increased the receptiveness of members to share and receive information, thoughts, feelings, and support from other members. There is an expansion of *presencing*, which deepens the connection between individual group members (agents) and enhances their understanding of the interconnected nature of various systems. This allows the groups to ideate or envision deeper possibilities. The deeper understanding allows the group to become more *active* through more focus and clarity.

Stage 4 Focus, Momentum and Correction

The Focus, Momentum and Correction Stage is meant to bridge the gap between the aspirations and goals of Stage 3 and the realities of the system in Stage 2. Here systems level interventions are applied. The deeper understanding of the system, the system structure (resources), and resulting behaviors allows for more focused approaches. Rather than making many changes, target changes are applied with a focus on sustainability and long-term impact.

- Introduce, implement, and evaluate **high-leverage systems interventions** and tools. The leverage tools identified earlier can be applied in key areas identified through the systems map. The leverage tools can be increasing people's awareness of the system's structure and function, shifting mental models, increased incentives, new metrics or restructuring, and rewiring feedback. Higher level interventions through goal alignment, shifts in authority or rule structures, or a realignment of funding can also be applied. The interventions can be coordinated and scaled as part of a layered or integrated intervention approach. Increased awareness highlights the key points within systems that need to be adjusted. Rewiring these feedback points shifts the causal relationships. New or realigned goals support the implementation of the changes in connections and beliefs. The foundation of these integrated interventions serves to support the other parts of the intervention strategies or plan, especially sustainability.

- Systems by their nature will continue to evolve and change, let alone respond to the systems interventions and strategies that the group chooses to apply. To support and respond to the continuous systems change, a **continuous process of learning and outreach** needs to be established. The continued learning and outreach (connections) serves to actively shape the evolving systems. The partnership service connects the systems to new mental models (understanding of the current system), new information, and new resources. The continuous learning helps in the implementation and sustainability plans for the group. As high-leverage plans are applied to the system, there should be a clear understanding of how the whole group will be informed and new members will be on-boarded upon joining. The system's feedback and information gathered from the different outputs and outcomes developed from the new goals and metrics should continue to be refined to increase the quality of data. The new data should be regularly evaluated with the information used to evaluate and revise the plans, using the feedback and input from the various partners; revisions may include shifting the scope or scale of the interventions or plan. The continuous process of learning and outreach is the ability to respond to the dynamic complexity of systems. These continual growth models, themselves, can ultimately be seen as the development of a new system or new paradigm.

Systemic change is building understanding about the multiple systems inter-actions that raise issues, create problems, or trigger unforeseen outcomes. The work between systems requires cross-systems approaches. Effective cross systems work is built on effective communication, collaboration, and targeting and coordinating goals. The Four Stage Model of Systemic Change is a great design tool for collective impact, or cross-systems impact, to create lasting change.

FIVE-STAGE DESIGN THINKING PROCESS WITH EQUITABLE PRINCIPLES

A traditional design model can be helpful in the development of equitable systemic interventions and supports. Particularly when a range of equitable principles are interwoven, the Equitable Design Model serves as a useful tool for systemic change. The design model is a human-centered process of iden-tifying challenges and goals through the gathering of information to gener-ate ideas (ideate) and build and refine strategies and solutions. The approach can be seen as a marrying of critical thinking and creativity, highlighting skills like empathy, collaboration, and systems thinking (Dam, 2023).

In the first step, Empathize, the designer or design-team connects with their clients to better understand their goals and their concerns. This collaborative process is done through monitoring, observing, and listening to make deep and informative connections. The equitable principles to incorporate into this process can be found in many community-based practices, where collab-orative partnerships are formed focused on the sharing of information and power. The connections would be made with clients but also with those most affected or impacted by the system or design. A deep inquiry should be made to identify, connect, and incorporate the feedback of those most shaped by systemic change, prioritizing the voices of the marginalized or minoritized prior to implementation. The expertise of subject matter experts that are consulted for insight into the issues is balanced by the lived experiences of those most impacted. The design should also hold a deep knowledge of historic oppression and patterns of systemic oppression to avoid the design flaws of recreating oppressive systems, even unintentionally.

In the next stage, Define, the designer or design team then works with the group to focus on key topics of themes and patterns to find clarity. This may involve shifting perspectives or prioritizing issues to be clear and actionable. The work is distilled down to being a problem statement or an action statement to be further developed.

In the Ideate stage, curiosity and imagination lead to collaborative brainstorming of potential solutions and possibilities. The generation of ideas will not be the same as the evaluation of the ideas. Discussion prompts like "how might we . . . " allow a solution-focused imagining of prospects.

The Prototype Stage is the actual development and implementation of the plans, approaches, intervention, or supports designed. The best solution or strategy developed in the Ideate Stage is shared and analyzed by the team or implemented as a real-world scenario as a "proof of concept" design.

The prototype is assessed in the Test & Evaluate Stage, a feedback-focused process. Data is collected based on metrics that may have been established from the goals of the Define State or the development during the Prototype phase. For plans or strategies involving real-world individuals, their experience and perceptions are necessary qualitative data to be understood during the Test Stage. Notably, the weighing of feedback is human-centered. Historically, prototype development has focused on cost or resource consumption over human experience. Human-centered approaches will prioritize the impact of systemic outcomes on humans (people) over the effect on systems or products (things). Quantitative and qualitative data is used to evaluate and refine the prototype, which is then redesigned and reassessed to achieve optimization.

ALIGNED EQUITABLE SYSTEMS FRAMEWORK

In examining models and frameworks that promote equity, there is often difficulty identifying practical steps in the implementation of the models. From grassroots movements to larger national organizations, there is sometimes a lack of clarity or direction in the trainings, programs, or results from the groups. There is also sometimes a lack of clarity in the definitions and language used. "Diversity, equity, inclusion, justice, antiracism, bias, social justice, cultural competence" are sometimes used interchangeably, although they can and should have different meanings and applications.

Through systems thinking, we can see that the systemic design of many models, frameworks, and initiatives often take a narrow approach, focusing on individuals (their internal thoughts and beliefs), on raising awareness of historic oppression or present-day trauma, or healing the trauma that is occurring now. Systems that don't consider complexity have more unforeseen and negative consequences.

When exploring race, we understand that all people have the capacity to be rich or poor, good or bad, right or wrong. People are multifaceted, and the denial of that complexity in systems, distilled to black and white, isn't simply ineffective and unjust—it's counterintuitive to the reality of existence. The systemic change approach is the ability to make practice and policy decisions that embrace complexity rather than narrowly dismiss or simplify them.

Antiracism is the design of equitable systems that address or counteract racism or racist practices or policies; mitigate racists systems, practices, or policies; or create new systems of liberation outside of racists systems. Historically, race has been treated like a single biological construct. In the analysis of the coding and recoding of race through history, we can see race is a set of biological characteristics that were applied to different social and legal conditions in the context of specific ways. As such, there wasn't a single system of race applied across multiple settings, but rather a system of race in criminal justice, in housing, in education, and many more systems occurred separately and concurrently. Just as a physical house is different from a picture of a house, a billing address, a mailing address, a blueprint, and a Zillow listing; race is also different from the various systems which reference it.

Systems that consider more equitable principles are capturing the complexity that already exists. There are ways to make models that address complexity. These models can be accessible as long as the framework is coherent. The purpose of the model, "equity," is going to be described as the systemic outcomes that can no longer be predicted in areas such as race, gender, class, sexuality, and more. As we design an equity framework, we identify the purpose (to create a comprehensive conceptual framework that promotes equity), identify the elements, and the relationships between the elements. To capture the complexity of the system in a systems model, the increased intensity or scope needs to be reflected or represented in the interrelationships. The scope of the interrelationships gives the model depth, conceptually making the model three-dimensional. Similarly, once the structure, changes, or interventions of a system are modeled across a continuum, reflecting the differences each action (or function) does to a system, this creates dynamic (or time) changes. And this kind of dynamic action adds a fourth dimension to the model.

Equitable principles should be clearly defined and aligned, not just to each other but also the inequitable or oppressive principles that they're trying to impact. Too often there are initiatives that try to address systemic problems by taking individualized approaches or see the systemic impact on individuals without recognizing the underlying systemic drivers at play. The Aligned Equitable Systems Framework (see Figure 29) identifies the elements of equity and oppression. From a systems framework, the equitable principles are aligned, scaled to reflect the **scope of the system**—the extent each equitable principle describes and influences the overarching system structure, creating a three dimensional model. Each equitable principle is also scaled across a continuum in order to understand which oppressive concept the equitable principle is trying to address and the equitable practices (or equitable functions) that are the mechanism for change. The **continuum of change** reflects the dynamics of the framework.

As we move up and down the **continuum of change,** the degree of complexity increases, likely needing higher levels or increased training, planning, support or intervention. Through a systems lens we understand that simple or less complex designs, planning, or insights can create many unforeseen outcomes that could have rippling (and detrimental) effects across multiple systems. Similarly, we know racist systems with simple or complex designs have lasting and widespread outcomes, needing higher levels of complex design to promote equity (either to manage the rippling outcomes or to address the racist system directly). Understanding the impact of the equitable practices (or equitable functions) can be a place to use strategies such as modeling to analyze and predict changes over time.

As we move across the **scope of the system** (from left to right), we see that actions begin with the individual and end with systemic change. As the interaction both internally and interconnectedly increases, the scope also expands; however, this expansion leads to a greater reduction in the interaction and influence over the whole system. The degree of intensity across the scope of the system reflects that individual awareness, while helpful, will be far from any systemic change—true systemic change needs a high degree of capacity building and resources to be meaningful and sustainable achieved.

The Aligned Equitable Systems Framework aligns equitable principles with the scope of the system, moving away from individual (agents) toward systemic change. Specific equitable principles are also contrasted with oppressive principles or concepts that need to change through an equitable function (or practice).

Imagine the model as a swimming pool, and the length of the pool (continuum of change) runs from shallow to deep. Similarly, the shallow end identifies oppressive concepts or principles that were derived or can be sustained with little or no systems intervention or complex system design. The deep end reflects the equitable principles that are sustained through intentional actions, practices, or designs to address or manage the complexity. Each equitable principle is in its own lane, and each principle is interrelated with others, just as water flows underneath each lane. But each lane is meant to have its own separate direction. Each lane reflects equitable principles from the self through the whole system and the many different ways to progress in awareness and influence to achieve systemic change.

FIGURE 29   THE ALIGNED EQUITABLE SYSTEMS FRAMEWORK, A SWIMMING POOL

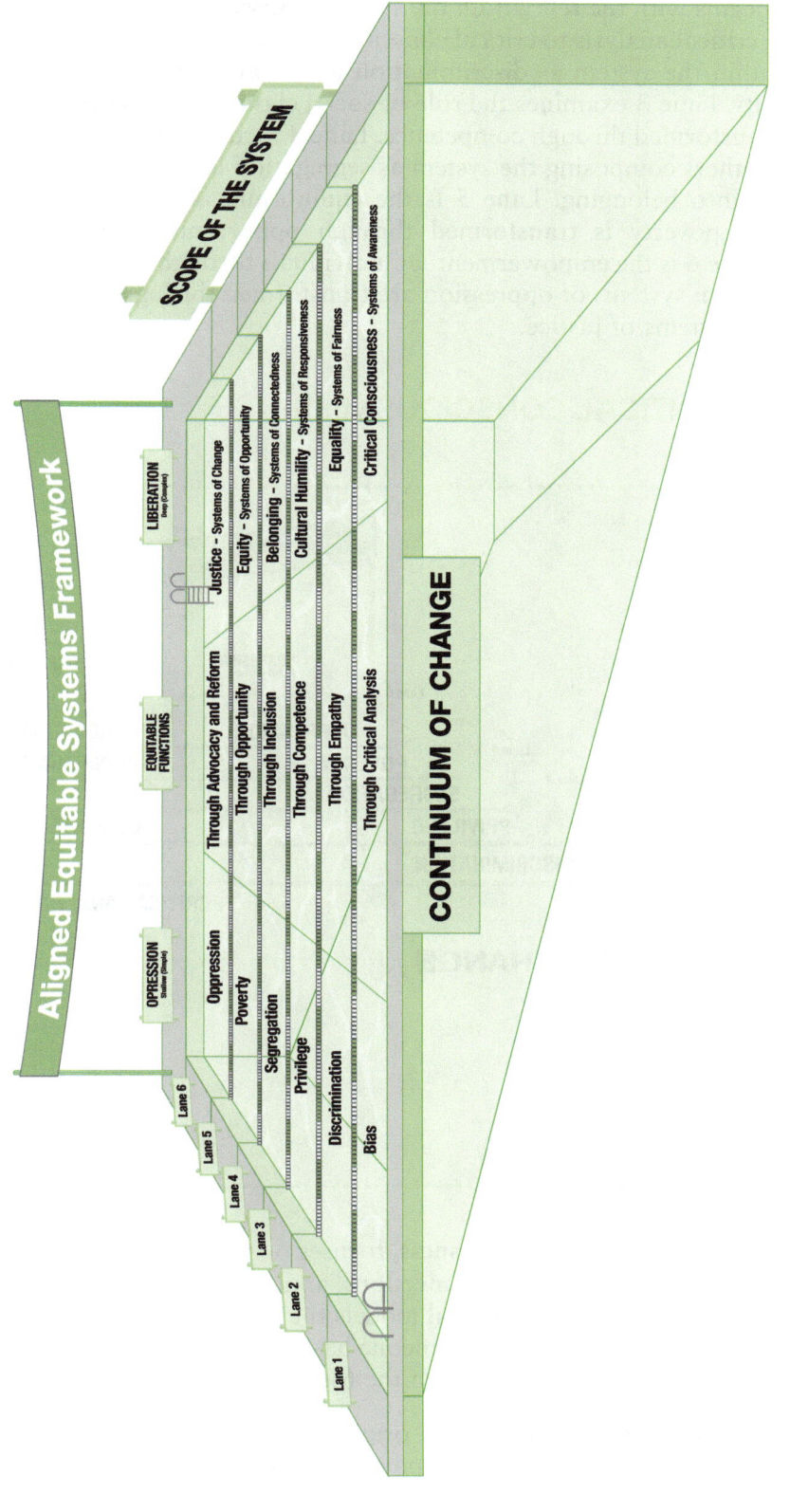

Aligned Equitable Systems Framework

SCOPE OF THE SYSTEM

OPPRESSION
Shallow (Simple)

EQUITABLE
FUNCTIONS

LIBERATION
Deep (Complex)

Oppression

Poverty

Segregation

Privilege

Discrimination

Bias

Through Advocacy and Reform

Through Opportunity

Through Inclusion

Through Competence

Through Empathy

Through Critical Analysis

Justice – Systems of Change

Equity – Systems of Opportunity

Belonging – Systems of Connectedness

Cultural Humility – Systems of Responsiveness

Equality – Systems of Fairness

Critical Consciousness – Systems of Awareness

CONTINUUM OF CHANGE

Lane 6

Lane 5

Lane 4

Lane 3

Lane 2

Lane 1

Lane 1 begins with the self within the system where bias can be transformed through critical analysis to critical consciousness. Lane 2 focuses on relationships within the system as discrimination is transformed through empathy to equality. Lane 3 examines the role of social class and the system as privilege is transformed through competence. Lane 4 focuses on the interrelationships of others composing the system as segregation is transformed through inclusion into belonging. Lane 5 is the equilibrium and sustaining of the system as poverty is transformed through opportunity towards equity. Finally, Lane 6 is the empowerment of individuals through dynamic changes of the system; systems of oppression are transformed through advocacy and reform to systems of justice.

BIAS TO CRITICAL CONSCIOUSNESS

FIGURE 30

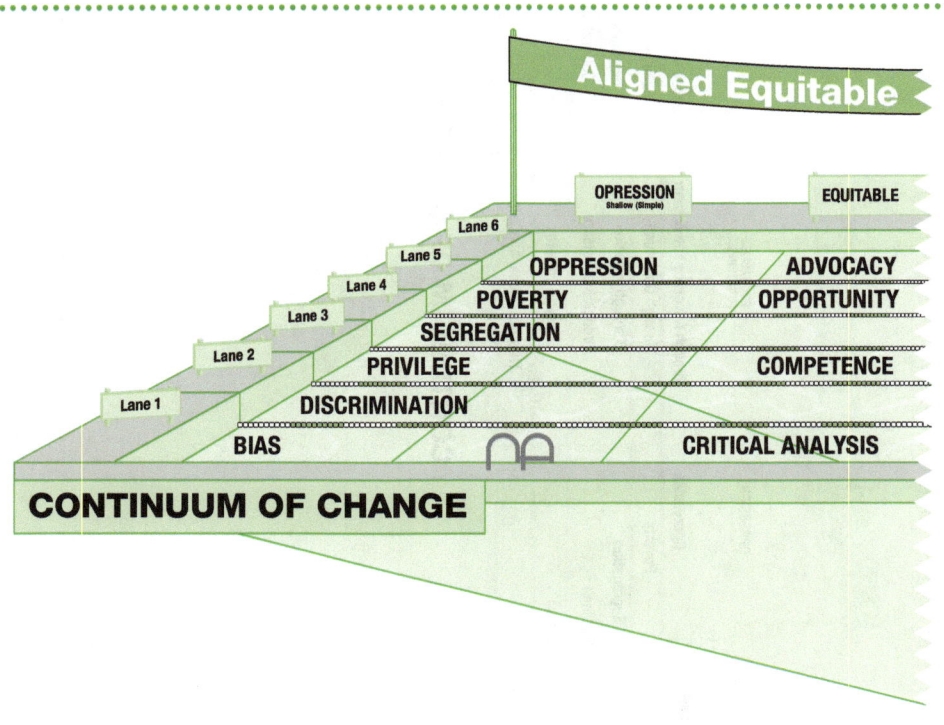

Lane 1, Bias to Critical Consciousness, focuses on the awareness an individual has about themselves, interconnections, and the system. Bias is the individual systems of beliefs, the mental models they hold. The bias includes the attitudes, knowledge, and beliefs someone has about themselves, groups, and the system. Examining biases is often the focus of much equity work.

Critical Consciousness is a concept originally identified by Freire (1970). Critical Consciousness is the development and application of at least three cognitive and social skills: social analysis, political agency, and social action.

Social analysis is the ability to name the social, economic, and political forces that contribute to inequality and inequity and further analyze them. Political agency is the attitude and belief that one has the ability to impact social or political change. Social action is the willingness to engage in activities or events that confront or challenge oppression or other unequal conditions (Seider & Graves, 2020).

The **Critical Analysis** skills needed to foster the skills in Critical Consciousness are rich. While the lists of activities to examine and explore biases is inexhaustible, there are several areas to highlight when exploring Critical Analysis skills. Enhancing knowledge of historic and systemic structures of oppression and opportunity can be foundational to Critical Analysis, involving identifying patterns and themes and illustrating the current realities of the world. There is extensive research on outcomes of the various practices that foster critical analysis skills. The practices range from formal training or classroom experiences to less formal opportunities, such as classroom discussions during an advisory period or student/teacher mentorship. (El-Amin et al., 2017). Key strategies support support Critical Analysis skills, an essential component in developing Critical Consciousness (El-Amin et al., 2017).

- **Teach the language of inequality.** Developing cross-cultural language and vocabulary as well as having language to understand inequality supports critical analysis. Frameworks like the Three I's, which give participants the language to identify and understand institutional, interpersonal, and internalized racism have been demonstrated to be successful tools to foster growth.

- **Create a safe space for analysis.** The ability to explore complex and emotional topics like racism benefits from continuing to promote emotional and psychological safety in the discussions and interrogation about race. Individuals and groups benefit from having a focal point such as a book, curriculum, or other media to work as a lens to facilitate discussion. The facilitated discussion is best done with individuals who have both training and experience with topics such as race, oppression, and trauma and have understanding of the developmental behavior and needs of the groups they are working with.

- **Empowering to take action.** As the level of awareness increases, individuals may be inclined to take action. This may include simply seeking additional learning, increased advocacy, formal protest or activism, or other adaptive strategies sparked by the new understanding and knowledge.

The fostering of Critical Consciousness is the process of building **Systems of Awareness.** While the broader system may remain unchanged, the increased awareness is the foundation for intergroup work, increased systems awareness, and systemic change.

DISCRIMINATION TO EQUALITY

Lane 2, Discrimination to Equality, focuses on the attitudes and behaviors between others. Discrimination is the treatment of a person or group differently due to characteristics such as race, gender, sexuality, and so forth. Discrimination is highly focused in equity work.

Equality is the fair and equal treatment of others without discrimination or bias. Equality is a founding principle for the United States and a legal principle and foundational to the rule of law (United Nations General Assembly, 2012). Equality is different from "sameness" where objects or individuals are thought to be identical (Gosepath, 2021). The practices of equality are often parallel with the use of policy language, such as the term nondiscriminatory. Through this lens, equality among individuals focuses on attitudes, treatment, and behavior.

There are different strategies and tools to promote **Empathy**. There are a range of practices and techniques to address discrimination and discriminatory behavior, but empathy encompasses many of the practices, strategies, and techniques. Empathy is sometimes mischaracterized as the ultimate goal of the interventions when actually it is a tool to affect behavioral change. There are two aspects to empathy: cognitive (thinking) and affective (feeling) empathy (Guthridge et al., 2023). Cognitive empathy is the understanding of others through ourselves. Affective empathy is our emotional or feeling response when observing the emotions of another person. Empathy builds intersubjectivity, the bidirectional response of being connected and wanting to respond to others, as we identify aspects or characteristics of ourselves within them (Guthridge et al., 2023). The reality is that a deep web of interconnection exists within all of humanity. Strategies to foster empathy can include the following:

- **Intergroup Dialogue is** the process of bringing together small- to medium-sized groups, consisting of ten to twenty individuals each who identify with different social groups. The groups typically focus on those with a noted history of two or more groups (e.g., race or gender). Trained facilitators lead discussion on perceptions and attitudes about prejudice, stereotypes, and discrimination as well as relevant current topics or themes. The dialogues allow participants to listen, ask questions, and share the experiences. Facilitators or group members may identify patterns, themes, or other common narratives found in the group discussion (Stephan & Finlay, 1999).

- **Values-based Messaging** can be a powerful narrative tool. Values such as equality, opportunity, respect, dignity, and safety can be powerful conversation anchors, specifically regarding social justice issues like race, gender, and sexuality. Creating a common language is also important. The shared values allow audiences to be more receptive to the message delivered and promote further dialogue (Opportunity Agenda, 2019).

There are many other strategies that promote empathy and lead individuals to respond to others with more fairness and equality. These **Systems of Fairness** serve as a rooted network for deeper work. The increased awareness of the impact on others can help individuals change their approaches with the system, as well.

PRIVILEGE TO CULTURAL HUMILITY

Lane 3, **Privilege to cultural humility,** is the awareness of the impact that relationships of individuals and groups have on the system. Privilege can be seen as the benefits that certain groups or individuals in a system have over others. First, Peggy McIntosh (1990) first wrote about the concept, as she explored privilege through lenses of masculinity and whiteness. Through the analysis of inequality, it's clear we are all damaged by systems of inequality (racism), just not equally. Similarly, there needs to be keen awareness of how we as individuals or groups may be perpetuating oppressive systems and of the ways we are maintaining the systems we are trying to change. Key to the understanding of privilege is the identification and acknowledgement of the imbalances that are created and maintained in resources, power, and influence.

Cultural humility in the incorporation of a lifelong commitment to self-examination and self-reflection, addressing power imbalances between oneself and others in the system, and forming partnership with other individuals (agents) or groups within the system. Tervalon and Murray-Garcia (1998) originally named the concept. Inherent in cultural humility is the approach to cultural conflicts. Those who show cultural humility apply flexibility and learning to groups when in the dominant position. Cultural ambivalence or cultural destruction to the nondominant groups are the other approaches that lead to negative outcomes (Foronda, 2020). The lens of cultural humility seeks to separate ourselves as agents from the reinforcing behaviors of the system.

Through cultural competence, individuals and groups engage in lifelong learning to not only increase their knowledge, understanding, and appreciation of other groups but also to gain increased awareness of the ways they, as individuals, support the broader systemic structure. Cultural competence should focus on increasing cultural awareness, knowledge, and skill; this should include broad knowledge (e.g., Latin, history, and culture in the United States) and local and systems specific information (e.g., related issues in education or health care). There are a range of available courses and training focused on cultural competence and cultural humility as well as diverse media to learn from.

- **Cultural immersion** programs are some of the most widespread benefits to individuals with their cultural competence. Cultural knowledge, attitudes, and skills appeared to grow broadly and deeply, specifically in fields such as health care, education, and counseling. Immersive technology like augmented reality and virtual reality can be leveraged to scale and increase accessibility to these types of experiences (Kuo et al., 2023).

- McIntosh's **Invisible Knapsack** has been adapted into several different exercises where the original framing of privilege is analyzed to explain a broader, more intersectional, understanding of privilege. This is done in small or large group discussions, scaled surveys, or other related group exercises. The is most successful when led by a facilitator who either has training or experience in the activity and has connections to a larger set of learning activities.

To truly make systemic change, we need to more fully understand how we contribute to system behavior. Through these **Systems of Responsiveness**, there is now the ability to work directly with the system's structure. Understanding power imbalances and developing skills to better respond with individuals and groups within the system equip us for systemic change.

SEGREGATION TO BELONGING

FIGURE 31

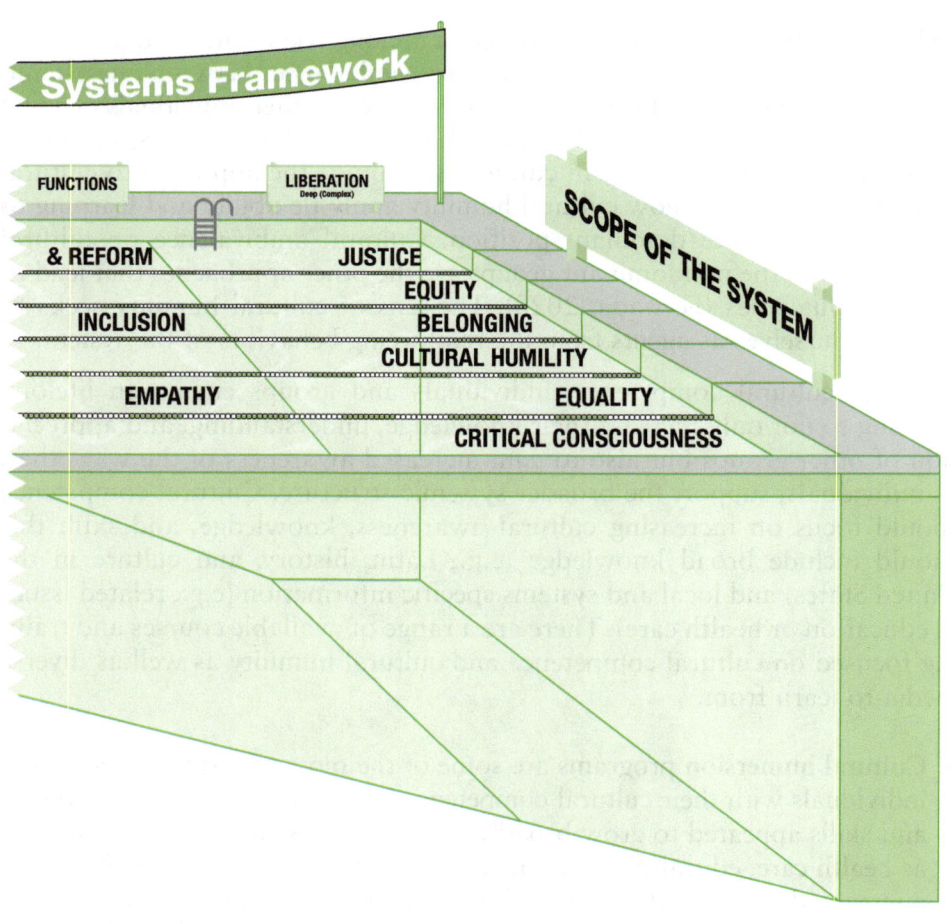

Lane 4, **Segregation to Belonging**, is the connection between others within the system. The ability to understand and enhance the interrelationships between individuals and groups within the system strengthens the system. **Segregation** is the exclusion or marginalization of individuals or groups from parts of the system. The segregation in the system creates (power) imbalances, competing goals, and decreases efficiency with less collective impact. The history of segregation in the United States is currently reflected in housing, education, employment, health care, and much more.

Belonging is often described as a feeling of appreciation, acceptance, or validation by a group (Cobb & Krownapple, 2019). Through systems thinking, Belonging refers to deeper connections, a convergence between agents (people or groups). Convergence is the alignment of goals, functions (actions), and behaviors. In social systems, convergence is extremely difficult. Belonging isn't an aspirational emotional state but rather the conditions that need to be present to achieve convergent behavior.

Inclusion is the practice of changing a system's inputs and connections so that the subpopulation of a system reflects the broader population from which the system draws, or so that the subpopulation has unrestrained and equal access to the system's other elements and agents. Simply, inclusion is changing the system, so all parties have equal access to all the relevant parts of the system.

Inclusion is different from diversity as diversity doesn't necessarily describe action or the benefits of the action on the system or people. The need for diversity arises from segregated systems that provide individuals or groups unequal access to the system and its benefits. The term diversity refers to the subpopulation represented in a system that reflects the broader population that it draws from.

Inclusive practices thrive when scaffolded with the following:

- Physically and psychologically safe environments (Cobb & Krownapple, 2019)
- Promotion culture of respect, dignity, and appreciation (Pless & Maak, 2004)
- Clear and open communication strategies and pathways (Pless & Maak, 2004)

There are a range of inclusive practices that help to shape systems. Inclusive practices should be intentionally designed with the specific system you're working with, but there are some practices that can be highlighted.

- **Universal Design is** a highly effective design approach that can incorporate inclusion from the onset. Universal Design not only focuses on inclusion but targets inclusion as part of the feedback to the design model.

- **Affinity Spaces** can serve as a powerful tool to promote inclusion. Affinity spaces are small groups for individuals who self-identify into the same groups (race, gender, sexuality, or professional) (Pless & Maak, 2004). The parallel system can help to support individuals or groups to build agency or collective power within a system. This can strengthen relationships between individuals and can also deepen their understanding and engagement with a system through their collective knowledge.

- **Situation crafting** is an inclusive design process that leads to transformative experiences (Cohen, 2022). Situation crafting (Cohen, 2022) relies on five resources to build the experiences:
  - **Time is** the introduction or administration of an opportunity, experience, or resource at a salient point for the individual. Short of serendipity, these are opportune moments or situations that can be responsive with the appropriate amount of awareness of an individual's state.
  - **Participatory processes** are the ability for an individual to have agency or responsibility in their change.
  - **Reference groups** are individuals identified with a new group or groups. The referencing is the mental model adopted from the social surrounding. As new groups are referenced, new models are added.
  - **Self-affirmation** is the response of individuals to situations created to share their thoughts, beliefs, or mindsets and be valued for it.
  - **New roles** are the shifts in how a person self-identifies as their roles in the situation or group is adopted.

Through inclusion, **Belonging** can be built within systems, moving past **segregation** from or within systems and creating **Systems of Connectedness**.

POVERTY TO EQUITY

Lane 5, **Poverty to Equity**, is creating equilibrium or balance to a system with the goal of transforming systems to maximize the benefits for all the agents. This focuses on the flow between the different parts of a system and subsystem. **Poverty** is not a lack of resources but rather a lack of effective distribution of resources within a system. Understanding poverty through a distributive systems lens helps to embrace many deeper and historical views of poverty. The distributed definition helps to capture why income alone doesn't fully reflect the scope or impact of poverty, while inequality seems to better capture societal effects related to poverty (Shaffer, 2001). Poverty is often defined in broader terms, but aspects of poverty (income, education, health, political power, etc.) remain closely correlated (Kanbur & Squire, 1999). Similarly, targeted policies and intervention in one area often show benefits to another (e.g. improving health increases income earnings;

improving education improves health outcomes). These demonstrated and redemonstrated parallel benefits reflect the interconnected or distributive nature of systems.

Equity is the system outcomes that can no longer be predicted in areas such as race, gender, class, sexuality, and the like. This operational definition of equity is different from most definitions found in practice and in literature. Here the definition specifically and narrowly defines equity in terms of the outputs (outcomes) of system function and behavior but is consistent with basic understanding and beliefs of race.

Opportunity, as a mechanism of equity, is the intentional and strategic distribution of access to resources, education, and other connections in systems. These provisions serve to enable and empower individuals and groups to more fully benefit and engage with the systems. Policy advocacy in areas or funding, educational programming, and acceleration tools like technology can be powerful opportunity bridges.

- **Equity audits** are tools to analyze and bridge opportunity gaps. The systematic review of policies, culture, practices, and outcomes by organization can identify imbalances and disparities and become foundational in the development of strategic opportunity or equity plans. The process can include surveys, interviews, data collection, and other reviews. Notable audit tools include Mid-Atlantic Equity Consortium (MAEC) Equity Audit; Government Alliance on Race & Equity - Race Equity Action Plans; the Alliance for Resource Equity - Resource Equity Diagnostic; and Annie E. Casey Foundation - Advancing the Mission.

- **Resource Mapping** can be a powerful practice of identifying, curating, and then visually charting the available resources for a region, community, organization, institution, or group (Lever et al., 2019). The resources include not only material assets but also services, skills, relationships, and other aids, both tangible and intangible. The collaborative process involves identifying and fostering partnerships, categorizing and classifying the resources, understanding the decision-making mechanism for the resources, and continually monitoring and assessing the maps developed. This allows for the appropriate support or system to be applied in a timely or responsive manner, promoting higher efficiency and the best outcomes.

Designing **opportunity** to promote **Equity** is a continual process of monitoring, strategic implementation, and evaluation. The imbalances that create **Poverty** are embedded in the structure of systems. Through careful analysis of system structure, assets can be identified and strategies can be applied intentionally to remove silos or provide equilibrium to unbalanced resource networks creating **Systems of Opportunity**.

OPPRESSION TO JUSTICE

Lane 6, Oppression to Justice, is the fundamental change to the structure of the system. While patterns of poverty are feedback loops that are reflected in excessive gains, siloed resources, or slow comparative growth, this is not the only negative outcome that can be found in social systems or system behaviors. Oppression found in the system is the predictable or patterned benefit for certain individuals or groups, while for others it is detrimental. These are written in policies and laws, which were shown to be recorded throughout history. As noted in this design model, in a careful and critical analysis and synthesis of the system dynamics (or history) the elements are needed. Specifically, with racists systems, as previously noted, each appearance of race in a different system is in fact a separate version of racism, a separate racist system.

Justice is the fair and reasonable allocation (Eckhoff, 1974) and management of the system and system behavior to create collective benefit. Through the recognition of complexity and the response to feedback loops, imbalances, and other structural issues, justice creates equitable access, engagement, and distribution sustainably. Justice contributes to the overall well-being of the system, prioritizing the agents, the ultimate beneficiaries of the system.

To achieve justice, the tools of advocacy and reform are best used. Advocacy is the application of multifaceted tools to raise awareness of the system, system behavior, and outcomes, specifically imbalances and silos. Reform is direct action of the system, redesigning system structure and flow, or creating alternate systems to compliment, counteract, or transcend the current system.

Advocacy has a series of competencies to help truly be impactful (Trusty & Brown, 2005). The first competency is the advocates' disposition. Here advocates motivated by social equity, empowerment, support of others, or by ethics and values embrace their agency as those who can influence the system and other actors within the system. They build knowledge—the second competency—of the system parameters (laws, policies, roles, and procedures), find available resources, and set the goals for both the system and for change. Finally, advocates build skills, the third competency. The skills include practical skills in collaboration, communication, and organization. As systems change, working across various systems becomes necessary, making having intergroup skills essential. The skills also include critical analysis and problem-solving skills. As a disposition is developed, coalitions and partnerships can be formed. The coalition can build a collective goal, which can drive an action plan. The action plan involves applying the group's skills and resources to identify and shift systems behavior. The process is monitored and evaluated, refining the action plan and approaches.

Reform is the collective and comprehensive approach to change the interdependencies, feedback loops, or dynamics relationship of a system or other holistic approaches to address or manage a system. As in the word itself, *re* and *form*, the definition means to make again or design new or better systems. System reform remakes racist systems, utilizing the equitable design principles and models presented in this chapter to overhaul the system.

Systems can be designed to have unequal outcomes,\ or unintentionally can lead to oppression as the system can have magnifying effects on certain individuals or groups. Through advocacy and reform, awareness can be raised and systems can be redesigned for Justice, focusing the system on the well-being and benefit of its agents, the primary beneficiaries. Through this process, we can create Systems of Change.

The Aligned Equitable Systems Framework can serve to fundamentally design equitable supports, interventions, tools, and systems. The Framework can also serve to complement or expand existing equitable work. To address complex and adaptive systems like racism, this complex and adaptive framework can guide more fair experiences, heal the trauma of systems of oppression, build equitable outcomes, and design unbounded futures.

CHAPTER 6 DISCUSSION QUESTIONS

- How does viewing racism through a systems lens help us understand its complexity and dynamics? Discuss specific examples from educational settings where systemic racism manifests and its impact on students and communities.

- How can educational leaders ensure that equity-focused interventions or supports are effectively integrated across different levels (individual, classroom, school/building, district)? What are some challenges and opportunities in implementing antiracist strategies at different levels of the educational system? Discuss specific strategies or frameworks that could enhance the sustainability and scalability of these initiatives.

- Several different equity-focused models and frameworks were introduced. How do these differ in their approaches to defining and addressing systemic racism? What implications do these differences have for designing equitable educational practices?

- Discuss the concept of "reverse engineering racism" in educational contexts. How can this approach help us understand and redesign

(Continued)

(Continued)

systems to promote equitable outcomes for all students? How can we leverage system dynamics and analysis to reverse engineer racist systems in education and other areas? Provide specific examples where this approach may be effective.

- How does Stroh's Four-Stage Change Process facilitate collective action for systemic change in educational institutions? What are the key stages in this process that are crucial for achieving equitable outcomes?

- Discuss the effectiveness of initiatives that start by raising individual awareness about equity issues versus those that directly target systemic change. What are the benefits and limitations of each approach, and how can they complement each other?

- Discuss the role of dynamic changes within systems, such as continuum of change, in promoting sustainable equitable outcomes. What strategies can individuals or organizations adopt to manage and leverage these dynamic changes effectively over time?

- How can organizations ensure clarity and alignment among diverse terms like diversity, equity, inclusion, justice, and cultural competence within their frameworks? What are the challenges in defining and operationalizing these terms across different contexts?

CHAPTER 7

....

HUMAN DESIGN

Future Systems

A THIN LAYER ACROSS THE WATER

Understand the world as a group of interconnected and interrelated systems with elements, agents, inputs and outputs, and stocks and flows, for most sounds like highly specific technobabble and not as the commonplace observation that we have watching people going about their routine business while walking down the street. Truly our world runs and functions through incalculable invisible systems which may feel incomprehensible, at first. The notion of changing the vast and varying systems may range from daunting to unimaginable, while many welcome the interaction of the digital systems we use daily. The systems of our phone, tablets, computers, and more are used with no hesitation, and when the systems change through updates, upgrades, and new adoptions, most never notice, remain unphased, or welcome the predicted and regular changes to the digital systems.

The language to understand and describe modern systems was birthed in MIT's Project Whirlwind. Project Whirlwind was a research project at the Massachusetts Institute of Technology and funded by the United States Navy to create a computer that was fast enough to track air traffic. The project created Whirlwind I, the world's first digital computer. Magnetic (random access) core memory, interactive displays, multiprocessing, and computer networks were created from the project (Waldrop, 1993). The first person trained as an operator for Whirlwind would be a recent high school graduate, a young Black man named Joe Thompson. Project lead Jay Forrester noted (Stern et al., 1981) the following:

> This is not a technical engineering history. Rather, it is the story of how technical, financial, and administrative problems vied for solution in an enterprise conducted in war and peace, the outcome of which was by no means foreordained or routine.

Jay Forrester was an engineer and MIT professor. Forrester rose to prominence developing several significant innovations, not only MIT's first digital computer but also North America's air defense system. Forrester shifted his focus to corporate leadership, understanding from his own experiences, as a manger, that complexity of social systems were much more difficult to understand than physical systems he helped to design. Forrester focused on organizational management and other industrial analysis before shifting to broader social structures. Next, he concentrated on mapping, simulating, analyzing systemic structure of cities (Forrester, 1970) before turning his attention to broader complex societal problems such as ecology, pollution, and the economy (Forrester, 1971). Simply, Forrester realized that many of the same strategies and frameworks that designed digital systems could be applied to complex real-world systems.

John Holland was a senior at MIT when he began to work on Project Whirlwind. He would take the experience in computing to explore and define complex systems and complexity science, which he applied to genetics, the environment, psychology, and public policy (Waldrop, 1993).

The applications of systems thinking and systems design created great digital computing systems to track aircrafts and allow us to view Earth from outer space, able to zoom down to views of schools and streets. Systems thinking, system dynamics, and complexity science would describe humanity as a thin layer across the water. The thin layer that we inhabit daily is a tiny set of systems spanning the surface of a vast blue world, nestled in a sprawling universe of infinite systems.

Still, across the blue waters, Black bodies were trafficked for labor in a developing country. The new country over time would create systems of bondage, segregation, exploitation, and discrimination. Yet, as told throughout history, there would be many systems created by humanity, not encoded in laws, but reflecting our shared beliefs, aspiration, and connectedness.

THE LANGUAGE OF OUR HUMANITY

Digital computing systems, policies, and laws are some of our most visible systems. These **bounded** systems are evident as they are written rules, policies, and descriptions that describe or embody the system, the structure and its functions. The majority of the systems we interact with are **unbounded**, unconstrained by clear language or rules, although still rooted in systems behavior nonetheless. Long before there were digital computers, computer coding languages, and even written languages, humans were coding. From early architecture, AfroFractals to Indigenous designs like those of Yupik Parka or Navajo Rug patterns, there is evidence of deep, complex, and historical cultural systems design (Eglash et al., 2006).

While the United States was coding and recoding racism in laws and policies, the people were coding, too. Music, language, cuisine, fashion, beauty, dance, sexuality, faith, mourning, and even celebrations were the encoding of resistance, freedom, community, and independence during periods of enslavement, segregation, and exploitation (Camp, 2002). The invisible codes of the deeper parts of our shared humanity would continue to adapt and recode across generations to challenge evolving systems of oppression.

Now is the time to meet modern design with the deeper parts of our humanity and elevate and design systems of connectedness, equity, and justice so that all can benefit. The tension exists where there are more tools to share information, store knowledge, and communicate ideas; still, there are new tools that challenge equity and encode oppression in new ways.

The digitized world has given way to accelerated learning, information, connections, and access. The bounded laws started in the colonial era had rippling effects echoing into the future. The digitized world has bounded but invisible systems with spanning reach. Algorithms are the set of rules that guide a series of actions toward an established goal. These are the guiding frameworks for digital (and quantum) computing frameworks for the innumerable apps, web services, and programs we use. These frameworks are not color-blind; they are no more color-blind than the centuries of laws reviewed that encoded racism. Algorithms reflect the framework that they are provided with, which will likely reflect the mental models of the designers or the real-world systems or practices that the digital systems attempt to replicate, support or replace. Unfortunately, there are many visible and invisible systems to be digitized.

The systems thinking skills, frameworks, and design tools are not just aspirations for a science fiction future but they comprise the essential knowledge needed in our digitized world. Through these tools, we have developed more awareness of how systems like algorithms can be analyzed and how they may produce oppressive results, and have the tools to create systemic change for equity.

EDUCATION TIES TO OUR FUTURES

For the stymied and antiquated model of education in our schools, the ideals of education persist as a universal language of hope, growth, and aspiration. As the rapid digitized evolution continues to create systemic societal pressures, our unbridled investment and innovation in our education systems can be the stabilizing factor.

Just as Freedmen knew education was the key to freedom, opportunity and healing as we reimagined our polarized and strained country, we must acknowledge that our schools can evolve into the design labs for our ideals for democracy, community, progress, and equity. Schools are not just the launching pad for our students—they can be a launching pad for broader systemic change, particularly when the work is centered on our youth.

From sit-ins to Birmingham's Children's Crusade to the Marches from Selma to Montgomery and on Washington, our youth have been part of the collective work to shape our collective nation. How will we design equitable futures for and with our youth?

We can mirror an equitable systems design process. Using the history of the systems of racism in the United States, we analyze how exploitation was and is encoded. We can see the ways racism is maintained through changing definitions and systems. The lasting results of the continued systems of inequality carry the highest levels of concern not just in the past, but for our present and future. Through understanding systems thinking and systems behavior, we can then learn to create systemic change with a range of different design tools.

Through our understanding of systems thinking and behavior, we know that changes to parts of the system could have rippling effects through the whole system. Small changes could lead to big results. The efforts toward equity With the skills, strategies, and tools provided, the efforts toward equity here can build capacity toward broader systems reform or be the transformative change that could have enormous, far-reaching consequences. As systems designers, we know our systems (things) may or may not be for the benefit of people, ultimately. The goal, well intended or not, if not focused and centered on our humanity, will eventually miss. As such, equitable systems are the result of being designers of humanity. The goals are not focused on material outputs but rather are centered on human experience, well-being, and collective prosperity. Deep analysis of our connections, the distance measured between our shared humanity, is how we get closer to equity.

Where can we deepen equity? We look to our schools. Schools are the design centers to prepare our youth for the future. Schools are also the design centers to prepare our futures for ourselves and our youth.

Schools, like all systems, have cycles. The beginning of each year for students and staff has a buzz of excitement and anxiety for change and newness. The opening doors reveal the interconnected systems within the schoolhouse walls, and past the doors a greater world of systems lies within the school. Kids talk to kids, teachers teach their students, counselors comfort children, families talk to teachers, principals talk to staff, and endless connections are made either stifling dreams or shaping futures between bells, report cards, schoolwide announcements, and graduation days. Seeing the interconnections, sharing visions of opportunity, and committing to the ongoing designs of equity is not about avoiding spiraling inequality or technological fears. It is a commitment to moving toward the best parts of what we are and have, the encoded parts of our humanity that are community, hope, joy, liberty, and progress, to build a sustainable and more perfect future.

Design a collective future. With systemic awareness, embrace the cycles of design, continuously redesigning and adapting to bridge the gap toward a more just world and the excitement of newness that comes with systemic change. Design a radical future, where unbounded systems of imagination, become real policies centered in empathy and focused on opportunity. Today, design to meet the challenges of now, informed by the struggles of yesterday, with our eyes set toward tomorrow. Design futures.

GLOSSARY

Adaptive Systems: A feature of complex systems, the adjustment and response to changes over time.

Causal Loop Diagram: A visual tool that shows the relationships and feedback loops between elements or agents in a system, illustrating how different behaviors and changes occur over time.

Delays: The effects of time on a system, including the time lag between awareness of a change and the implementation of actions, and the subsequent impact on the system.

Dynamic: The nature of systems to change over time, reflecting the ongoing evolution of structure, behavior, and relationships.

Dynamic Equilibrium (Equilibrium): A state where there is an equal flow of elements in and out of a stock, maintaining a stable condition.

Dynamics: The changing of stocks over time due to their flow, reflecting the evolving state of the system.

Emergence: A behavior or property that arises unpredictably from the interaction of elements within a system.

Feedback: The system's interaction and resulting change in behavior or structure within the same system.

Feedback Control: The process of identifying leverage points in a system's feedback loop and introducing interventions, supports, or policies to influence or change the feedback loop.

Feedback Loop: A cycle where the output of a system feeds back into the system, influencing future behavior or structure.

Flow: The change of the stock over time within a system.

Intervention: An action or strategy introduced into a system to influence its behavior and improve outcomes. Interventions can target specific leverage points to create desired changes.

Leverage Points: Specific areas within a system that, when targeted, can lead to significant changes and improvements. These points are often key to implementing effective systemic change.

Mental Models: The thoughts, beliefs, and perceptions that people hold about systems, influencing their understanding and actions.

Negative Feedback (Self-correcting): A type of feedback that counteracts or opposes change within a system.

Nonlinearity: A characteristic of complex systems where changes in one part can lead to unpredictable or disproportionate effects in another part.

Positive Feedback (Self-reinforcing): A type of feedback that promotes growth, amplification, or increasing returns within a system.

Self-organization: The process by which new systems or structures spontaneously form and create patterns of behavior within a system.

Stock: The quantity, amount, or accumulation of an element within a system.

Stock and Flow Models: A representation of systems using stocks (quantities or reservoirs of elements) and flows (the changes to these stocks over time). These models help visualize and understand the dynamics of a system.

Subsystems: Smaller, interrelated systems within a larger system that interact and influence each other.

System: A description of the interaction of different interrelated or interconnected agents (people) or elements (parts or things) working toward a function or purpose.

System Modeling and Simulation: The use of models and simulations to understand, predict, and optimize the behavior and structure of a system. These tools can be used for education, communication, and strategy development.

Systemic Change: The process of applying systems thinking to create effective and sustainable changes within a system, focusing on relationships and feedback rather than just individual elements.

Systems Characteristics: The fundamental traits and behaviors that define and influence systems, particularly in terms of their structure, relationships, and changes over time.

Systems Thinking: A perspective that views the world as a series of interconnected complex systems, emphasizing the interrelationships between elements rather than just the elements themselves.

Unintended Consequences: Unpredictable or unintended effects that result from systemic change or interventions.

REFERENCES

Du Bois, W. E. B. (1903). *The talented tenth*. Teaching American History. https://teaching americanhistory.org/document/the-talented-tenth/

INTRODUCTION

Blad, E., & Najarro, I. (2023, November 28). Race is a big factor in school closures. What you need to know. *EdWeek*. https://www.edweek.org/leadership/race-is-a-big-factor-in-school-closures-what-you-need-to-know/2023/11

Gaebe, A. (n.d.). *Black schools and colleges*. Lynchburg Museum & College. https://www.lynchburgmuseum.org/digital-exhibit-black-schools-and-colleges

Gordon, B. (2023, August 31). Lynchburg city school board committee recommends two school closures to full board. *The News and Advance*. https://newsadvance.com/news/local/lynchburg-city-school-board-committee-recommends-two-school-closures-to-full-board/article_af10282c-4746-11ee-8a84-6b2c07dc8fde.html

Johns Hopkins Center for Gun Violence Solutions and Johns Hopkins Bloomberg School of Public Health, Department of Mental Health. (2023). *Still ringing the alarm: An enduring call to action for Black youth suicide prevention*. https://publichealth.jhu.edu/center-for-gun-violence-solutions/2023/still-ringing-the-alarm-an-enduring-call-to-action-for-black-youth-suicide-prevention

Kendi, D. I. X. (2016). *Stamped from the beginning*. Avalon Publishing Group.

Love, B. (2023, September 5). American education hurt black students. We deserve reparations. *Education Week*. https://www.edweek.org/leadership/opinion-american-education-hurt-black-students-we-deserve-reparations/2023/09

Redelmeier, R. (2023, August). *A school closure cliff is coming. Black and Hispanic students are likely to bear the brunt*. The Hechinger Report. https://hechingerreport.org/a-school-closure-cliff-is-coming-black-and-hispanic-students-are-likely-to-bear-the-brunt/

Schmidt, S. L. (1994). *Talking about race facilitation guide*. Iris Films.

PART I

Chapter 1

Anastaplo, G. (1989). Slavery and the constitution: Explorations. *Texas Tech Law Review, 20*, 677.

Battalora, J. (2013). *Birth of a white nation: The invention of white people and its relevance today*. Routledge.

Black Teacher Archive. (2023). *Harvard graduate school of education*. https://curiosity.lib.harvard.edu/black-teacher-archive

Blackwell, S. (2023, February 11). *The importance of public education in the Massachusetts Bay Colony*. The Blackwell Firm. https://curiosity.lib.harvard.edu/black-teacher-archive/feature/black-education-timeline

Bowen, E. (1747). A new & accurate map of Negroland and the adjacent countries: also upper Guinea, showing the principle European settlements & distinguishing wch. belong to England, Denmark, Holland & c: the sea of the rivers being drawn from surveys & the best modern maps and charts, & regulated by astron. observns [Map].

Library of Congress. https://www.loc.gov/item/2018585377/

Chaffin, R. J. (2000). The Townshend Acts crisis, 1767–1770. In J. P. Greene & J. R. Pole (Eds.), *A companion to the American revolution* (pp. 134–150).

Comminey, S. (1999). The society for the propagation of the gospel in foreign parts and Black education in South Carolina, 1702–1764. *The Journal of Negro History, 84*(4), 360–369. https://doi.org/10.2307/2649037

Continental Congress. (1777). *US articles of confederation and perpetual union between the states of New Hampshire, Massachusetts Bay, Rhode Island, and providence plantations, Connecticut, New York, New Jersey, Pennsylvania, Delaware, Maryland, Virginia, North Carolina, South Carolina, and Georgia.* Library of Congress. https://www.loc.gov/resource/rbpe.17802600/?st=pdf&pdfPage=1

Cooley, W. D. (1841). *The Negroland of the Arabs examined and explained; or, an inquiry into the early history and geography of Central Africa.* J. Arrowsmith.

De Witte, M. (2020, July 1). When Thomas Jefferson penned 'all men are created equal,' he did not mean individual equality, says Stanford scholar. *Stanford News Services.*

The Education of African Americans. (n.d.) *African-American years: Chronologies of American history and experience.* In encyclopedia.com. https://www.encyclopedia.com/history/news-wires-white-papers-and-books/education-african-americans

General Assembly. (2020a, December 7). *An act for preventing Negroes insurrections (1680).* Encyclopedia Virginia. https://encyclopediavirginia.org/primary-documents/an-act-for-preventing-negroes-insurrections-1680

General Assembly. (2020b, December 7). *English running away with Negroes (1661).* Encyclopedia Virginia. https://encyclopediavirginia.org/primary-documents/english-running-away-with-negroes-1661

General Assembly. (2020c, December 7). *Runaway servants (1643).* Encyclopedia Virginia. https://encyclopediavirginia.org/primary-documents/runaway-servants-1643

General Assembly. (2020d, December 7). *Treaty ending the third Anglo-Powhatan war (1646).* Encyclopedia Virginia. https://encyclopediavirginia.org/primary-documents/treaty-ending-the-third-anglo-powhatan-war-1646

General Court. (2020, December 7). *General court responds to runaway servants and slaves (1640).* Encyclopedia Virginia. https://encyclopediavirginia.org/primary-documents/general-court-responds-to-runaway-servants-and-slaves-1640

Georgia. (1978). *The earliest printed laws of the province of Georgia, 1755-1770.* Michael Glazier. https://archive.org/details/earliestprintedl0002geor/page/14/mode/2up?view=theater

Gerlach, D. R. (1966). A note on the quartering act of 1774. *The New England Quarterly, 39*(1), 80. https://doi.org/10.2307/363643

Landers, J. (1984). Spanish sanctuary: Fugitives in Florida, 1687-1790. *The Florida Historical Quarterly, 62*(3), 296–313.

Laws of Virginia, 1662 Act XII; Latin added by William Henig, The Statutes at Large, 1819.

Little, B. (2022, September 22). *How the coercive acts helped spark the American revolution.* https://www.history.com/news/intolerable-coercive-acts-american-revolution

Maryland State Archives. (1637-1664). Proceedings and Acts of the General Assembly January 1637/8-September 1664, Vol. 1, 533.

Maryland State Archives. (2000, November 14). *Blacks before the law in colonial Maryland.* https://msa.maryland.gov/msa/speccol/sc5300/sc5348/html/chap2.html

Maryland State Archives, University of Maryland, College Park History Department, Historic St. Mary's City, & Hampton National Historic Site. (2020). *A guide to the history of slavery in Maryland.* [Online] Retrieved from https://slavery.msa.maryland.gov/pdf/md-slavery-guide-2020.pdf

Maryland State Archives. (2023, October 6). *Proceedings and Acts of the General Assembly, April 26, 1715-August 10, 1716.* Author. https://msa.maryland.gov/megafile/msa/speccol/sc2900/sc2908/000001/000030/html/am30--289.html

McCartney, M. (2020, December 7). *Virginia's first Africans*. In Encyclopedia Virginia. https://encyclopediavirginia.org/entries/africans-virginias-first

Morgan, J. L. (2018). Partus sequitur ventrem: Law, race, and reproduction in colonial slavery. *Small Axe: A Caribbean Journal of Criticism, 22*(1), 1–17.

National Archives. (n.d.a.). *The Declaration of Independence: A history*. National Archives. https://www.archives.gov/founding-docs/declaration-history

National Archives. (n.d.b.). United States. (1776). *Declaration of Independence: A transcription*. America's founding documents. National Archives. https://www.archives.gov/founding-docs/declaration-transcript

New England Historical Society. (n.d.). *How the Old Deluder Satan act made sure puritan children got educated*. New England Historical Society. https://newenglandhistoricalsociety.com/old-deluder-satan-act-made-sure-puritan-children-got-educated

Niven, S. J. (2016). The Stono slave rebellion was nearly erased from US history books. *The Root*.

Ostler, J. (2020, February 8). The shameful final grievance of the declaration of independence. *The Atlantic Monthly*.

Robinson, Y. (2016, July 14). *Elizabeth Key Grinstead (1630–1665)*. BlackPast. https://www.blackpast.org/african-american-history/grinstead-elizabeth-key-1630/

Roos, D. (2022, September 6). *What school was like in the 13 colonies?* History.com. https://www.history.com/news/13-colonies-school

Sewall, S. (1700). The selling of Joseph. Printed by Bartholomew Green and John Allen, 1700 in Boston. The archived URL: https://ia600701.us.archive.org/17/items/SellingOfJoseph/Selling%20of%20Joseph.pdf

Simba, M. (2022, January 13). *The evolution of slavery in Virginia, 1619 to 1661*. BlackPast.org. https://www.blackpast.org/african-american-history/perspectives-african-american-history/the-evolution-of-slavery-in-virginia-1619-to-1661/

Slavery Law and Power. (n.d.). *Butts v. Penny (1677)*. Author. https://slaverylawpower.org/butts-v-penny-1677/

South Carolina Slave Code. *West's encyclopedia of American law*. (n. d.) https://www.encyclopedia.com/law/encyclopedias-almanacs-transcripts-and-maps/south-carolina-slave-code

Statutes at Large of Pennsylvania. (n.d.). Better regulating of Negroes in the Province. Act 292. Vol. 4. 1726. Legislative Reference Bureau of Pennsylvania. https://www.palrb.gov/Preservation/Statutes-at-Large/ViewDocument/17001799/1726/0/act/0292.pdf

Thorpe, F. N. (Ed.). (1909). *The federal and state constitutions, colonial charters, and other organic laws of the states, territories, and colonies now or heretofore forming the United States of America*. Government Printing Office. https://avalon.law.yale.edu/17th_century/art1613.asp

Tiffany, M. (2017). *Bound in Bermuda and Virginia: The first century of slave laws and customs* [Master's thesis]. Central Washington University.

Triber, J. (2024, January 9). *Slavery and law in 17th century Massachusetts*. Boston National Historical Park, Boston African American National Historic Site. https://www.nps.gov/articles/000/slavery-and-law-in-early-ma.htm

Virginia Assembly. Laws, statutes, etc. (1814–1823). *The statutes at large; being a collection of all the laws of Virginia, from the first session of the legislature, in the year 1619*. (W. Waller Hening, Ed., Vols. 1–13).

Virginia General Assembly. (2020, December 7). *An act for suppressing outlying slaves (1691)*. Encyclopedia Virginia. https://encyclopediavirginia.org/primary-documents/an-act-for-suppressing-outlying-slaves-1691

Ward, N. (1641). *The Massachusetts body of liberties*. General Court of Massachusetts. Hanover Historical Texts Project. https://history.hanover.edu/texts/masslib.html#back

Wilson, J. (1866). Civil rights speech delivered in the House of Representatives Debates. *Congressional Globe*.

Wood, B. (2021, July 27). Slavery in colonial Georgia. *New Georgia Encyclopedia*. https://www.georgiaencyclopedia.org/articles/history-archaeology/slavery-in-colonial-georgia/

Chapter 2

Anderson, J. D. (1988). *The education of Blacks in the south, 1860-1935* (p. 19). University of North Carolina Press. http://www.jstor.org/stable/10.5149/9780807898888_anderson

Annals of Congress. (n.d.) *A century of lawmaking for a new nation: U.S. Congressional documents and debates, 1774–1875*. Annals of Congress, Senate, 16th Congress, 1st Session. pp. 427–428.

Bacow, L. (2022). *The legacy of slavery at Harvard: Report and recommendations of the presidential committee*. Harvard University Press.

Black Codes of Mississippi. (1865, October 31). *Teaching American history*. Retrieved March 1, 2024, from https://teachingamericanhistory.org/document/black-codes-of-mississippi/

Brown, A. (2020, February 25). *The changing categories the U.S. census has used to measure race*. Pew Research Center.

Brown, D. L. (2015, March 27). Black towns, established by freed slaves after the Civil War, are dying out. *The Washington Post.*

National Constitution Center. (n.d.) *Civil rights cases, 109 U.S. 3. (1883)*. https://constitutioncenter.org/the-constitution/supreme-court-case-library/the-civil-rights-cases

Claybaugh, A. J. (2010. December 20). Public education and the welfare state: The case of the freedmen's schools. *Occasion: Interdisciplinary Studies in the Humanities.* http://occasion.stanford.edu/node/45

Digital History. (2021). *Secession ordinances of 13 confederate states*. Digital History. https://www.digitalhistory.uh.edu/disp_textbook.cfm?smtID=3&psid=3953

Douglass, F. (1892). *Life and times of Frederick Douglass* (p. 460). De Wolfe & Fiske.

Dred Scott v. Sandford, 60 U.S. 393, 15 L. Ed. 691, 15 L. Ed. 2d 691 (1857).

Du Bois, W. E. B. (1901, March). The freedmen's bureau. *The Atlantic Monthly.*

Feldman, N. J. (2017). Madison's lesson on racism. *The New York Times Opinion.*

Foner, E. (1996). *Freedom's lawmakers: A directory of Black officeholders during reconstruction* (2nd ed.). LSU Press.

Glynn, J. C., Jr. (2011). *William Whipple.* Descendants of the Signers of the Declaration of Independence.

Goodman, B. F. (1912). The black codes, 1865-1867. [Master's Thesis]. University of Illinois. https://www.ideals.illinois.edu/items/51542/bitstreams/149621/data.pdf

Hackney, H. E. (1969). Racial discrimination and the Civil Rights Act of 1866. *Sw. L. J, 23,* 373.

Harris, W. T. (1889). 'Introduction', In T. J. Morgan (Ed.), *U.S. bureau of education bulletin no.1. Indian education*. Government Printing Office.

Hochschild, J., & Weaver, V. (2007). Policies of racial classification and the politics of racial inequality. In J. Soss, J. Hacker, & S. Mettler (Eds.), *Remaking America: Democracy and public policy in an age of inequality* (pp. 159–182). https://scholar.harvard.edu/jlhochschild/publications/policies-racial-classification-and-politics-racial-inequality

Hoffer, P. C. (2017). *John Quincy Adams and the gag rule, 1835–1850*. Johns Hopkins University Press.

Inskeep, S. (2021, June 7). *The supreme court justice who made history by voting no on racial segregation*. NPR - National Public Radio.

Jackson, F. J. (2011). Dred Scott v. Sandford: A prelude to the Civil War. *Rich. J. L & Pub. Int., 15,* 377.

Katz. (1976). *A history of compulsory education laws*. Fastback Series (No. 75). Bicentennial Series. Phi Delta Kappa Educational Foundation.

Kendi, I. X. (2017). *Stamped from the beginning: The definitive history of racist ideas in America*. Nation Books.

Lado, M. L. (1995). A question of justice: African-American legal perspectives on the 1883 civil rights cases - Freedom: Constitutional law. *Chicago-Kent Law Review, 70,* 1123. https://scholarship.kentlaw.iit.edu/cklawreview/vol70/iss3/9

Lai, K. K. R., & Medina, J. (2023, October 16). An American puzzle: Fitting race in a box. *The New York Times*. https://www.nytimes.com/interactive/2023/10/16/us/census-race-ethnicity.html

Loewen, J. W. (2011). Using confederate documents to teach about secession, slavery, and the origins of the Civil War. *OAH*

Magazine of History, 25(2), 35–44. https://doi.org/10.1093/oahmag/oar002

Louisiana Separate Car Act, 1890. https://www.studythepast.com/weekly/louisianacaract.html

Murray, P. (Ed.). (1997). *States' laws on race and color.* University of Georgia Press.

National Archives. (n.d.). *The constitution of the United States: A transcription.* Author. https://www.archives.gov/founding-docs/constitution-transcript

National Archives. (2022, May 10). *13th amendment to the U.S. Constitution: Abolition of slavery (1865).* Author. https://www.archives.gov/milestone-documents/13th-amendment#:~:text=The%2013th%20Amendment%20to%20the%20United%20States%20Constitution%20provides%20that,place%20subject%20to%20their%20jurisdiction.%22

National Archives. (2024a, January 12). *15th amendment to the U.S. constitution: Voting rights (1870).* National Archives.

National Archives. (2024b, March 6). *14th amendment to the U.S. constitution: Civil rights (1868).* Author.

National Constitution Center. (n.d.) *Civil rights cases, 109 U.S. 3. (1883).* https://constitutioncenter.org/the-constitution/supreme-court-case-library/the-civil-rights-cases

National Education Association of the United States. Committee on Secondary School Studies. (1894). *Report of the committee of ten on secondary school studies: With the reports of the conferences arranged by the committee.* National Education Association.

Newman, N., & Gass, J. J. (2004). *A new birth of freedom: The forgotten history of the 13th, 14th, and 15th amendments.* Brennan Center for Justice at NYU School of Law.

Parry, M. (2017, March 19). How U.S. law inspired the Nazis. *Chronicle for Higher Education.*

Perea, J. F. (2012). *Race and constitutional law casebooks: Recognizing the proslavery constitution.* https://repository.law.umich.edu/mlr/vol110/iss6/12

Plessy v. Ferguson (1896) 163 U.S. 537 (1896). https://constitutioncenter.org/the-constitution/supreme-court-case-library/plessy-v-ferguson

Police Regulations of Saint Landry Parish, Louisiana. (1865). *Dictionary of American History.* https://www.encyclopedia.com/history/dictionaries-thesauruses-pictures-and-press-releases/police-regulations-saint-landry-parish-louisiana-1865

Rawley, J. A. (1979). *Race and politics: Bleeding Kansas and the coming of the civil war* (Vol. 714). University of Nebraska Press.

Schmidt, R. W. (2011, January). American Indian identity and blood quantum in the 21st century: A critical review. *Journal of Anthropology, 2011,* 1–9. 10.1155/2011/549521.

South Carolina Convention. (1860). *Declaration of the immediate causes which induce and justify the secession of South Carolina from the federal union; and the ordinance of secession.* Evans & Cogswell, printers to the convention. Yale Law School. https://avalon.law.yale.edu/19th_century/csa_scarsec.asp

Stowe, H. B. (1879). The education of freedmen. *The North American Review, 128*(271), 605–615.

Tarter, B. (2020, December 7). *Vagrancy Act of 1866.* Encyclopedia Virginia. https://encyclopediavirginia.org/entries/vagrancy-act-of-1866

Teaching American History. (n.d.). *Black Codes of Mississippi. October 31, 1865.* Retrieved March 1, 2024 from, https://teachingamericanhistory.org/document/black-codes-of-mississippi/

Trammell, V. (2022, May). *The one drop rule: Its origin and history as an instrument of American racism.* Black Then. https://blackthen.com/the-one-drop-rule-its-origin-and-history-as-an-instrument-of-american-racism/

United States Congress. (n.d.) A century of lawmaking for a new nation: U.S. congressional documents and debates, 1774–1875. *Annals of Congress,* Senate, 16th Congress, 1st Session, pp. 427, 428. Library of Congress.

United States Congress. (1865). *An act to establish a bureau for the relief of freedmen and refugees - law creating the freedmen's bureau.* Freedmen and Southern Society Project.

United States Congress. (1866, April 9). *The civil rights act of 1866.* Teaching American

History. Retrieved March 1, 2024, from https://teachingamericanhistory.org/document/the-civil-rights-act-of-1866/

United States House of Representatives. (1866). A century of lawmaking for a new nation: U.S. congressional documents and debates, 1774–1875. *Congressional Globe,* House of Representatives, 39th Congress, 1st Session, p. 1117.

United States Senate. (2023, August 8). *The confiscation acts of 1861 and 1862.* Author. https://www.senate.gov/artandhistory/history/common/generic/ConfiscationActs.htm

Weaver, V. W. (1969). The failure of civil rights 1875–1883 and its repercussions. *The Journal of Negro History, 54*(4), 368–382. https://ctdigitalnewspaperproject.org/wp-content/uploads/2017/06/Failure-of-Civil-Rights-1875-1883-Journal-Negro-History.pdf

Zeitz, J. M. (2000). The Missouri compromise reconsidered: Antislavery rhetoric and the emergence of the free labor synthesis. *Journal of the Early Republic, 20*(3), 447. https://doi.org/10.2307/3125065

Chapter 3

Allen, J., & Daugherity, B. (2020, December 7). *Green, Charles C. et al. v. County School Board of New Kent County, Virginia.* Encyclopedia Virginia. Virginia Humanities. https://encyclopediavirginia.org/entries/green-charles-c-et-al-v-county-school-board-of-new-kent-county-virginia/

Beman, L. T. (Ed.). (1924). The Towner-Sterling Bill: US Department of Education. H. W. Wilson Company. *The Reference Shelf, 11*(5), 340–342.

Blank, R. K. (2011). *Closing the achievement gap for economically disadvantaged students? Analyzing change since no child left behind using state assessments and the national assessment of educational progress.* Council of Chief State School Officers.

Bolotnikova, M. N. (2020, January 12). Appeals court rules in Harvard's favor in admissions lawsuit. *Harvard Magazine.* https://harvardmagazine.com/2020/01/appeals-court-rules-in-harvards-favor

Bowen, E. (1747). A new & accurate map of Negroland and the adjacent countries: also upper Guinea, showing the principle European settlements & distinguishing wch. belong to England, Denmark, Holland & c: the sea of the rivers being drawn from surveys & the best modern maps and charts, & regulated by astron. observns [Map]. Library of Congress. https://www.loc.gov/item/2018585377/

Bradley v. Milliken, 338 F. Supp. 582. (E.D. Mich. 1971).

Branton, W. A. (1983). Little Rock revisited: Desegregation to resegregation. *The Journal of Negro Education, 52*(3), 250–269.

Brown v. Board of Education. (1955). 349 U.S. 294, 75 S. Ct. 753, 99 L. Ed. 1083.

The U.S. Government Brief as Amicus Curiae for Brown v. Board of Education: The interest of the United States. 347 U.S. 483 (1954). https://ia803106.us.archive.org/22/items/brownvboardamicuscuriemcgranery/brown%20v%20board%20amicus%20curie%20mcgranery.pdf

Brown-Nagin, T. (2022, January 20). Rescuing the civil rights movement and children of Birmingham. *Harvard Gazette.* https://news.harvard.edu/gazette/

Caldera, C. G., Franklin, D. R., & Zwickel, S. W. (2019, October 2). Federal judge rules Harvard's admissions policies do not discriminate against Asian American applicants. *The Crimson.* https://www.thecrimson.com/article/2019/10/2/admissions-suit-decision/

Casalaspi, D. (2017). The making of a "Legislative Miracle": The Elementary and Secondary Education Act of 1965. *History of Education Quarterly, 57*(2), 247–277. https://doi.org/10.1017/heq.2017.4; https://sci-hub.se/10.1017/heq.2017.4

Chang, A., Brown, A., & Marquez Janse, A. (2021, July 13). *The right to vote: The impact of Shelby County V. Holder on voting rights.* All Things Considered. NPR

Cineas, F. (2023, July 25). *Affirmative action for white college applicants is still here.* Vox. https://www.vox.com/politics/2023/6/30/23778906/affirmative-action-white-applicants-legacy-athletic-recruitment

Darling-Hammond, L., & Marks, E. L. (1983). *The new federalism in education: State responses to the 1981 education consolidation and improvement act.* RAND.

Darling-Hammond, L., Noguera, P., Cobb, V. L., & Meier, D. (2007). Evaluating "no child left behind." *The Nation, 284*(20), 11.

Driver, J. (2018). *The schoolhouse gate: Public education, the Supreme Court, and the battle for the American mind.* Pantheon.

Emeka, T. Q. (2023, July 16). Detroit riot of 1967. *Encyclopedia Britannica.* https://www.britannica.com/event/Detroit-Riot-of-1967

English-Reif, T. (2020, September 15). *Four girls forever lost: 57 years ago, 16th Street Baptist Church bombing awakened nation to deadly consequences of hate.* Southern Poverty Law Center.

Farinde, A. A., Adams, T., & Ewis, C. W. L. (2014). Segregation revisited: The racial education landscape of Charlotte Mecklenburg schools. *Western Journal of Black Studies, 38*(3), 177–183. https://research.ebsco.com/c/ypghjh/viewer/pdf/gj3oe6gref

Federal Housing Administration, Underwriting Manual: Underwriting and Valuation Procedure Under Title II of the National Housing Act, 1938, § 937. https://www.huduser.gov/portal/sites/default/files/pdf/Federal-Housing-Administration-Underwriting-Manual.pdf

Fiscella, K., & Kitzman, H. (2009). Disparities in academic achievement and health: The intersection of child education and health policy. *Pediatrics, 123*(3), 1073–1080.

Fox, E. E. (2022, February 1). *The civil rights act of 1964.* The JFK Library Archives: An Inside Look. https://www.jfklibrary.org/archives/search-collections

Galton, F. (1904). Eugenics: Its definition, scope, and aims. *American Journal of Sociology, 10*(1), 1–25.

Gamson, D. A., McDermott, K. A., & Reed, D. S. (2015). The Elementary and Secondary Education Act at fifty: Aspirations, effects, and limitations. *RSF: The Russell Sage Foundation Journal of the Social Sciences, 1*(3), 1–29. https://www.rsfjournal.org/content/rsfjss/1/3/1.full-text.pdf

Garver, K. (1991). *Eugenics: Past, present, and the future.* https://www.ncbi.nlm.nih.gov/pmc/articles/PMC1683254/pdf/ajhg000820206.pdf

Gilbert, R. E. (1982). John F. Kennedy and civil rights for Black Americans. *Presidential Studies Quarterly, 12*(3), 386–399.

Gobitis, L. (1993). The courage to put god first. https://wol.jw.org/en/wol/d/r1/lp-e/101993526

Graff, M. (2021). *50 years after the Swann decision: What worked and what didn't.* Axios. https://www.axios.com/local/charlotte/2021/04/20/50-years-after-the-swann-decision-what-worked-and-what-didnt-255177

Green v. County School Board, 391 U.S. 430, 88 S. Ct. 1689, 20 L. Ed. 2d 716 (1968).

Hannah-Jones, N. (2013, October 10). *A colorblind constitution: What Abigail Fisher's affirmative action case is really about.* ProPublica.

Herbold, H. (1994/1995, Winter). Never a level playing field: Blacks and the GI bill. *The Journal of Blacks in Higher Education,* (6), 104–108. http://dx.doi.org/10.2307/2962479

Hershman, J. (2020, December 7). Massive resistance. *Encyclopedia Virginia.* https://encyclopediavirginia.org/entries/massive-resistance

Hinger, S. (2018, October 18). *Meet Edward Blum, the man who wants to kill affirmative action in higher education.* ACLU.

Hirschman, C., & Mogford, E. (2009). Immigration and the American industrial revolution from 1880 to 1920. *Social Science Research, 38*(4), 897–920.

Hunt, T. C. (2023, August 26). National Defense Education Act. *Encyclopedia Britannica.* https://www.britannica.com/topic/National-Defense-Education-Act

Kennedy, J. F. (1963). *Radio and television report to the American people on civil rights, June 11, 1963.* John F. Kennedy Presidential Library and Museum. https://www.jfklibrary.org/archives/other-resources/john-f-kennedy-speeches/civil-rights-radio-and-television-report-19630611

Kirchgaessner, S. (2023, July 12). Lawyers with Supreme Court business paid Clarence Thomas aide via Venmo. *The Guardian.*

Klein, A. (2015, April 10). No child left behind: An overview. *Education Week.* https://www.edweek.org/policy-politics/no-child-left-behind-an-overview/2015/04

Klibaner, I. (1983). The travail of southern radicals: The Southern Conference educational fund, 1946-1976. *The Journal of Southern History, 49,* 179–202.

Ko, L. (2016, January 29). Unwanted sterilization and eugenics programs in the United States. *Independent Lens Blog.* PBS. https://www.pbs.org/independentlens/blog/unwanted-sterilization-and-eugenics-programs-in-the-united-states/

Kotlowski, D. (2005). With all deliberate delay: Kennedy, Johnson, and school desegregation. *Journal of Policy History, 17*(2), 155–192. https://doi.org/10.1353/jph.2005.0013

Krieg, J. M. (2011). Which students are left behind? The racial impacts of the No Child Left Behind Act. *Economics of Education Review, 30*(4), 654–664.

Lawrence, C. R., III. (2006). *Who is the child left behind? The racial meaning of the new school reform.* Georgetown Law Faculty Publications and Other Works. https://scholarship.law.georgetown.edu/facpub/341

Levy, P. B. (2019). *The civil rights movement: A reference guide.* Bloomsbury Publishing USA.

Liptak, A. (2017, November 19). Affirmative action lawsuits. *The New York Times.*

Marcus, M. L. (1992). Symposium: Brown v. Board of Education and its legacy: A tribute to Justice Thurgood Marshall, learning together: Justice Marshall's desegregation opinions. *Fordham Law Review, 61*(1), 69.

Mayer, M. S. (1989). The Eisenhower administration and the civil rights act of 1957. *Congress & the Presidency, 16*(2), 137–154. https://doi.org/10.1080/07343468909507929

McCallister, J. L. (2023, October 20). *Racial and sexual exclusion in World War II-era military and veterans' policy: An excerpt from "Ambivalent affinities."* UNC Press.

Meinke, S. (2011, September). Milliken v. Bradley: The northern battle for desegregation. *Michigan Bar Journal,* 20-22. https://www.michbar.org/file/journal/pdf/pdf4article1911.pdf

Meschede, T., Eden, M., Jain, S., Jee, E., Miles, B., Martinez, M., Stewart, S., Jacob, J., & Madison, M. (2022, December). *IERE research brief final report: GI bill study.* Institute for Economic and Racial Equity. The Heller School for Social Policy and Management at Brandeis University. https://heller.brandeis.edu/iere/pdfs/racial-wealth-equity/racial-wealth-gap/gi-bill-final-report.pdf

Milliken v. Bradley, 418 U.S. 717, 94 S. Ct. 3112, 41 L. Ed. 2d 1069 (1974).

Milliken v. Bradley, 433 U.S. 267, 97 S. Ct. 2749, 53 L. Ed. 2d 745 (1977).

Mitchell, W. A. (1949). Religion and federal aid to education. *Law & Contemp. Probs., 14,* 113

Minersville School Dist. v. Gobitis, 310 U.S. 586, 60 S. Ct. 1010, 84 L. Ed. 1375 (1940).

Murray, P. (Ed.). (1997). *States' laws on race and color.* University of Georgia Press.

NAACP Legal Defense Fund. (2020). Brown v. Board of Education | The case that changed America. NAACP Legal Defense and Educational Fund, Inc. https://www.naacpldf.org/brown-vs-board/

National Archives. (2022, February 8). *Civil rights act of 1964.* Author. https://www.archives.gov/milestone-documents/civil-rights-act

Ngai, M. M. (2017). The architecture of race in American immigration law: A reexamination of the immigration act of 1924. In I. H. López (Ed.), *Race, law and society* (pp. 351–376). Routledge.

OECD. (2019). *Health at a Glance 2019: OECD Indicators.* OECD Publishing. Paris. https://doi.org/10.1787/4dd50c09-en.

Orfield, G., Frankenberg, E., Ee, J., & Kuscera, J. (2014, May 15). *Brown at 60 - UCLA civil rights project.* Civil Rights Project. https://civilrightsproject.ucla.edu/research/k-12-education/integration-and-diversity/brown-at-60-great-progress-a-long-retreat-and-an-uncertain-future/Brown-at-60-051814.pdf

Paul, D. B. (2003). Darwin, social Darwinism and eugenics. In J. Hodge & G. Radick (Eds.), *The Cambridge companion to Darwin* (pp. 214–239). Cambridge University Press.

Popenoe, P., & Johnson, R. H. (1918). *Applied eugenics.* DigiCat.

Reardon, S. F., Kalogrides, D., & Shores, K. (2013, August 12). *The widening achievement gap between high-and low-income youth: New evidence from the ECLS-K.* Center for Education Policy Analysis, Stanford University.

Reisner, E. H. (1922). *Nationalism and education since 1789: A social and political history of modern education.* Macmillan.

Roberts, S. (2022, April) We know the pledge. Its author, maybe not. *New York Times.* https://www.nytimes.com/2022/04/02/us/pledge-of-allegiance-author.html

Rothstein, R. (2017). *The color of law: A forgotten history of how our government segregated America.* Liveright Publishing.

Runyan, J., Gianopoulos, E., & Mogk, J. (2022, January). School desegregation: 50 years after Milliken v. Bradley. *Michigan Bar Journal.* https://www.michbar.org/journal/Details/School-desegregation-50-years-after-Milliken-v-Bradley?ArticleID=4318

Seddiq, O., & Epstein, J. (2022, October 31). *Clarence Thomas says 'I don't have a clue' what 'diversity' means as the Supreme Court confronts the role of race in university admissions.* Business Insider.

Slade, S. (2023, February 23). *The KKK's push for compulsory schooling and a federal education department.* Reason. https://reason.com/2023/01/23/the-kkks-push-for-a-federal-education-department/

Stoskopf, A. (2002). Echoes of a forgotten past: Eugenics, testing, and education reform. *The Educational Forum, 66*(2), 126–133. https://doi.org/10.1080/00131720208984814; https://sci-hub.se/https://www.tandfonline.com/doi/epd/10.1080/00131720208984814?needAccess=true

Students for Fair Admissions, Inc. v. President and Fellows of Harvard College, 142 S. Ct. 895 (2022).

Sturkey, W. (2018, February 8). *The hidden history of the civil rights act of 1960.* Black Perspectives. African American Intellectual History Society. https://www.aaihs.org/the-hidden-history-of-the-civil-rights-act-of-1960/

Sutherland, A. E. (1955). Segregation by race in public schools retrospect and prospect. *Law and Contemporary Problems, 20*(1), 169–183.

https://scholarship.law.duke.edu/cgi/viewcontent.cgi?article=2629&context=lcp

Swann, J. E., et al. v. Charlotte-Mecklenburg Board of Education. (1971). 402 U.S. 1, 91 S. Ct. 1267, 28 L. Ed. 2d 554.

U.S. Department of Defense (DOD). (2020, October 22). *75 years of the GI bill: How transformative it's been.* https://www.defense.gov/News/Feature-Stories/story/Article/1727086/75-years-of-the-gi-bill-how-transformative-its-been/

U.S. Department of Housing and Urban Development. (1938). Federal housing administration underwriting manual: Underwriting and valuation procedure under title II of the National Housing Act, 1938, § 937. https://www.huduser.gov/portal/sites/default/files/pdf/Federal-Housing-Administration-Underwriting-Manual.pdf

Wellington, P., & Clifton, L. (1926). *A debate handbook on a national department of education: Being a discussion of the proposal for a national department of education, with a Compilation of Articles on the Subject* (Vol. 5 No. 6). University of Kentucky.

West, C. (2017, October 8). Clinton desegregation crisis. *Tennessee Encyclopedia.* Tennessee Historical Society. http://tennesseeencyclopedia.net/entries/clinton-desegregation-crisis/

Whitman, J. Q. (2017). *Hitler's American model: The United States and the making of Nazi race law.* Princeton University Press.

Winfield, A. G. (2007). *Eugenics and education in America institutionalized racism and the implications of history ideology and memory.* Peter Lang.

Woods, L. L., II. (2013). Almost "no negro veteran . . . could get a loan": African Americans, the GI bill, and the NAACP campaign against residential segregation, 1917–1960. *The Journal of African American History, 98*(3), 392–417.

Ziemer, G. (1941). *Education for death: The making of the Nazi.* Oxford University Press.

Chapter 4

Abdullah, A., Doucouliagos, H., & Manning, E. (2015). Does education reduce income inequality? A meta-regression analysis. *Journal of Economic Surveys, 29*(2), 301–316.

Carter, K. N., Blakely, T., Collings, S., Gunasekara, F. I., & Richardson, K. (2009). What is the association between wealth and mental health? *Journal of Epidemiology & Community Health, 63*(3), 221–226. https://doi.org/10.1136/jech.2008.079483

Castagno, E., Corvino, R., & Ruggiero, F. (2023). *Skills, education and wealth inequality.* SSRN 4539267. https://papers.ssrn.com/sol3/papers.cfm?abstract_id=4539267

Daly, M., Wilson, M., & Vasdev, S. (2001). Income inequality and homicide rates in Canada and the United States. *Canadian Journal of Criminology, 43*(2), 219–236.

Derenoncourt, E., Kim, C. H., Kuhn, M., & Schularick, M. (2022). *Wealth of two nations: The U.S. racial wealth gap, 1860-2020* (NBER Working Paper No. 30101). National Bureau of Economic Research. http://www.nber.org/papers/w30101

Fajnzylber, P., Lederman, D., & Loayza, N. (2002). Inequality and violent crime. *The Journal of Law and Economics, 45*(1), 1–39.

Fontana, J., Kim, D., & Lapp, D. (2020, January). *Unequal access to educational opportunity in high school: A national analysis of the civil rights data collection.* Research for Action. https://www.researchforaction.org/wp-content/uploads/2021/07/CRDC-National-Jan2020.pdf

Foster, A. C., & Rojas, A. (2018). Program participation and spending patterns of families receiving government means-tested assistance. *Monthly Labor Review.* U.S. Bureau of Labor Statistics. https://doi.org/10.21916/mlr.2018.3

Garrett, B., & Gangopadhyaya, A. (2016, December). *Who gained health insurance coverage under the ACA, and where do they live?* Robert Wood Johnson Institute. Urban Institute. https://www.urban.org/sites/default/files/publication/86761/2001041-who-gained-health-insurance-coverage-under-the-aca-and-where-do-they-live.pdf

Government Accountability Office. (2022). *K-12 education: Student population has significantly diversified, but many schools remain divided along racial, ethnic, and economic lines* (Report No. GAO-22-104737). https://www.gao.gov/assets/gao-22-104737.pdf

Heckman, J., Pinto, R., & Savelyev, P. (2013). Understanding the mechanisms through which an influential early childhood program boosted adult outcomes. *American Economic Review, 103*(6), 2052–2086.

Hopkins, H. (2020, June 8). Racism is killing the planet. *Sierra.* https://www.sierraclub.org/sierra/racism-killing-planet

Illing, S. (2019, March 19). *How the politics of racial resentment is killing white people.* Vox. https://www.vox.com/2019/3/19/18236247/dying-of-whiteness-trump-politics-jonathan-metzl

Kuhfeld, M., Soland, J., & Lewis, K. (2022). *Test score patterns across three COVID-19-impacted school years.* EdWorkingPaper: 22-521. Annenberg Institute at Brown University. https://doi.org/10.26300/ga82-6v47

Massie, V. (2023, June 29). *White women benefit most from affirmative action—and are among its fiercest opponents.* Vox. https://www.vox.com/2016/5/25/11682950/fisher-supreme-court-white-women-affirmative-action

Pew Research Center. (2016). *On views of race and inequality, Blacks and Whites are worlds apart.* Pew Research Center.

Raudenbush, S. W., & Eschmann, R. D. (2015). Does schooling increase or reduce social inequality? *Annual Review of Sociology, 41*, 443–470.

Schaeffer, K. (2020, February 7). *6 facts about economic inequality in the U.S.* Pew Research Center. https://www.pewresearch.org/short-reads/2020/02/07/6-facts-about-economic-inequality-in-the-u-s/

Schenkman, S., & Bousquat, A. (2021). From income inequality to social inequity: Impact on health levels in an international efficiency comparison panel. *BMC Public Health, 21*, 1–17.

Shaw-Amoah, A., & Lapp, D. (2022, October). *Unequal access to educational opportunity among pennsylvania's high school students.* Research for Action.

World Economic Forum. (2017). *The global risks report 2017, 12th edition.* The Global Competitiveness and Risks Team.

World Economic Forum. (2024). *The global risks report 2024.* The Global Competitiveness and Risks Team.

Wilkinson, R. G., & Pickett, K. E. (2006). Income inequality and population health: A review and explanation of the evidence. *Social Science & Medicine, 62*(7), 1768–1784. https://doi.org/10.1016/j.socscimed.2005.08.036

Yu, S. (2018). Uncovering the hidden impacts of inequality on mental health: A global study. *Translational Psychiatry, 8*, 98. https://doi.org/10.1038/s41398-018-0148-0

Chapter 5

Meadows, D. H. (2008). *Thinking in systems: A primer*. Chelsea Green Publishing.

Stroh, D. P. (2015). *Systems thinking for social change: A practical guide to solving complex problems, avoiding unintended consequences, and achieving lasting results*. Chelsea Green Publishing.

Chapter 6

Anyon, Y., Bender, K., Kennedy, H., & Dechants, J. (2018). A systematic review of youth participatory action research (YPAR) in the United States: Methodologies, youth outcomes, and future directions. *Health Education & Behavior, 45*(6), 865–878. https://doi.org/10.1177/1090198118769357

Cammarota, J., & Fine, M. (2010). Youth participatory action research: A pedagogy for transformational resistance. In J. Cammarota & M. Fine (Eds.), *Revolutionizing Education* (pp. 9–20). Routledge.

Castro, F. G., Barrera, M., Jr., & Holleran Steiker, L. K. (2010). Issues and challenges in the design of culturally adapted evidence-based interventions. *Annual Review of Clinical Psychology, 6*, 213–239. https://doi.org/10.1146/annurev-clinpsy-033109-132032

Center for Antiracist Education (CARE). (2021). *Stand for children*. https://antiracistfuture.org/web-series/principles/

Cobb, F., & Krownapple, J. (2019). *Belonging through a culture of dignity*. Mimi & Todd Press, Inc.

Cohen, G. L. (2022). *Belonging: The science of creating connection and bridging divides*. W. W. Norton & Company.

Cowan, K. C., Vaillancourt, K., Rossen, E., & Pollitt, K. (2013). *A framework for safe and successful schools* [Brief]. National Association of School Psychologists.

Dam, R. F. (2023, October 16). *The 5 stages in the design thinking process*. Interaction Design Foundation - IxDF. https://www.interaction-design.org/literature/article/5-stages-in-the-design-thinking-process

Delgado, R., & Stefanic, J. (2017). *Critical race theory: An introduction*. New York University Press.

Eckhoff, T. (1974). *Justice: Its determinants in social interaction*. Rotterdam University Press.

El-Amin, A., Seider, S., Graves, D., Tamerat, J., Clark, S., Soutter, M., Johannsen, J., & Malhotra, S. (2017). Critical consciousness: A key to student achievement. *Phi Delta Kappan, 98*(5), 18–23.

Evans, C. (2021). *Culturally sensitive, relevant, responsive, and sustaining assessment*. National Center for the Improvement of Educational Assessment.

Foronda, C. (2020). A theory of cultural humility. *Journal of Transcultural Nursing, 31*(1), 7–12. https://doi.org/10.1177/1043659619875184

Forrester, J. W. (1971). *World dynamics* (1973, 2nd ed.). Pegasus Communications.

Freire, P. (1970). *Pedagogy of the oppressed*. Continuum.

Gosepath, S. (2021, April 26). Equality. *Stanford Encyclopedia of Philosophy*. https://plato.stanford.edu/entries/equality/

Guthridge, M., Penovic, T., Kirkman, M., & Giummarra, M. J. (2023). The role of affective empathy in eliminating discrimination against women: A conceptual proposition. *Human Rights Review, 24*(3), 433–456.

Johnson, B. (1992). *Polarity management: Identifying and managing unsolvable problems*. Human Resource Development.

Kanbur, R., & Squire, L. (1999). *The evolution of thinking about poverty: Exploring the interactions*. https://ecommons.cornell.edu/server/api/core/bitstreams/e6c7717f-179c-4ecd-95be-772d3db7dd01/content

Kendi, I. X. (2019). *How to be an antiracist*. One World.

Kuo, B. C., Hussein, N., Makhzoum, N., Sabhnani, P., & Zvric, M. (2023). Evaluating the effects of cultural immersion on counselor trainees' multicultural development and intercultural competence: A metasynthesis of qualitative evidence. *International Journal of Intercultural Relations, 94,* 101798.

Learning for Justice. (2022). *Social justice standards: The Learning for Justice anti-bias framework, second edition.* Southern Poverty Law Center. https://www.learningforjustice.org/frameworks/social-justice-standards

Lever, N., Castle, M., Cammack, N., Bohnenkamp, J., Stephan, S., Bernstein, L., Mann, A., Whitaker, A., Torres-Gullien, S., Morton, M., Jordan, H., Coyle, S., & Sun, W. L. (2019). *Cops & no counselors: How the lack of school mental health staff is harming students.* https://www.aclu.org/publications/cops-and-no-counselors

McIntosh, P. (1990). *White privilege: Unpacking the invisible knapsack.* https://files.eric.ed.gov/fulltext/ED355141.pdf#page=43

Moir, T. (2018). Why is implementation science important for intervention design and evaluation within educational settings? *Frontiers in Education, 3,* 61.

Opportunity Agenda. (2019). *A communications toolkit.* Toolkit. The Opportunity Agenda. https://opportunityagenda.org/wp-content/uploads/2022/12/2019.05.06-Toolkit-Without-Comic-Book.pdf

Otto, K. N., & Wood, K. L. (1996, August). *A reverse engineering and redesign methodology for product evolution* [Conference session]. International Design Engineering Technical Conferences and Computers and Information in Engineering Conference (Vol. 97607, p. V004T04A016), American Society of Mechanical Engineers, Irvine, California, USA.

Pless, N., & Maak, T. (2004). Building an inclusive diversity culture: Principles, processes and practice. *Journal of Business Ethics, 54,* 129–147.

Seider, S., & Graves, D. (2020). *Schooling for critical consciousness: Engaging Black and Latinx youth in analyzing, navigating, and challenging racial injustice.* Harvard Education Press.

Shaffer, P. (2001). *New thinking on poverty: Implications for poverty reduction strategies.* Paper Prepared for the United Nations Department for Economic and Social Affairs (UNDESA).

Shelton, R. C., Adsul, P., & Oh, A. (2021). Recommendations for addressing structural racism in implementation science: A call to the field. *Ethnicity & Disease, 31*(Suppl 1), 357–364. https://doi.org/10.18865/ed.31.S1.357

Shortell, S. M. (2004). Increasing value: A research agenda for addressing the managerial and organizational challenges facing health care delivery in the United States. *Medical Care Research and Review, 61*(3_suppl), 12S–30S.

Singleton, G. E. (2014). *Courageous conversations about race: A field guide for achieving equity in schools.* Corwin.

Stephan, W. G., & Finlay, K. (1999). The role of empathy in improving intergroup relations. *Journal of Social Issues, 55*(4), 729–743. https://doi.org/10.1111/0022-4537.00144

Stern, N., Redmond, K. C., Smith, T. M., & Lavington, S. H. (1981). Project whirlwind: The history of a pioneer computer. *Technology and Culture, 22*(3), 644. https://doi.org/10.2307/3104418

Stroh, D. P. (2015). *Systems thinking for social change: A practical guide to solving complex problems, avoiding unintended consequences, and achieving lasting results.* Chelsea Green Publishing.

Sue, D. W., Sue, D., Neville, H. A., & Smith, L. (2022). *Counseling the culturally diverse: Theory and practice.* John Wiley & Sons.

Toraif, N., Augsberger, A., Young, A., Murillo, H., Bautista, R., Garcia, S., Sprague Martinez, L., & Gergen Barnett, K. (2021). How to be an antiracist: Youth of color's critical perspectives on antiracism in a youth participatory action research context. *Journal of Adolescent Research, 36*(5), 467–500. https://doi.org/10.1177/07435584211028224

Trusty, J., & Brown, D. (2005). Advocacy competencies for professional school counselors. *Professional School Counseling, 8,* 259–265.

United Nations General Assembly. (2012, November 30). *Declaration of the high-level* meeting of the general assembly on the rule of law at the national and international levels: Resolution / adopted by the general assembly, A/RES/67/1. https://www.refworld.org/legal/resolution/unga/2012/en/89696

U.S. Government (1953). Brief of the United States as amicus curiae in support of petitioners. Amicus brief filed in *Brown v. Board of Education*. 347 U.S. 483, 74 S. Ct. 686, 98 L. Ed. 873. https://ia803106.us.archive.org/22/items/brownvboardamicuscuriemcgranery/brown%20v%20board%20amicus%20curie%20mcgranery.pdf

Valdez, E. S., Skobic, I., Valdez, L., O Garcia, D., Korchmaros, J., Stevens, S., Sabo, S., & Carvajal, S. (2020). Youth participatory action research for youth substance use prevention: A systematic review. *Substance Use & Misuse, 55*(2), 314–328. https://doi.org/10.1080/10826084.2019.1668014

Waldrop, M. M. (1993). *Complexity: The emerging science at the edge of order and chaos.* Simon and Schuster.

Woo, A., Lawrence, R. A., Doan, S., & Kaufan, J. H. (2022). *A snapshot of anti-bias education in US K–12 schools. Findings from the 2021 American instructional resources surveys.* RAND.

Chapter 7

Camp, S. M. H. (2002). The pleasures of resistance: Enslaved women and body politics in the plantation South, 1830-1861. *The Journal of Southern History, 68*(3), 533. https://doi.org/10.2307/3070158

Eglash, R., Bennett, A., O'donnell, C., Jennings, S., & Cintorino, M. (2006). Culturally situated design tools: Ethnocomputing from field site to classroom. *American Anthropologist, 108*(2), 347–362.

Forrester, J. W. (1970). Urban dynamics. *IMR; Industrial Management Review (pre-1986), 11*(3), 67.

Forrester, J. W. (1971). *World dynamics* (1973, 2nd ed.). Pegasus Communications.

INDEX

achievement gap, 99–100, 109
Adequate Yearly Progress (AYP), 100
admission, 61, 76, 87, 102, 107
advocacy, 81, 169–70, 178–79
African descent, 17, 19, 22, 31, 39–40
agencies, 92–93, 176, 178
algorithms, 183
American Revolution, 21, 26–27, 29, 31
antiracism, 2, 4–5, 147, 155, 166–67
antiracist policy, 155
antiracist systems, 157
assault, 24
attendance zones, 90
attitudes, 4, 151, 170–73
AYP (Adequate Yearly Progress), 100

balance, racial, 85–86, 90, 95–96
bathtub, 134–35
biases in educational policies, 64
Black Americans, 55, 64, 113
Black and Indian, 60–61
Black and white schools, 79
Black Codes, 46–49, 52, 55, 64
Black education, 44, 80
Black people, 10, 20–21, 23–24, 36, 53–54, 59
Black population, 18, 21, 76, 92
Blacks and whites, 114
Black soldiers, 73
Black students, 1, 76, 80, 87, 99, 105, 117
Black veterans, 73, 76
Blackwell, S.,16
Blum, Edward, 101–2
Bradley v. Milliken, 91, 94–97, 100, 109
British colonies, 10, 17–18, 21, 23, 25, 28, 31
Brown v. Board of Education, 77–79, 108–9

Casalaspi, D., 86
census, 35
change systems, 126, 142, 169, 179

Charlotte-Mecklenburg Schools (CMS), 89, 91
Chief State School Officers, 100
Civil Rights Act, 49–50, 52, 64, 80–82, 84–87, 102, 109
civil rights cases, 52, 54–55, 59, 64
Civil Rights Commission, 81
Civil War, 42, 44, 47, 54–55, 64, 103
class citizenship system, 80
CMS (Charlotte-Mecklenburg Schools), 89, 91
coded language of race and racism, 157
coded race, 37
coded systems, 123
coding, 108, 167, 182–83
coding race, 108
college admissions, 61–63, 103–7
colonists, 14, 21, 27–28
colored persons, 54
colored races, 55–56
common school, 38, 71
competence, 71, 130, 169–70
   cultural, 166, 173, 180
competency, 56, 178
complex systems, 123–26, 143, 147–48, 182
compulsory school attendance laws, 78
Confederation, 15, 29
continuum of change, 168–70, 180
contracts, 12, 46, 48, 50, 75
costs of change, 163
Council of Chief State School Officers, 100
Courageous Conversations Compass, 151–52
Court of Appeals, 94, 98
critical analysis, 142, 169–71, 178
Critical Race Theory, 154
CRT, 154
cultural humility, 173–74
curriculum, 2, 61, 117, 141, 156, 171

data, qualitative, 132–33, 166
Declaration of Independence, 27–28, 31, 63

delays, 79, 124–25, 127, 130, 132, 134, 140
Department of Education, 67
Department of Justice, 81, 105
desegregation, 79, 81, 89–90, 96, 98
design
    complex system, 168
    equitable system, 123
design centers, 184
designers, 161, 165–66, 183–84
design of education systems, 120
design of equitable systems, 167
design tools, 165, 183–84
Detroit Public Schools, 92, 96
Detroit School Board, 98
digital computing systems, 182
digital systems, 181, 183
dismantling systems of equity, 107
disparities, 113, 120, 148, 158, 177
dissent, 78, 94, 96, 103–4
District Court, 79, 90, 94–95, 97–98
diversity, 106, 109, 150, 153, 156,
    166, 175, 180
Dred Scott, 38–39, 64
dual systems, 88, 123
    operating state-compelled, 88

ECIA (Education Consolidation and
    Improvement Act), 99
Education Act, 86–87
Education Consolidation and Improvement Act
    (ECIA), 99
education reform, 38, 118
education separation, 56, 59
education systems, 25, 60, 76, 80, 92, 94,
    119–20, 150, 183
    broader, 86
    exclusive, 63
    racist, 98
    unequal, 77
Elementary and Secondary Education Act.
    See ESEA
emancipation, 27, 34, 42
encoded races, 27
enslaved individuals, 30–31, 64
enslaved people, 17–18, 20–25, 28, 31,
    33–34, 42
enslaved person, 26, 33, 42
enslavement, 11, 14–15, 20–23, 26, 183
equality of rights, 57–58, 103
Equal Protection Clause, 95, 102–3

equitable outcomes, 156, 179–80
equitable principles, 142, 158, 165, 167–68
equitable system designs and systemic change, 123
equitable systems, 6, 9, 120, 157, 160, 167, 184
equity, educational, 64, 99, 108, 120
ESEA (Elementary and Secondary Education
    Act), 86–87, 99–100, 109
eugenics, 63, 65, 67, 69–70
explicit choice, 160–61, 163–64

Federal Housing Administration. See FHA
feedback loops, 125, 127, 129, 135, 143, 178–79
Ferguson, J., 54–55, 59, 64, 95
FHA (Federal Housing Administration),
    74–75, 92
fidelity, 149–50
flag, 68–71
flow, 125, 132, 134–35, 140, 176, 178, 181
flow models, 134–35
forced servitude, 43, 47–48
Forrester, J., 182
foundation for systemic change, 161
Fourteenth Amendment, 51–53, 56, 64, 66, 77,
    79, 102, 104–5
freedmen, 44–45, 48–49, 52, 183
Freedmen's Bureau, 44, 46–47, 49, 64
Freedmen's Schools, 44
freedom of choice, 88
freemen of other races, 54
free schools, 25, 38, 46
funds, 2, 34, 67, 86–87, 100, 159
    federal, 87

gender, 154, 167, 172, 176–77
Georgia Slave Code, 25–26
German school system, 69
GI Bill, 73, 75–76, 108
goal of equity, 148
Goddard, H., 66
Goodman, B. F., 46–48
grades, 62, 134–35, 137
graphing, 133–34
groups
    dominant, 151
    identified, 115, 151
    minoritized, 151, 154
    new, 176

Harvard, 63, 101–2, 105
Harvard College, 101–2, 104

HBCUs (Historically Black Colleges and Universities), 76
health care, 59, 173, 175
Herbold, H., 73, 76
higher education, 1, 73, 76, 103, 106–7, 113, 115
Hispanic students, 117
Historically Black Colleges and Universities (HBCUs), 76
HOLC (Home Owners' Loan Corporation), 74–75, 92
housing segregations, 74, 91

IASA (Improving America's Schools Act), 99
imbalances, 148, 153, 173, 175, 177–78
Immigration Restriction Act, 66
immunities, 30, 40, 50, 52–54, 56
imprisonment, 20, 47–48
Improving America's Schools Act (IASA), 99
inclusion, 63–64, 148, 166, 169–70, 174–76, 180
income, 114–15, 117, 157, 176
Indians, 13–14, 19–20, 23, 33, 35, 49, 60–61, 63
Indian servants, 14
Indigenous people, 13–15, 23–24, 28, 31
inequality
    bridging, 119
    educational, 116
    racial, 104–5, 107
inequality in education, 143
inequity, racial, 155
infidels, 20
information practices, 149
initiatives, 64, 117–18, 162, 166–67, 179–80
integration, 79–81, 89, 91–92, 108, 148
interconnected systems, 9, 184
interrelationships, 124, 157, 167, 170, 175
interventions
    equitable systemic, 165
    systems level, 135, 164
invisible systems, 63, 183

Jamestown, 10, 17
Jim Crow laws, 49, 54–55, 59, 64–65
Johnson, L. B., 84–86
Justice Harlan, 53, 78, 103–4
Justice Marshall, 96, 104

Kendi, I. X., 4, 42, 155

language and tools of systems design, 120
laws
    first compulsory education, 24
    first education, 16
    passing, 49, 66
    restrictive education, 25
    supreme, 58, 103
    vagrancy, 48
Learning for Justice Anti-Bias Framework, 153
legislation, 20, 46, 52–53, 57, 81–86, 109, 150
lens of equity, 148
leverage tools, 141–42, 164
liberty
    civil, 71–72, 78
    personal, 57–58
Lincoln, A., 41–42

Maryland's anti-miscegenation laws, 18, 31
masters, 12–13, 15, 18, 20, 22, 25
McCartney, M., 10–11
Milliken v. Bradley, 91, 94–97, 100, 109
Minersville School Dist, 70–71
minoritized individuals, 151
Missouri state courts, 38
models
    conventional, 128–29
    conventional problem-solving, 128–29
    nationalized, 69
momentum, 84, 160–61, 164
motivation, 2, 84, 104, 136–39
mulatto, 19–20, 35
multitiered systems, 159
Murray, P., 59, 66, 76–77

NAACP (National Association for the Advancement of Colored People), 77, 91–92
National Association for the Advancement of Colored People (NAACP), 77, 91–92
National Constitution Center, 53
National Education Association, 61–62, 68
nationalized model of education, 69
Naturalization Act, 35–36, 63
Nazi-German era education system, 70
NCLB (No Child Left Behind), 1, 99–101, 109
negro education, 44, 46
Negroland, 10–11, 31
Negro servant, 13
New England education system, 25
New England Historical Society, 16

New Kent County, 87–88, 109
No Child Left Behind. *See* NCLB

oppressive systems, 80, 142, 157, 166, 173
outreach, 164–65

Partus Sequitur Ventrem, 16–17
Pennsylvania Slave Codes, 22
people of color, 47, 67, 74
plantation, 20, 24–25
Plessy, 56, 59, 78, 95, 104
Plessy v. Ferguson, 54–55, 59, 64
pool, 168–69
prejudice, 3–5, 172
prisoner, 14–15
private schools, 59, 70, 79
process of law, 52–53, 56
Project Whirlwind, 181–82
public schools, 59, 68, 79, 90, 93–94,
    96–97, 100

race-conscious admissions policies, 101, 106
Race Equity Action Plans, 177
race laws, 59
    previous, 107
race neutrality, 104, 107
racial group, identified, 151
racism and race, 3, 9, 154
racist structures, countering, 147
racist systems, reverse engineer, 180
rebellion, 17, 23, 28, 37, 44
reconstruction, 44, 49, 52, 54, 64–65
redesign, 9, 151, 158, 179
refugees, 44–45
Reisner, E. H., 67–69
religion, 20–21, 49, 71–72, 85, 90, 154
residential patterns, 90, 93
rights, political, 50, 52, 56
Runyan, J., 91–92

safety, 28, 30, 118, 139, 148, 150, 172
school administration, 80, 93
school authorities, 88–91, 93
school boards, 87–88, 98, 109, 141
school climate, 117, 160
    positive, 116–17
school counselors, 139, 148, 158
school culture, 138–39
school integration, 80, 89
school segregation, 59, 77, 91, 93, 101
    public, 77, 93

secession, 41–42
segregated system, 87, 90, 97, 175
segregation in public education, 82, 104
selectmen, 16
self-organization, 124, 141
separation, 54, 56, 59, 90, 113, 118
servants, 12–13, 15–17, 20, 48
servicemen, 73, 75
servitude, 10–15, 17, 26–27, 35, 37, 47,
    52–53, 78
    lifelong, 12–14
shared language of race and systems, 3
slave codes, 20–22, 24, 33
slave-holding States, 36–37, 41–42
slavery
    expanse of, 21–22
    re-establishment of, 48–49
Snow White, 3
social structures and systems of race and
    racism, 31
social systems, 59, 113, 175, 178, 182
South Carolina Slave Code, 23
state action, 53, 95–96
state laws, 54, 67, 88
state legislation, 53
state officials, 91–92, 97–98
states
    free, 33, 36
    individual, 46, 59
    slaveholding, 37, 41–42
    southern, 37, 42, 64, 73, 87
stock and flow models, 134–35
strategies, effective, 127, 150
Stroh, D. P., 124, 132, 160–61, 180
student enrollment, 96, 134
student motivation, 135–39
students
    graduate, 2
    minoritized, 99
    special education, 99
students and accountability measures, 99
Students for Fair Admissions, 101–2, 104
students of color, 1, 105
Sturkey, W., 81
subpopulation, 175
subsystems, 127–28, 130, 132, 141, 157, 161, 176
sustainability, 149, 164, 179
Swann v. Charlotte-Meclenburg, 89, 91, 94, 97
systemic change in education systems, 150
systemic change models, 129, 148
systemic inequalities, 109, 113

systemic issues of housing and segregation, 89
systemic structures of oppression and
    opportunity, 171
systems change, 124, 141, 163, 178, 181
systems design process, 164
systems dynamics, 143, 156, 178, 182
systems framework, 168
systems function, 139, 177
systems interventions, 140–41, 164, 168
systems lens, 128, 147, 168
systems map, 163–64

teacher training, 67, 138–39
territories, 36–38, 41, 44, 50
Third Anglo-Powhatan War, 13–14
Thirteenth Amendment, 43–44, 47, 51, 53
tools for systemic change, 142, 165
Townshend Acts, 26–27

unitary system, 88, 96, 98
United Colonies of New England, 15
United States Congress, 37, 44, 49
United States House of Representatives, 50–51
United States Navy, 181

United States Senate, 42
United States Supreme Court, 38, 93
US attorney, 84–85

veterans, 73, 76
violent crime, 115, 118–19
Virginia General Assembly, 12, 17, 19–20
Virginia Slave Code, 17, 20–21, 31
vote, 50–52, 68, 83

water, 134–35, 181–82
wealth, 10, 76, 114–15, 117, 120
wealth inequality, 115
whiteness, 23, 40–41, 173
white schools, 76, 79, 87, 89, 95
white students, 87, 90, 117
Wilson, J., 50–51

youth, 2, 119, 153–54, 156, 184
YPAR (Youth Participatory Action Research),
    153–54, 156

zero sum, 103, 107, 131
Ziemer, G., 69–70

A Sage Company

CORWIN HAS ONE MISSION: to enhance education through intentional professional learning.

We build long-term relationships with our authors, educators, clients, and associations who partner with us to develop and continuously improve the best evidence-based practices that establish and support lifelong learning.